AN INTRODUCTION TO
THE BAHA'I FAITH

e Baha'i Faith has some five million adherents around the world.
reaches the oneness of God, the unity of all faiths, universal edu-
tion, and the harmony of all people, but has no priesthood and few
rmal rituals. In this book, Peter Smith traces the development of the
Baha'i Faith from its roots in the Babi movement of mid-nineteenth-
century Iran to its contemporary emergence as an expanding worldwide religion.

- Explores the textual sources for Baha'i belief and practice, theology
  and anthropology, and understanding of other religions.
- Covers the concept of the spiritual path, Baha'i law, and administration and aspects of community life.
- Examines the Baha'is' social teachings and activities in the wider
  world.

This introduction will be of particular interest to students of new
religious movements, Middle East religions, and comparative religion
and for those studying short courses on the Baha'i Faith.

PETER SMITH is Chairman of the Social Sciences Division, Mahidol
University International College, Bangkok. He is author of several
books in the field of Baha'i studies, including *The Bahá'í Faith: A
Short History, Second Edition* (1999) and *A Concise Encyclopedia of the
Bahá'í Faith, Second Edition* (2002).

AN INTRODUCTION TO THE BAHA'I FAITH

PETER SMITH

Mahidol University International College

CAMBRIDGE
UNIVERSITY PRESS

CAMBRIDGE UNIVERSITY PRESS
Cambridge, New York, Melbourne, Madrid, Cape Town, Singapore, São Paulo, Delhi

Cambridge University Press
32 Avenue of the Americas, New York, NY 10013-2473, USA

www.cambridge.org
Information on this title: www.cambridge.org/9780521681070

First published 2008

Printed in the United States of America

A catalog record for this publication is available from the British Library.

Library of Congress Cataloging in Publication Data
Smith, Peter, 1947 Nov. 27–
An introduction to the Baha'i faith / Peter Smith.
p.   cm. – (Introduction to religion)
Includes bibliographical references and index.
ISBN 978-0-521-86251-6 (hardcover) – ISBN 978-0-521-68107-0 (pbk.)
1. Bahai Faith.   I. Title.   II. Series.
BP365.S655   2008
397.9′3–dc22   2007045453

ISBN   978-0-521-86251-6 hardback
ISBN   978-0-521-68107-0 paperback

For Anne, Corinne, James, William, and Lua

Contents

x   *Contents*

List of Map, Figures, and Tables

Preface

Emerging out of the earlier Babi movement in the 1860s, the Baha'i Faith has since developed into a religion of considerable scope and dynamism. Now established throughout the world, the Faith has attracted several million adherents from a variety of religious and cultural backgrounds, its followers lauding this multiplicity as a demonstration of the Faith's claims to be a universal religion able to unite all the peoples of the world.

Baha'is are followers of Bahá'u'lláh (1817–92), an Iranian nobleman who spent much of his life as an exile in the Ottoman Empire, and whose teachings provide the core elements of their beliefs. For Baha'is, Bahá'u'lláh is the latest in a series of divine messengers and as such is God's prophet for the present age, summoning all humanity to unite and establish the millennial peace promised in the religions of the past. Regarding the world's major religions as various aspects of the same truth and all human beings as members of a single race and nation, Baha'is believe that their religion provides the ideas and structures for a new world order.

The present book provides first a brief survey of the historical development of the Baha'i Faith and of the Babi movement out of which it emerged (Section I), followed by overviews of the major beliefs and practices of present-day Baha'is (Sections II and III). There is also a select bibliography and an appended list of recent Baha'i leaders.

In preparing this book, I have drawn extensively from my *Concise Encyclopedia of the Bahá'í Faith* (2000; 2nd ed. 2002), and I extend my particular thanks to Oneworld Publications for permitting me to reuse material from that earlier work. I also acknowledge the kind assistance of the Baha'i Office of Public Information in Haifa, the Baha'i National Office in London, and my friends on the 'Tarikh' internet Baha'i history discussion group for responding to particular queries. Very special thanks are due to Dr. Moojan Momen and Dr. Stephen Lambden for reading and commenting on the manuscript before publication – such faults as remain of course are entirely my responsibility. My thanks also to my colleagues and friends at Mahidol University International College and to Kate Brett, my editor at Cambridge University Press, for their encouragement and support.

Peter Smith
Bangkok
December 2006

Chronology

I. THE EARLY BABI PERIOD, 1844–53

1843/44 Death of Sayyid Kázim Rashtí (31 December/1/2 January) leads to a leadership crisis in the Shaykhi movement.

1844 The Báb's declaration of mission to Mullá Husayn (22–23 May). The beginning of an organized movement.

1845 Trial of Mullá 'Alí Bastámí, the Báb's emissary in Iraq (13 January). First persecution of Babis in Iran.

1846 The Báb escapes from Shíráz (23 September) and proceeds to Isfahán, where he is favourably received by the governor, Manúchihr Khán.

1847 Following the death of Manúchihr Khán (21 February), the Báb is taken to the fortress-prison of Mákú (July). Táhirih returns to Qazvín (July) and is accused of involvement in her uncle's murder (August–September?). The first killings of Babis occur. The Báb begins his composition of his book of laws, the *Bayán*.

1848 The Báb is brought for trial in Tabríz, where he makes public claim to be the Mahdi (July/August). Mullá Husayn leads a growing band of followers in a proclamatory march from Khúrasán (July). Following the death of Muhammad Sháh (4 September), the conflict of Shaykh Tabarsí begins (10 October–10 May 1849).

1849 The Tabarsí conflict ends (10 May).

1850 Seven leading Babis in Tehran are executed (19/20 February). Vahíd's preaching in Yazd leads to disturbances (January–February), and when he goes to Nayríz, an armed struggle between the Babis and their opponents follows (27 May–21 June). An armed struggle also occurs in Zanján

(c. 13 May–c. 2 January 1851). The Báb is executed at the instructions of Amír Kabír (8/9 July).

1851   The Zanján conflict ends (January). Several Babis are killed in Yazd and elsewhere.

1852   Amír Kabír is killed at the order of the king (January). One Babi faction makes an attempt on the life of Náṣiri'd-dín Sháh (15 August). Many Babis are killed, including Ṭáhirih. Bahá'u'lláh is arrested (16 August) and imprisoned in the 'Black Pit' (August–December), where he experiences his initiatory vision.

1853   Renewed conflict in Nayríz (March–October).

2. THE DEVELOPMENT OF BABISM, 1853–66

1853   Bahá'u'lláh is exiled from Iran. He and his family journey from Tehran to Baghdad (12 January–8 April).

1854–56   Bahá'u'lláh leaves Baghdad for Kurdistan (10 April 1854–19 March 1856).

1856–63   Bahá'u'lláh gradually revivifies the Babi community and becomes the dominant Babi leader, overshadowing Ṣubḥ-i Azal, who remains in hiding.

1863   Bahá'u'lláh stays in the garden of Riḍván (22 April–3 May) prior to his journey to Istanbul (3 May–16 August). He remains in Istanbul until his journey to Edirne (1–12 December). Claims to divinely bestowed authority become prominent in his writings.

c. 1865   Bahá'u'lláh is poisoned by Azal, but survives. Western scholarly interest in Babism begins.

3. THE EMERGENCE OF THE BAHA'I FAITH, 1866–92

1866   Bahá'u'lláh makes formal announcement to Azal to be He Whom God Shall Make Manifest. Most of the local Babi community choose to follow him (as 'Baha'is') rather than Azal. The first Baha'i missionaries begin to convert the Babi remnant in Iran.

1867   Bahá'u'lláh begins his proclamation to the rulers. Persecutions in various parts of Iran.

1868   Arrest of Baha'is in Egypt and Baghdad. Conversion of first Baha'i of Christian background. Bahá'u'lláh is banished to

Akka under an order of life imprisonment (he and his companions leave Edirne on 12 August and reach Akka on 31 August). Azal and some others are sent to Famagusta (arr. 5 September).

1869   Bahá'u'lláh's letter to Násiri'd-dín Sháh is delivered and its bearer tortured and killed.

1870   Bahá'u'lláh leaves the Akka barracks and lives in the city (October).

1873   Bahá'u'lláh completes the *Kitáb-i Aqdas*.

1875   'Abdu'l-Bahá writes the *Secret of Divine Civilization* (lithographed, 1882). First Baha'i missionary teacher sent to India.

1876   Deposition of Sultan Abdulaziz (30 May).

1877   Bahá'u'lláh leaves Akka, residing in country houses in the region.

1889   Murder of a Baha'i in Ashkhabad by Shi'is (8 September) prompts Russian intervention. The Baha'is in Russian Turkestan henceforth emerge as a separate religious community free of persecution.

1892   Death of Bahá'u'lláh (29 May). He designates 'Abdu'l-Bahá as his successor as head of the Faith.

4. THE PERIOD OF 'ABDU'L-BAHÁ'S LEADERSHIP, 1892–1921

1894   Ibrahim Kheiralla begins Baha'i teaching activity in Chicago. Conversion of the first American Baha'is.

1896   Assassination of Násiri'd-dín Sháh by a follower of Jamálu'd-dín 'Al-Afghání' (1 May).

1897   Consultive council of Hands of the Cause in Tehran prepares for the formation of a Baha'i Assembly (1899).

1898   Tarbíyat Baha'i school for boys established in Tehran. The first Western pilgrims arrive in Akka (December).

1899   Baha'i activities begun in Paris and London. Kheiralla returns to America. A leadership crisis develops, finally marked by Kheiralla renouncing 'Abdu'l-Bahá (1900).

1902   Construction of the Baha'i temple in Ashkhabad begins.

1905   Baha'i activities begin in Germany. The Constitutional Revolution begins in Iran.

1908   The Young Turk Revolution transforms Ottoman government and releases political and religious prisoners.

	'Abdu'l-Bahá is released from Ottoman confinement and subsequently moves his family to Haifa (1909).
1909	The remains of the Báb are interred in a shrine on Mount Carmel (21 March). American Baha'is start their project to build a temple in Chicago.
1910	'Abdu'l-Bahá travels to Egypt (10 August). Establishment of a Baha'i girls school in Tehran.
1911	'Abdu'l-Bahá completes his first tour of Europe (August–December). A systematic teaching campaign is launched in India.
1912	'Abdu'l-Bahá begins his second Western tour (North America, 11 April–5 December; Europe, 13 December–13 June 1913). He returns to Haifa on 5 December.
1914	World War I begins. Baha'i activity started in Japan.
1918	British take Palestine from the Turks, ensuring 'Abdu'l-Bahá's safety. World War I ends.
1919	The *Tablets of the Divine Plan* are ceremonially 'unveiled' in New York. Martha Root travels to Latin America to teach the Baha'i Faith. 'Abdu'l-Bahá composes his *Tablet to the Hague*.
1920	First Baha'i pioneers arrive in Australia and South Africa. Work begins at the site of the proposed Baha'i House of Worship at Wilmette, Illinois. The first All-India Baha'i Convention is held. 'Abdu'l-Bahá is knighted by the British.
1921	Shi'is seek to gain possession of the House of Bahá'u'lláh in Baghdad (January), leading to a long-running legal dispute. The first pioneer arrives in Brazil. 'Abdu'l-Bahá dies (28 November).

5. THE GUARDIANSHIP OF SHOGHI EFFENDI, 1922–57

1922	Shoghi Effendi is publicly named as Guardian (January). He calls a conference of leading Baha'is to discuss the future of the Faith. His first general letter on Baha'i administration is sent to the West (5 March).
1923	Baha'i national assemblies are elected in Britain, Germany, and India.
1925	The International Baha'i Bureau is established in Geneva. A Baha'i Esperanto magazine begins publication in Germany. An Egyptian court declares the Baha'i Faith to be separate from Islam. Shoghi Effendi establishes definite qualifications

	for Baha'i membership. Qájár rule in Iran formally comes to an end, and Reza Khan becomes Shah.
1926	Queen Marie of Romania meets Martha Root and pays public tribute to the Faith.
1928	Persecution of the Baha'is in Soviet Asia. The case of Bahá'u'lláh's House in Baghdad is brought before the Permanent Mandates Commission of the League of Nations, which finds in favour of the Baha'is (but to no effect).
1932	Bahiyyih Khánum dies (15 July).
1934	Baha'i schools in Iran closed. Purge of Baha'is in government employment. Mounting campaign of official persecution (–1941). National assembly established for Australia and New Zealand. The Egyptian assembly secures legal incorporation.
1937	First American Seven Year Plan (–1944) marks beginning of a systematic campaign to establish the Faith in Latin America. Other national plans follow (1938–53). The Baha'i Faith is banned in Nazi Germany.
1938	Mass arrests and exile of Baha'is in Soviet Asia. The Ashkhabad temple is turned into an art gallery.
1939–45	World War II.
1946	Systematic campaign begins to establish the Baha'i Faith throughout Western Europe.
1948	Establishment of the 'Baha'i International Community' (BIC), affiliated with the United Nations. The state of Israel comes into being. Construction of the superstructure of the Shrine of the Báb begins (–1953).
1951	International Baha'i Council inaugurated. A systematic campaign to establish the Faith in Africa begins. Shoghi Effendi's first appointment of Hands of the Cause.
1953	Ten Year Crusade begins (–1963). The Baha'i temple in Wilmette is dedicated for worship.
1954	Women become eligible to serve on Baha'i assemblies in Iran. Shoghi Effendi establishes the Auxiliary Boards.
1955	Construction of the International Archives Building begins (–1957). National campaign of persecution against the Baha'is in Iran.
1957	Death of Shoghi Effendi in London (4 November). The Hands of the Cause assume leadership of the Baha'i world.

6. THE CUSTODIANSHIP OF THE HANDS, 1957–63

1960	Charles Mason Remey makes claim to be the second Guardian and is declared a Covenant-breaker. All Baha'i activities in Egypt are banned by presidential decree (August).
1961	The Baha'i temples in Kampala and Sydney are dedicated for worship. 'Mass teaching' begins in India.
1962	Persecution of Baha'is in Morocco (–1963). Baha'i institutions are banned in Indonesia.

7. THE UNIVERSAL HOUSE OF JUSTICE, 1963–

1963	Establishment of the Universal House of Justice (21–22 April) as head of the Faith. It announces that it knows of no way in which further guardians can be appointed (6 October). First Baha'i world congress held in London (28 April–2 May).
1964	The Baha'i temple in Frankfurt is dedicated for worship. The Universal House of Justice declares that there is no way to appoint further Hands of the Cause. The Nine Year Plan begins (–1973). Other international plans follow.
1967	Permanent BIC office established in New York. Global proclamation campaign begins.
1968	Establishment of the Continental Boards of Counsellors.
1970	All Baha'i institutions and activities are banned in Iraq. The BIC gains consultative status with the United Nations' Economic and Social Council (ECOSOC).
1972	The Panama temple is dedicated for worship. The Universal House of Justice adopts its Constitution.
1973	Establishment of the International Teaching Centre.
1976	The Baha'i Faith is banned in Vietnam. BIC is granted consultative status with the United Nations' Children's Fund (UNICEF).
1977	First Baha'i radio station established in Latin America (Ecuador). The first of a series of international Baha'i women's conferences are held.
1979	Islamic revolution in Iran. Major persecution of Baha'is begins. The House of the Báb is destroyed.

1983	Seat of the Universal House of Justice comes into use. Office of Social and Economic Development established. The Baha'i Faith is officially banned in Iran.
1984	Baha'i temple in Apia dedicated for worship. International Baha'i Refugee Office established.
1985	The Universal House of Justice issues its statement, *The Promise of World Peace.*
1986	The Baha'i temple in New Delhi is dedicated for worship.
1989	The Baha'i Office of the Environment is established as part of BIC. Collapse of communist rule in Eastern Europe.
1990	A special teaching plan for former Eastern Bloc countries is launched (–1992).
1992	Second Baha'i world congress in New York. Baha'i involvement in the 'Earth Summit' in Rio de Janeiro. BIC Office for the Advancement of Women is established. Publication of the English-language translation of the *Kitáb-i Aqdas.*
2001	Official opening of the Terraces of the Shrine of the Báb (May).

Prologue: The Middle East in the Nineteenth Century

The Babi and Baha'i religions originated in the Middle East in the mid-nineteenth century, but they developed in significantly different contexts. The Babi movement of the 1840s was largely confined to the Iranian Empire at a time when it was still relatively isolated from the wider world, whilst the Baha'i Faith developed from the 1860s in the more cosmopolitan Ottoman world at a time when even Iran was experiencing greater foreign influence and ideological debate.

In the mid-nineteenth century, the dominant Middle Eastern power was the Ottoman Empire, which then incorporated much of the Balkans and the Arab world as well as the Ottoman heartlands in what is now the Republic of Turkey. To its east was Iran, and to the south Egypt, the later still technically an Ottoman vassal. All three states were monarchies with theoretically autocratic rulers, albeit local governors and landowners, and, in Iran, leaders of the numerous nomadic tribes, often enjoyed considerable power. Traditional Islamic religious leaders were also important, with official state-controlled hierarchies in the Ottoman Empire and Egypt and a powerful independent clerical order in Iran – a Shi'i state, unlike its Sunni neighbours. More heterodox forms of Islam were also present, notably various branches of Sufism, as well as large Christian and Jewish minorities, and, in Iran, Zoroastrians.

Throughout the region, European interference and the threat of colonial expansion was a reality (the Ottoman and Iranian empires had already lost considerable territory to Russia by the early nineteenth century; Egypt was effectively incorporated into the British Empire in 1882). European cultural influence was already strong in the Ottoman Empire and Egypt by the early nineteenth century and increased after the Crimean War (1853–56) and the completion of the Suez Canal (1869), both countries seeing major movements of Western-influenced modernization. Iran was more isolated and less economically developed than its western neighbours, but even there a modernist movement emerged, albeit it lagged behind its Ottoman and Egyptian counterparts.

Linguistically, the region was dominated by three languages: Ottoman Turkish, the official language of the Ottoman Empire; Persian, the language of Iran – but also widely known as a literary language in British India; and Arabic, the language of Islam, studied by all Islamic scholars everywhere and spoken in various popular forms in Egypt and the rest of the Arab world.

It should be noted that during the whole Babi and early Baha'i periods (1844–92), transportation in the Middle East was generally poor. Steamship companies provided the first modern transportation links from the 1830s onwards, with a network of sailings eventually being established across the waters linked to both the Eastern Mediterranean and the Arabian Sea, as well as river services up the Nile and Tigris-Euphrates, but small sailing ships remained the main form of water transportation throughout the period. On land, apart from railway construction in Egypt (from 1851), a few miles of railway in Anatolia, and some short stretches of modern roads, the means of transportation remained traditional, with travellers riding or walking along ill-maintained tracks or across open land. There were few bridges. Given the great distances involved (Iran is some 1.6 million square kilometres in extent, three times the size of France; the modern road from Baghdad to Haifa – only completed in 1941 – is 616 miles [919 kilometres]; the direct distance from Tehran to Akka is 1,532 kilometres), journey times between the major cities and towns referred to in this book might then take weeks or even months. Modern communication, in the form of the electric telegraph, was established between the main centres in the 1850s.

PART I

History

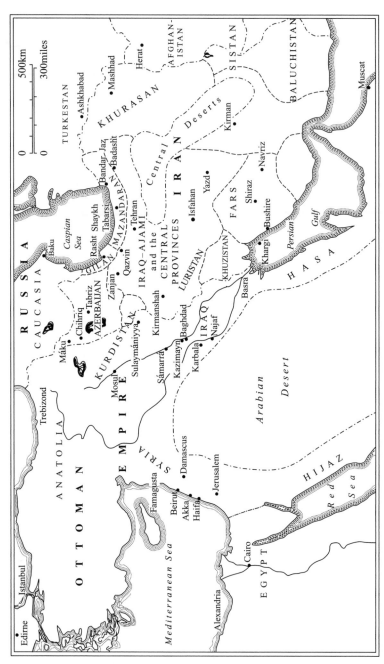

Map 1 Iran and the Ottoman Empire in the mid-nineteenth century. The international boundaries to the east of Iran were not defined or demarcated until the late nineteenth century. Iran's internal provincial boundaries varied over time.

CHAPTER I

The Babi Movement

I. SHI'ISM AND SHAYKHISM

Shi'ism

The Baha'i Faith developed out of the earlier Babi religion, and Babism in turn emerged as a movement within Shi'i Islam, particularly as it had developed in Iran.[1] Shi'i Muslims are those who believe that the rightful successors of the Prophet Muḥammad were a series of *Imáms* drawn from the Prophet's own family. These claims are rejected by the majority of the world's Muslims (the Sunnis), but Shi'ism has come to predominate in several parts of the Middle East, most notably Iran, where 'Twelver' Shi'ism has been the state religion since the sixteenth century.

Twelver Shi'ism is characterized by its belief in a series of twelve Imáms, beginning with 'Alí (d. 661), Muḥammad's young cousin and son-in-law and continuing through his immediate descendants by his marriage to the Prophet's daughter Fáṭima to the last of the Imáms, who disappeared

---

[1] The best English-language introduction to Shi'ism is Moojan Momen, *An Introduction to Shi'i Islam: The History and Doctrines of Twelver Shi'ism* (Oxford: George Ronald, 1985). See also Seyyed Hossein Nasr, Hamid Dabashi, and Seyyed Vali Reza Nasr (eds.), *Expectation of the Millennium: Shi'ism in History* (Albany: State University of New York Press, 1989); A. Abdulaziz A. Sachedina, *Islamic Messianism: The Idea of the Mahdi in Twelver Shi'ism* (Albany: State University of New York Press, 1981); and 'Allámah Sayyid Muḥammad Ḥusayn Ṭabáṭabá'í, *Shi'ite Islam*. Trans. S.H. Nasr (London: Allen and Unwin, 1975).

On the Iranian religious context, see Hamid Algar, *Religion and State in Iran, 1785–1906: The Role of the Ulama in the Qajar Period* (Berkeley and Los Angeles: University of California Press, 1969); idem. 'Religious forces in eighteenth- and nineteenth-century Iran'. In *The Cambridge History of Iran. Vol. 7. From Nadir Shah to the Islamic Republic*, Peter Avery, Gavin Hambly, and Charles Melville (Cambridge: Cambridge University Press, 1991), pp. 705–31; Said Amir Arjomand, *The Shadow of God and the Hidden Imam: Religion, Political Order, and Societal Change in Shi'ite Iran from the Beginning to 1890* (Chicago and London: University of Chicago Press, 1984); Nikki R. Keddie, *Roots of Revolution: An Interpretive History of Modern Iran* (New Haven, CT: Yale University Press, 1981); and Roy Mottahedeh, *The Mantle of the Prophet: Religion and Politics in Iran* (Harmondsworth: Penguin Books, 1985).

mysteriously whilst still a boy in the Iraqi city of Sámarrá in AH 260 (AD 873–4). According to the Twelvers, these twelve Imáms were the rightful rulers of the Islamic world as well as a source of divinely transmitted knowledge. The Twelvers also believe that whilst the last Imám is now hidden from the eyes of men, he continues to exist in a mysterious state of occultation, whence he will eventually reappear as the *Mahdí* (rightly guided one) and *Qá'im* (he who will arise), battle the forces of evil in a final apocalyptic battle, and herald the day of judgement.

In addition to this strong millenarian expectation, the Twelvers are also distinguished by their particular devotion to the Third Imám, Husayn, the younger son of 'Alí, who was killed along with a small band of his followers by an army of the Umayyad caliph in 680 at what later became the Iraqi shrine-city of Karbalá. This killing of the grandson of the Prophet gives Shi'ism a cult of sacrificial martyrdom, and constitutes a strong emotional base for Shi'i identity, renewed annually in dramatic commemorative displays of self-mortification. Other distinctive features of modern Twelver Shi'ism include the continuance of the tradition of Islamic theosophical philosophy and the enormous power that has accrued to the higher-ranking members of the Islamic learned, the *'ulamá*, effectively a clerical order unparalleled in the Sunni world.

Shaykhism

Of crucial importance for the future emergence of Babism was the development of the Shaykhí school of Shi'i theosophy.[2] The Shaykhis followed the teachings of Shaykh Ahmad al-Ahsá'í (1753–1826), an Arab from what is now the Gulf region of Saudi Arabia, who gained a reputation for piety and learning as well as a large and influential following amongst both Arab and Iranian Shi'is and also some powerful opponents who accused him of deviating from Islamic orthodoxy. His immediate successor, the Iranian Sayyid Kázim Rashtí (c. 1790s–1843/4), consolidated his master's movement

---

[2] On the Shaykhi background to Babism, see Amanat, *Resurrection and Renewal*, pp. 48–69, and Denis MacEoin, 'Early Shaykhí reactions to the Báb and his claims'. In *Studies in Bábí and Bahá'í History*, *Vol. 1*, ed. M. Momen (Los Angeles CA: Kalimát Press, 1982), pp. 1–47. See also Mangol Bayat, *Mysticism and Dissent: Socioreligious Thought in Qajar Iran* (Syracuse, NY: Syracuse University Press, 1982), pp. 37–86, and Momen, *Shi'i Islam*, pp. 225–31. The standard Baha'i account is in Nabil, pp. 1–46. For some account of the Shaykhi movement in general, see Henry Corbin, *En Islam iranien: Aspects spirituels et philosophiques*. 4 vols. (Paris: Gallimard, 1971–72). On the early Shaykhis, see Vahid Rafati, 'The Development of Shaykhí Thought in Shi'i Islam' (Ph.D. dissertation. University of California at Los Angeles, 1979).

into a distinctive Shi'i sect centred in Karbalá in what by then was Ottoman territory.

Early Shaykhi doctrine was complex and subtle and remains subject to differing interpretations. Again, some elements seem deliberately obscure, or to involve the Shi'i practice of pious dissimulation (*taqiyya*), so as to conceal more controversial ideas from the Shaykhis' opponents and avoid persecution. Certainly, one emphasis was on the mystical dimension of religious faith rather than mere obedience to its outer laws. The early Shaykhi leaders also claimed to be able to unveil deeper esoteric truths for their true followers. Thus, given that God was absolutely unknowable and transcendent, human beings not only had to approach the divine through the Prophets and the Imáms, but should seek the 'Perfect Shi'i' of the age in which they lived who would act as an intermediary between the Hidden Imám and the faithful. By implication, Shaykh Aḥmad and Sayyid Káẓim occupied this role, Shaykh Aḥmad himself stressing that his own authority derived from intuitive and inspired knowledge which he derived directly via visionary experiences of the Imáms. Babi and Baha'i accounts also identify a major emphasis by Sayyid Káẓim on messianic expectation and the return of the Hidden Imám.

The Babi movement emerged in the immediate context of the Shaykhi succession crisis which followed the death of Sayyid Káẓim (around 1 January 1844). With no appointed successor, a leadership struggle developed between rival Shaykhi clerics in different cities, all of whom came in time to present a more conservative image of their master's teachings, deemphasizing the more radical aspects which had brought opprobrium upon the movement. By contrast, the growing number of Shaykhis who became Babis had a more radical vision in which millenarian expectation and the immediacy of divine guidance were paramount.

2. SAYYID ʿALÍ-MUḤAMMAD, THE BÁB

The Babi movement centred on Sayyid ʿAlí-Muḥammad Shírází (1819–1850), a young Iranian merchant from the southern city of Shíráz with no clerical training but with a growing reputation as a local holy man.

Following the early death of his father (c. 1826), ʿAlí-Muḥammad had grown up with his mother Fáṭima Bagum, and under the guardianship of one of her brothers, Ḥájí Mírzá Sayyid ʿAlí, a prominent local merchant.[3]

---

[3] See Smith, *Concise Encyclopedia of the Bahá'í Faith* (hereinafter CEBF), 'Báb'; 'Báb, family', loc. cit. H. M. Balyuzi, *Khadíjih Bagum: The Wife of the Báb* (Oxford: George Ronald, 1981).

He was an only child. Little is known about his early years other than that he received an elementary education at a local Qur'ánic school and gained the commercial training necessary to join the trading operations run by members of his mother's family. In 1835, he began to work as a merchant in the port city of Bushire on the Persian Gulf.

Later accounts emphasize 'Alí-Muḥammad's extreme piety as a youth, and religious concerns eventually impelled him to close his office in Bushire (1840) and embark on an extended pilgrimage to the Shi'i shrine cities in Iraq, remaining there for about a year. During this time he attended some of the classes of Sayyid Káẓim and attracted the attention of some of the Sayyid's disciples by his great piety. He did not embark on any formal course of religious training, however, and eventually returned to Shíráz where he married one of his mother's cousins, Khadíjih (August 1842), and established a household. The young couple had one son, Aḥmad, who died in infancy (1843).

During these years in Shíráz, 'Alí-Muḥammad experienced a number of visionary dreams, in the most dramatic of which he later described how he saw the severed head of the Imám Ḥusayn, drops of whose blood he drank, and from the grace of which he felt that his breast had been filled with 'convincing verses and mighty prayers': the spirit of God having 'permeated and taken possession of My soul', 'the mysteries of His Revelation were unfolded before my eyes in all their glory'.[4] He also began to write what, by the early months of 1844 if not earlier, he regarded as divinely inspired verses, and apparently began to gain a reputation as a holy ascetic and possible miracle-worker, blessed with the grace of the Hidden Imám.

The Báb's declaration and initial claims

The development of a distinct religious movement centring on 'Alí-Muḥammad is traditionally dated to the night of 22 May 1844, with the conversion of Mullá Ḥusayn Bushrú'í (c. 1814–49) as his first disciple.[5] It is of note that this declaration took place in the Islamic year 1260, that is, a full millennium after the disappearance of the Hidden Imám in 260 AH, thus giving the Babis a powerful linkage to popular religious expectations of the time.

Although there continues to be discussion as to what exactly 'Alí-Muḥammad was initially claiming to be, it is clear that a major and

---

[4] Denis MacEoin, 'From Shaykhism to Babism' (Ph.D. dissertation, University of Cambridge, 1979), p. 141; Nabil, p. 253.
[5] See Ruhu'llah Mehrabkhani, *Mullá Ḥusayn: Disciple at Dawn* (Los Angeles: Kalimát Press, 1987), and also CEBF, 'Ḥusayn Bushú'í, Mullá', loc. cit.

distinctive claim to authority was made and that this was widely understood to be that of being the *Báb* (Gate) to the Hidden Imám, 'Alí-Muḥammad hence coming to be frequently referred to by this title and his followers being labelled as 'Bábís'. One important text here was the *Qayyúmu'l-asmá*, a lengthy treatise of over 9300 verses (a third longer than the Qur'án).[6] Written in Arabic, and begun on the initial night of declaration, it was completed over the following forty days. Although the writer's exact status is presented enigmatically, the Báb's own claim to authority is central to the book. Thus, whilst he refers to himself as the exalted or greatest 'Remembrance' (*dhikr*) [of God] and as the 'Gate' of God or of the Hidden Imám, the book also includes passages in which the speaker is the Imám himself, or which express an identity between the Imám and the Báb, or even claim divine revelation: God had inspired the Báb as he had in the past inspired Muḥammad and other prophets and these were 'new verses from God' and 'the essence of the Qur'án'. Moreover, the book's style and format mirrored those of the Qur'án, paraphrasing its wording; replicating its 'rhyming, rhythmical cadences'; employing the same type of chapter and verse divisions and prefatory 'disconnected letters'; and making the same claims to inimitability. All human beings – including the 'rulers of the Earth' and the Islamic learned – were summoned to believe in the Báb. Obedience to him was the same as obedience to God. Those who rejected him were consigned to hell-fire. Extensively copied and widely distributed by his disciples, the *Qayyúmu'l-asmá* came to be regarded as the 'Qur'án' of the Babis. Unsurprisingly, most clerical readers saw it as heterodox and condemned it.[7]

3. THE ESTABLISHMENT OF A MOVEMENT

Following Mullá Ḥusayn's acceptance of the Báb, a small group of close disciples formed around the Báb, most of them like Mullá Ḥusayn former youthful followers of Sayyid Káẓim. After a period of association with the Báb in Shíráz, most of this inner circle of eighteen 'Letters of the Living'

---

[6] A few selected passages of the *Qayyúmu'l-asmá* have been translated into English (The Báb, *Selections from the Writings of the Báb*. Trans. Habib Taherzadeh et al. (Haifa: Bahá'í World Centre, 1976), pp. 41–74), but the book as a whole remains untranslated. On the Báb's early writings, see B. Todd Lawson, 'Interpretation as revelation: The Qur'án commentary of Sayyid 'Alí Muḥammad Shírází, the Báb (1819–1850)'. In *Approaches to the History of the Interpretation of the Qur'án*, ed. Andrew Rippin (Oxford: Oxford University Press, 1988), pp. 223–53; idem, 'The Qur'án Commentary of Sayyid 'Alí Muḥammad Shírází, the Báb' (Ph.D. dissertation, McGill University, 1987); idem, 'The terms "Remembrance" (*dhikr*) and "Gate" (*báb*) in the Báb's Commentary on the Sura of Joseph'. In *Studies in Honor of the Late Hasan M. Balyuzi*, ed. Moojan Momen (Los Angeles, CA: Kalimát Press, 1988), pp. 1–63. See also MacEoin, *Sources*, pp. 55–57, and CEBF, '*Qayyúmu'l-asmá*', loc. cit.

[7] Lawson, 'The terms'; MacEoin's 'Early Shaykhi reactions', and *Rituals*, p. 35.

(*Ḥurúfu'l-ḥayy*) dispersed, becoming a core missionary group for the further expansion of the Báb's cause throughout Iran and the Shi'i areas of Iraq.[8] Meanwhile, the Báb himself, together with one disciple and a servant, set out for Mecca (September 1844) to make a public proclamation of his mission in fulfilment of Islamic prophecy regarding the time of the return of the Imám Mahdí: in the event largely unheeded.

The Babis' initial missionary endeavour was largely covert, the disciples being instructed not yet to divulge the Báb's name. The mere circulation of extracts from the Báb's writings and the announcement of the near advent of the Hidden Imám sparked millenarian fervour, however, as well as strident opposition from leading clerics determined to snuff out what they saw as religious deviation. The first to suffer was the Báb's missionary to Iraq, Mullá 'Alí Basṭámí (d. 1845), who soon after his arrival in August/September 1844, was arrested as a spreader of false teachings and eventually tried before an unprecedented joint tribunal of Sunni and Shi'i clerics in January 1845. Subsequently transferred to Istanbul on instructions from the Ottoman government, he was sentenced to hard labour in the naval dockyard, in which he died shortly thereafter, gaining thereby the status of the first Babi martyr.[9]

The Báb had originally intended to proceed from Mecca to Iraq to join Mullá 'Alí, but was apparently dissuaded from this plan by news of the growing tumult there, as well as the possibilities for violent confrontation – many of his would-be followers flocking to Karbalá with weapons so as to assist the Imám on his expected arrival. Instead, he announced a change in the divine decree (the quasi-heterodox doctrine of *badâ*), and returned to Iran. There was also now tumult in Shíráz, however, one of the Báb's emissaries publicly identifying 'Alí-Muḥammad by the dramatic means of adding his name to the Muslim call to prayer. Outraged, the provincial governor severely punished those involved in this incident and sent a detachment of troops to arrest the Báb whilst he was en route to his native city. Following a stormy interview at the governor's court, the Báb was released into the charge of his uncle, and required to make a public recantation of the claim to be the *Báb* of the Imám.

Avoiding public attention and restricted in his activities at the governor's order, the Báb was still able to maintain contact and correspondence with his

---

[8] See CEBF, 'Letters of the Living', loc. cit. and Denis MacEoin, 'Hierarchy, authority, and eschatology in early Bábí thought'. In *In Iran*, ed. P. Smith, pp. 95–155 (Los Angeles CA: Kalimát Press, 1986). The only member not present was the only woman Letter of the Living, Ṭáhirih (see later).

[9] Moojan Momen, 'The trial of Mullá 'Alí Basṭámí: A combined Sunní-Shí'í *fatwá* against the Báb'. *Iran* 20 (1982), pp. 113–43, and also CEBF, ''Alí Basṭámí, Mullá', loc. cit.

followers and covertly to receive visitors in his home, whilst his disciples in the various provinces continued to gain new converts, consolidating a network of Babi cells throughout the country and in Iraq. Many Babi converts continued to be drawn from amongst the Shaykhis, but the leading Shaykhi clerics also now sought to clearly distance themselves from the Babis and their evident heterodoxy, the most prominent amongst them, Ḥájí Karím Khán (1810–71), particularly condemning the Báb as an infidel, dismissing those Shaykhis who had become Babis as ignorant, and resisting any Babi missionary endeavour in his own city of Kirmán.[10] As opposition to the Babis from the more 'orthodox' Shaykhis was consolidated, new converts were gained from outside Shaykhi circles, however, including two prominent non-Shaykhi clerics who would come to play a major role in subsequent events: Sayyid Yaḥyá Dárábí (known by his Babi title as *Vaḥíd*, the 'Peerless') (c. 1809–50) and Mullá Muḥammad-'Alí Zanjání (*Ḥujjat*, the 'Proof') (1812/3–1850).[11]

The Báb also continued to write extensively during this period, completing more than twenty new major works, including commentaries on Qur'ánic verses and Islamic traditions and treatises on theological and legal issues, in addition to prayers, homilies and letters. Indeed, the actual process of the revelation of verses was now seen as a miraculous proof of the Báb's divine power.

4. HOPES AND TENSIONS, SEPTEMBER 1846–JULY 1848

The relative quiet of the Báb's sojourn in Shíráz ended in September 1846 when he was rearrested for his religious activities. He was able to escape the city during the confusion caused by an ensuing outbreak of cholera, however, moving to the central city of Iṣfahán, then under the governorship of Manúchihr Khán (d. 1847), one of the most powerful men in the kingdom, who accorded the Báb his protection. Here the Báb continued to write treatises and correspond with his followers. Eventually, Manúchihr Khán himself is said to have become a Babi, seeking to arrange a meeting between the Báb and Muḥammad Sháh, so that the Báb could proclaim his claims directly to the king, a plan frustrated by the governor's death in February 1847.[12]

---

[10] See MacEoin, 'Early Shaykhí reactions', and also CEBF, 'Karím Khán Kirmání, Ḥájí (Muḥammad-)', loc. cit.

[11] See CEBF, 'Ḥujjat' and 'Vaḥíd', loc. cit.

[12] See CEBF, 'Manúchihr Khán'; and 'Muḥammad Sháh', loc. cit.

A major change in the Báb's fortunes now occurred. Muḥammad Sháh (reg. 1834–48), with a known liking for popular religiosity, appears to have been initially sympathetic towards the Báb, and the Báb wrote to him on a number of occasions, appealing to him to promote his cause and promising him great victories if he did so. By contrast, the Shah's chief minister and spiritual advisor, Ḥájí Mírzá Áqásí (c. 1783–1849), undoubtedly saw the Báb's growing national popularity as a religious leader as a potential threat to his own position. Thus, at Áqásí's order, the Báb was made an effective prisoner of state and transferred to the remote fortress of Mákú in Azerbaijan (July 1847–April 1848), close to the Ottoman and Russian borders, and later to another remote fortress in Chihríq (April 1848–June 1850).[13]

The period of the Báb's captivity in Azerbaijan was one in which both the Babi movement and its relationship with Iranian society were profoundly transformed. As Áqásí's enmity and the Shah's acquiescence at the Báb's imprisonment and internal exile became evident, the Báb ended his earlier praise, eventually condemned Áqásí unreservedly as Satan and consigning the Shah to hell. Early in 1848, he also made an open claim to his followers to be the Mahdi, and as such declared the abrogation of Islamic holy law, delineating a new order to replace that of Islam in his book, the *Bayán* ('Exposition').[14] This radical break with orthodox Shi'ism was reinforced in July, when, at Áqásí's order, the Báb was brought before a tribunal of clerics in the provincial capital of Tabríz presided over by the Crown Prince (the future Náṣiri'd-dín Sháh). Here the Báb made public his claim to be the Mahdi – being punished with the bastinado for his assertions before being returned to Chihríq.

Meanwhile, many of the Báb's followers were becoming increasingly strident in their promulgation and defence of their faith. A crucial catalyst here was Fáṭimih Baraghání (1814–52), variously known by the titles *Qurratu'l-'Ayn* ('Solace of the Eye') and *Ṭáhirih* (the 'Pure'), the only woman amongst the Letters of the Living, and a formidable charismatic personality.[15] Already known for her considerable learning (unusual for a woman of her day) and for her disregard for Islamic convention, she had generated opposition from more conservative Babis as well as orthodox Shi'is. Leaving her husband, she gained leadership of the Babis in Karbalá until she was deported by

[13] See CEBF, 'Áqásí, Hájí Mírzá'; 'Mákú'; and 'Chihríq', loc. cit.
[14] There are two *Bayáns*, a longer work in Persian and a shorter one in Arabic. See CEBF, '*Bayán*', loc. cit. Both are available in French translation by A. L. M. Nicolas: *Le Béyân arabe* (Paris: Ernest Leroux, 1905) and *Le Béyân persan*. 4 vols. (Paris: Librairie Paul Geuthner, 1911–14). Only a few extracts are available in English translation; see Báb, *Selections*, pp. 224–39.
[15] See CEBF, 'Ṭáhirih', loc. cit.

the Ottomans in March 1847. Returning to her home town of Qazvín in July, she refused to return to her husband, whom she declared to be an infidel, and came into verbal conflict with her Shaykhi-hating uncle and father-in-law, Mullá Muḥammad-Taqí Baraghání, one of the most prominent and powerful clerics in the region. Religious tensions in Qazvín escalated, culminating in Muḥammad-Taqí's murder (August/September 1847) by a Shaykhi with Babi sympathies.[16] Denying involvement in the killing, Ṭáhirih was nevertheless held to be complicit by her uncle's family and followers, and whilst Ṭáhirih was eventually able to escape to Tehran, several members of her entourage were killed in retaliation for Muḥammad-Taqí's death. For leading clerics throughout Iran, Baraghání's murder was a turning point, identifying the Babis as a dangerous threat to society.

5. CONFLICT AND THE QUESTION OF BABI RADICALISM

In Shi'i terms, the Báb's public claim to be the Mahdi was a profoundly radical act. In popular belief, the Mahdi was the rightful ruler of the faithful and the inaugurator of the final days prior to the Resurrection. The Babis themselves had various understandings of the meaning of the Báb's claim, with tensions between 'radicals' and 'conservatives' emerging at a secret conference of leading Babis held in June and July 1848 at the remote hamlet of Badasht. Here, Ṭáhirih voiced her own radical understanding, proclaiming the advent of a new age and the abrogation of Islamic holy law, and dramatizing her position by appearing unveiled, proclaiming that she was 'the Word' which the Mahdi was to utter on the day of judgement, and on another occasion allegedly brandished a sword. Many of the Babis present were scandalized and shocked, and some took the abandonment of Islamic law as a reason to engage in unspecified antinomian acts.

Meanwhile, Mullá Ḥusayn had left Mashhad in the northeastern province of Khúrasán (July 1848), where he been propagating Babism, and marched westward with a growing band of followers who were reportedly flying the messianic symbol of the Black Standard which announced the coming of the Mahdi. The purposes of this group remain unclear, and it has been speculated that they may have been intending to journey all the way to travel all the way to Azerbaijan to release the Báb. Whatever the case, the situation changed dramatically in September with the death of

---

[16] See Moojan Momen, 'Usuli, Akhbari, Shaykhi, Babi: The tribulations of a Qazvin family'. *Iranian Studies* 36/3 (2003), pp. 317–37, and also CEBF, 'Muḥammad-Taqí Baraghání, Ḥájí Mullá', loc. cit.

Muḥammad Sháh and the chaos and confusion which then ensued before his son could be installed as shah in Tehran. Travelling to the northern city of Bárfurúsh, close to the Caspian Sea, Mullá Ḥusayn and his companions were attacked by a mob led by a local cleric and fighting ensued, several Babis and their opponents being killed. The Babis, now several hundred strong, then repaired to the small regional shrine of Shaykh Ṭabarsí (12 October), round which they constructed crude fortifications and awaited developments.[17] Accused of rebellion by their opponents, they were subsequently attacked by various local and national forces, putting up ferocious resistance against enormous odds and killing many of their attackers. Finally, after seven months of siege and severely weakened by starvation and their own loss of men, they responded to sworn promises of a truce and were for the most part massacred (10 May 1849). It was a major blow to the new religion, half of the Báb's Letters of the Living dying in the struggle and its aftermath.

Little was then heard of the Babis until the early months of 1850, when there were disturbances in the southern city of Yazd which were exacerbated by the preaching of the Babi leader Vaḥíd (January–February), and accusations surfaced of a Babi conspiracy in Tehran itself, leading to the execution of seven socially prominent Babis purely on the basis of their faith (19/20 February). The Babis now clearly felt themselves under threat, and in May local tensions led to attacks on the large Babi communities of the towns of Zanján in the north and Nayríz in the south.[18] Led respectively by Ḥujjat and Vaḥíd, the Babis fought back vigorously, and as at Ṭabarsí, their fervour was such as to enable them to fight against greatly superior numbers before being falsely offered a truce and overwhelmed – in Nayríz after less than a month (27 May–21 June), but in Zanján only after seven-and-a-half months (c. 13 May–c. 2 January 1851). Fearful of further Babi actions, the new chief minister, Amír Kabír (1807/8–52), determined to cut off their inspiration, and ordered the execution of the Báb, who was accordingly

---

[17] See Siyamak Zabihi-Moghaddam, 'The Babi-state conflict at Shaykh Tabarsi'. *Iranian Studies* 35/1–3 (2002), pp. 87–112, and idem, 'The Bábí-state conflict in Mázandarán: Background, analysis and review of sources'. In *Studies in Modern Religions, Religious Movements and the Bábí-Baháʾí Faiths*, Moshe Sharon (ed.), pp. 179–225 (Leiden and Boston MA: Brill, 2004). See also Moojan Momen, 'The social basis of the Babi upheavals in Iran (1848–53): A preliminary analysis'. *International Journal of Middle East Studies* 15 (1983), pp. 157–83, and CEBF, Ṭabarsí, Shaykh', loc. cit.

[18] See Momen, 'Social basis', and CEBF, 'Nayríz'; and 'Zanján', loc. cit. On Zanján see Edward G. Browne, (trans.) 'Personal reminiscences of the Bábí insurrection at Zanján in 1850,...by Áqá ʿAbduʾl-Aḥad-i-Zanjání'. *Journal of the Royal Asiatic Society* 29 (1897), pp. 761–827; and John Walbridge, 'The Babi uprising in Zanjan: Causes and issues'. *Iranian Studies* 29/3–4 (1996), pp. 339–62.

brought again to Tabríz and placed before a firing squad together with one of his disciples (8/9 July).[19]

With the three major conflicts at Tabarsí, Zanján, and Nayríz, the Babis were accused at the time of insurrection by their enemies, a charge later repeated by various writers.[20] Purely revolutionary activity seems unlikely, however. In all three instances, the Babis were provocative in their assertion of their mission, but the fighting that ensued was defensive in nature, and in the case of the two urban struggles closely tied up with pre-existing social and political tensions within the towns. Again, there is no evidence of a coordinated plan of action. This does not necessarily mean that the Babis did not see their actions as hastening a new political order: an age of messianic fulfilment was approaching, the Mahdi had come, and the Iranian government had proven its illegitimacy by imprisoning him and allowing his followers to be persecuted. Death by martyrdom could be seen, perhaps, as a vivid proof of the reality of the Báb's new order. Certainly, the Babis were ferocious in their resistance and in the killing of their opponents, their fervour contributing to the awe which many of those who fought against them had of them: in a culture that glorified sacrificial martyrdom, the Babis evoked the memory of the Imám Husayn's death at Karbalá.

6. THE COLLAPSE OF BABISM AS AN ORGANIZED MOVEMENT, 1850–53

It is difficult to reconstruct developments within the Babi movement in any detail for the next several years. In the face of the realities of persecution, most of the surviving Babis seem to have following a secretive existence, concealing their activities and beliefs. Presumably, the execution of the Báb and the death of so many of their leaders caused some Babis to doubt their faith, whilst others despaired or dreamed of revenge. Others again hoped for the future, encouraged by the Báb's frequent references in the *Bayán* to the coming appearance of a further messianic figure of 'He Whom God Shall Make Manifest' (Ar. *Man-yuzhiruhu'lláh*).[21] Seemingly, the movement

---

[19] See CEBF, 'Amír Kabír', loc. cit. Also known as Mírzá Taqí Khán. Chief minister from October 1848 to November 1851, he was subsequently killed on the Shah's order.

[20] This view is taken by both Kurt Greussing, 'The Babi movement in Iran, 1844–52: From merchant protest to peasant revolution'. In *Religion and Rural Revolt*, ed. J. M. Bak and G. Benecke (Manchester: Manchester University Press, 1984), pp. 256–69, and M. S. Ivanov, *Babidski Vostanii i Irane, 1848–1852* (Moscow, 1939). For an English language review of the latter see V. Minorski in *Bulletin of the School of Oriental and African Studies*, vol. 11 (1946), pp. 878–80. See also Ivanov's articles 'Babism'; and 'Babi uprisings' in *The Great Soviet Encyclopedia*, loc. cit.

[21] See CEBF, 'He whom God shall make manifest', loc. cit.

began to break apart, as new leaders emerged to replace those who had been killed, and various local groups formed and developed different plans for action. With fewer clerics now leaders, claims to spiritual authority on the basis of some messianic or esoteric station multiplied.

The most prominent of the new leaders was initially Mullá Shaykh 'Alí Turshízí (d. 1852), better known by his Babi title, *Azím* ('Great'). Formerly a Shaykhi cleric, he had acted as the Báb's chief agent and intermediary in Azerbaijan during the period of the Báb's imprisonment there and subsequently assumed the role of the Báb's deputy in Tehran. Also of importance in the capital were two of the sons of Mírzá 'Abbás Núrí ('Mírzá Buzurg', d. 1839), a member of the landowning notability who had served for a while as a provincial governor: Mírzá Ḥusayn-'Alí (b. 12 November 1817), known by the Babi religious title of *Bahá* (later *Bahá'u'lláh* [the 'Glory of God']) and his young half-brother, Mírzá Yaḥyá (1831/2–1912), entitled *Ṣubḥ-i Azal* ('Morn of Eternity'). Capable and socially prominent, Bahá had already distinguished himself as a practical organizer, but by 1850, it was Azal, then still in his teens, who came to be widely regarded as in some way the Báb's successor on the basis of a letter from the Báb instructing him to preserve his religion. The future of the Babi religion eventually came to rest in the hands of these two men.[22]

Amongst the Tehran Babis, the group headed by Azím and supported by Azal began to plot revenge against the state, a policy opposed by Bahá. Any moderating influence which Bahá might have been able to exert was removed in June 1851, however, when at the chief minister's request he went into exile in Iraq, returning only after Amír Kabír's fall from power. The radicals now went ahead with their plans, making a botched attempt to assassinate Náṣiri'd-dín Sháh (reg. 1848–96) (15 August 1852).[23] Lightly wounded, the Shah embarked on a ruthless campaign of repression. Those linked to the conspiracy (less than thirty in number, and including Azím) were quickly rounded up and executed – many in gruesome public scenes of torture and dismemberment, but at the Shah's insistence, a general pogrom was also mounted against the Babis as a collectivity. Many were killed – about four hundred according to one account, but possibly more – despite their innocence of any involvement with the plotters. Azal escaped and

---

[22] 'Abbás had four full wives and three concubines, by whom he had a total of fifteen children, twelve of whom survived him. Bahá'u'lláh was the third child by the second wife, Khadíjih; Azal, the only child by the first concubine. Some of the siblings later became Baha'is, some Azalis, whilst others remained Muslims.

[23] See Abbas Amanat, *Pivot of the Universe: Nasir al-Din Shah Qajar and the Iranian Monarchy, 1831–1896* (London: I.B. Tauris, 1997).

went into hiding. Bahá, who had been staying with the new chief minister's brother at the time of the assassination attempt was arrested and thrown into the loathsome Síyáh Chál ('Black Pit') dungeon. Any hopes he may have had for forging a rapprochement with the new government were ended.

After August 1852, apart from renewed conflict in Nayríz in March 1853 (-October), which was again bloodily suppressed, the Babis were quiescent: the government's Babi 'problem' seemed to have been resolved, and the movement extirpated.

CHAPTER 2

Bahá'u'lláh and the Emergence of the Baha'i Faith

1. BAHÁ'U'LLÁH AND THE REANIMATION OF BABISM, 1853–66

The 'Babi episode' appeared to have ended with the total collapse of the movement. That this proved not to be the case was largely due to the activities of Mírzá Husayn-'Alí Núrí – Bahá'u'lláh. After four months of imprisonment in the Black Pit (August–December 1852), Bahá'u'lláh was released and ordered into exile, choosing to go again to Ottoman Iraq rather than taking up the offer of refuge in Russia (presumably suggested by a brother-in-law who was the Russian legation secretary). He left Tehran in mid-January with members of his family (his then two wives, eldest two children, and two of his brothers, Mírzá Músá and Mírzá Muhammad-Qulí) to make the difficult winter journey over the mountains, arriving in Baghdad in early April 1853.[1]

What happened next is difficult to establish in detail, and is coloured by the later partisan accounts of Baha'is and Azalis, but in essence it would seem that Bahá'u'lláh began to eclipse Azal as a leader of the remaining Babis. After the failure of the attempt on the life of the Shah, Azal, had gone into hiding, eventually secretly making his way to Baghdad to join his brother. Here Azal chose to maintain a hidden existence from most of the Babis

---

[1] Bahá'u'lláh eventually married three wives, and had eight children who survived childhood. The first marriage, to Ásíyih Khánum (*Navváb*) (1820–86), was in 1835, when Bahá'u'lláh was almost eighteen. Seven children were born to the marriage, but only three survived to adulthood: 'Abbás (*'Abdu'l-Bahá*) (1844–1921), Fátimih (Bahiyyih) Khánum (1846–1932), and Mihdí (1848–70). The second marriage, in 1848/9, was to Fátimih Khánum (*Mahd-i-'Ulyá*) (1828–1904), one of his cousins who had been recently widowed. By her, he had six children, four of whom survived to adulthood: a daughter, Samadiyyih (b. 1856/7), and three sons, Muhammad-'Alí (1853/4–1937), Díyá'u'lláh (1864–98), and Badí'u'lláh (1867–1950). The third marriage, was to a Gawhar Khánum, the sister of Mírzá Mihdí Kashání. The marriage occurred in Baghdad in c. 1862. Unlike the other wives, Gawhar remained in Baghdad after Bahá'u'lláh's departure, only rejoining him after his exile to Akka. She had only one child, a daughter, Furúghiyyih. Six of the children married – to relatives of prominent Baha'is, including in two cases to the offspring of Bahá'u'lláh's brother, Mírzá Musá. There were fifteen grandchildren. Bahiyyih chose to remain unmarried, whilst Mihdí died in his youth. According to tradition, 'Abbás ('Abdu'l-Bahá) was born on the very night of the Báb's declaration (23 May 1844).

16

for his own protection, relying on Bahá'u'lláh and Bahá'u'lláh's full brother Mírzá Músá (d. 1887) and their families for material support. By contrast, Bahá'u'lláh was outgoing, authoritative and accessible, and now began to be seen by an increasing number of Babis as a religious leader in his own right (rather than simply as a practical organizer) and as a focus for their devotion, a development increasingly resented by Azal. Tensions quickly mounted and barely a year after his arrival in Baghdad, Bahá'u'lláh decided to abandon the city to pursue the life of a solitary mystic in the mountains of Kurdistan, leaving his family in the care of Mírzá Músá. Departing the city on 10 April 1854, accompanied initially by a single servant, he later wrote that his 'withdrawal contemplated no return'.[2] Living first as a hermit in a cave in the mountains at Sar-Galú, he 'communed with [his own] spirit' oblivious of the world, later coming into contact with Sufi leaders in the regional centre of Sulaymáníyyih and establishing close relationships with them. Only in March 1856, after two years in Kurdistan, did he return to Baghdad at his family's urging (19 March 1856).

Back in Baghdad, Bahá'u'lláh found the Babi remnant in sorry disarray; dispirited and divided into factions, with Azal both unable to provide effective leadership and continuing a policy of militancy – now including against prominent Babis who challenged his position, most notably the learned Mírzá Asadu'lláh Khu'í (*Dayyán*, 'Judge'), whom he had denounced in bloodthirsty language, and whose murder he seems to have instigated (1856). Determined not to allow this situation to continue, Bahá'u'lláh now set to work to revive the Babi community, both in Iraq, and through correspondence, in Iran. Writing extensively, he began to give the Babis a new understanding of their religion, in the process attracting a growing band of dedicated disciples. He was soon recognized as the preeminent Babi leader, both by the Babis and by the Iranian and Ottoman authorities. Outside of the Babi community, he also gained increasing sympathy from both residents and visitors in Baghdad, including Ottoman officials, Iranian notables, and even Sunni clerics, coming to be widely regarded as an important personage. Finally, the Iranian government became concerned that Bahá'u'lláh's rising prestige and influence could reanimate the Babi movement in Iran (as in fact it was), and petitioned the Ottomans to extradite him back to his homeland. Refusing to comply with this request, the Ottoman government instead invited Bahá'u'lláh (now an Ottoman subject) to journey to Istanbul – and so leave the sensitive border region

[2] Bahá'u'lláh, *The Kitáb-i-Íqán*, p. 160.

with Iran. By the time of Bahá'u'lláh's departure from Baghdad (April 1863), the Babi community had been both revived and transformed.

2. THE VISION AND EARLY WRITINGS OF BAHÁ'U'LLÁH

Central to Bahá'u'lláh's rise as preeminent Babi leader and to the revival and transformation of the Babi community which he was able to affect were his writings, particularly those written after his return from Kurdistan. Dealing with a range of themes, these writings gave the Babis a renewed vision of their religion, but they also articulated a number of elements that were distinctively innovative in terms of the Babi tradition. More ambiguously, they revealed something of Bahá'u'lláh's own sense of the divine presence, and hence expressed their author's authority as a religious leader. Again, apart from subject matter, some of them were innovative within the Babi tradition in being very straightforward and accessible to the reader. Bahá'u'lláh sometimes wrote in the obscure and inaccessible manner of many of the Babis, but he could also write lucid prose and forceful religious poetry. Living in Iraq in a bilingual environment, he wrote very naturally in both Persian and a somewhat Persianized Arabic. Much of what became a substantial literary output took the form of letters to individuals, several of great length. Copyists ensured that a number of these works were widely distributed. Later, after Bahá'u'lláh had laid claim to be a divine revelator, all these early writings were retrospectively incorporated into the corpus of his revelation.[3]

Perhaps the most important theme in Bahá'u'lláh's writings at this time was his own sense of the divine presence. Although this was fundamental to his own vision and to his emerging position of leadership, it is not easy to define, in part because it was implicit rather than an open statement of authority. There is also the question of interpretation, with later Baha'i theologically-influenced accounts seeking to make his status as a divine theophany explicit at as early a date as possible. Academically, I think this question has to be left open: Bahá'u'lláh's writings of the time regarding his own 'station' can be understood in different ways, and it seems likely that there were a variety of attitudes towards them amongst contemporary Babis. In a movement in which there was a tradition of 'concealed truths' and of

---

[3] Only a fraction of the fifteen thousand letters and books by Bahá'u'lláh so far collected has been translated into English – albeit that the writings that have been translated include many of the most important works. *Bahá'í World*, vol. 18, pp. 833–4 provides a partial listing of titles. For summaries of some of the works see Browne, *Selections*, pp. 248–88; Shoghi, *God Passes By*, pp. 116–17, 120–21, 123, 137–41, 170–76, 205–20; Taherzadeh, *Revelation*; and CEBF, 'Bahá'u'lláh, writings of', loc. cit.

the progressive unveiling of perceived realities – as in the case of the Báb's early claims – we should not be surprised to encounter opaqueness regarding such a critical and sensitive issue, especially perhaps because Bahá'u'lláh's later explicit claims to be a Manifestation of God clearly nullified his own half-brother's position as Babi leader.

This said, many of Bahá'u'lláh's Baghdad writings clearly convey a powerful sense of his own encounter with the divine, sometimes personified in the figure of a luminous divine maiden, garbed in white, standing in the air before him or consoling him in her embrace. As he later made explicit, a key moment in the development of this sense was a series of visions which he had experienced during his four-month imprisonment in the Black Pit of Tehran. Subsequently recalling those months – when he was confined with other Babis deep underground in a former water cistern in conditions of appalling squalor and discomfort, under threat of execution, and personally weighted down by two chains which were so infamous that they actually had names (one weighed 51 kg) – Bahá'u'lláh was to write that in his 'infrequent moments of slumber', he had felt that something flowed from the crown of his head over his chest like 'a mighty torrent' streaming down from 'a lofty mountain', and causing every limb of his body to feel that it had been set afire. At such moments, he would recite 'what no man could bear to hear'. Again, this is when he first saw above and before him the vision of the divine maiden embodying the remembrance of God's name who rejoiced his soul with her words and proclaimed to 'all who are in heaven and all who are on earth' that he was 'the Best-Beloved of the worlds', the 'Beauty', 'Mystery' and 'Treasure' of God, and 'the power of His sovereignty'. Previously, 'a man like others', asleep upon his couch, 'the breezes of the All-Glorious' had been wafted over him, teaching him 'the knowledge of all that hath been'. Transformed by God's will, he was bidden to lift up his voice between heaven and earth and praise God 'amidst all people'.[4]

Informed by this sense of divine presence, Bahá'u'lláh's writings bore authority. Thus, he referred to one of his books, the *Hidden Words* (*Kalimát-i Maknúnih*, 1857–8), as having descended from the divine world, and as constituting what had been revealed to God's messengers in the past. He (Bahá'u'lláh) had taken its 'inner essence . . . as a token of grace unto the righteous', so that they might be faithful to God's Covenant, live according to his trust, and obtain 'the gem of Divine virtue'. Again, in his *Javáhiru'l-asrar* (*Gems of Divine Mysteries*; lit. 'The Essence of Mysteries', c. 1860–1),

---

[4] Bahá'u'lláh, *Epistle to the Son of the Wolf*, pp. 21–22; idem, *Summons of the Lord of Hosts*, pp. 5–6, 129.

Bahá'u'lláh wrote of having received 'the wonders' of God's knowledge, 'the gems of His wisdom' and 'the tokens of His power', but being 'forbidden' to divulge them. He could only relate the truths which God had vouchsafed to him to the extent that human souls and minds could bear them, but should it be his wish, he could recount all that had been revealed in the scriptures of the past.[5]

It also seems clear that, however individual Babis understood Bahá'u'lláh's 'station', there was a growing response to the spiritual authority which he expressed so strongly in his writings, and which was itself linked to his personal sense of the divine presence. In the difficult and confusing conditions of the time, he was someone to whom the Babis might turn, and it was probably only a secondary matter for most of them to define exactly who he was. Thus, when Bahá'u'lláh did begin to make explicit claims to authority, large numbers of Babis in both Iraq and Iran responded rapidly and readily: the way as it were had already been prepared.

Of the substantive themes in Bahá'u'lláh's writings at this time, three were particularly prominent: the spiritual-mystical path; the ethical demands of belief; and certain doctrinal concerns. Referring to the mystical path, whereon the religious seeker journeyed towards God, Bahá'u'lláh explicitly addressed the Sufi tradition of Islamic mysticism, as in the two short treatises, the *Seven Valleys* (*Haft Vádí*) and the *Four Valleys* (*Chahár Vádí*), which he composed for Sufi notables shortly after his return from Kurdistan in 1856 (the first described the seven stages ['valleys'] of the seeker's journey quest towards God and the second the four 'stations' which the mystic might attain in relationship to God).[6] It is clear from these works and others that Bahá'u'lláh had a deep knowledge of and empathy for much of the Sufi tradition – though also significant disagreements with some of the theological ideas linked to it: for Bahá'u'lláh the godhead was ultimately unknowable and distinct, and he rejected the conception of existential monism. It is also evident that in these 'Sufistic' writings, he was able to bridge the sectarian divide between Shi'is and Sunnis and that he was able to attract the admiration of religious notables who had no knowledge of Babism.

Bahá'u'lláh's conception of the path of the religious seeker also emphasized the ethical demands of belief, most notably at this time in the *Hidden Words* and the *Kitáb-i Íqán* (*The Book of Certitude*, 1861–2). This had immediate relevance in the revival of the Babi community, identifying practical morality as key to the religious life, but it is also interesting in the context

---

[5] Bahá'u'lláh, *Hidden Words*, p. 5; idem, *Gems of Divine Mysteries*, pp. 4, 10.
[6] Bahá'u'lláh, *Seven Valleys*.

of the Islamic thought of the time, in that Bahá'u'lláh can be seen as using ethics as a bridge between Islamic legalism and mysticism. Identifying both Islamic law, the *shari'a*, and the mystical path, the *tariqa*, as part of proper religiosity, he implicitly gave both an important moral dimension. He also explicitly rejected the antinomianism of those Sufis who believed that the mystic's path transcended the requirements of religious law, but at the same time assented that to be religious required more than simply a narrow following of the law.

As for Bahá'u'lláh's doctrinal concerns, a primary focus was the immediate past, Bahá'u'lláh effectively justifying the Báb's claim to be the *Qá'im* by reconciling it with traditional Shi'i expectations, whilst at the same time providing a general account of humanity's successive rejection of each of God's messengers. This focus was particularly expressed in two works completed in the 1860s: the *Javáhiru'l-asrár* and the *Kitáb-i Íqán* (above), written respectively in Arabic and Persian. Composed in response to questions by one of the as yet unconverted maternal uncles of the Báb (Hájí Mírzá Sayyid Muhammad), the *Íqán* was of particular importance, and was soon widely copied and circulated among the Babis in Iran. Written in a straightforward Persian prose style, it was extremely accessibly to ordinary Iranians who had not received a clerical education and became an important element in attracting Babis and others to Bahá'u'lláh (including the uncle for whom it was written).

Bahá'u'lláh's argument here was that the contemporary rejection of the Báb echoed similar rejections of God's messengers in the past. In every age, people had expected a divine messenger but had opposed him when he came. Religious leaders had ignored the truth, either through ignorance – judging the messengers' claims by their own limited understanding – or because they feared what they saw as a threat to their own leadership. Instead of seeing with their own God-given eyes and investigating truth for themselves, the mass of the people had then followed the foolish example of their leaders.

A persistent reason for this rejection was the literalistic interpretation of scripture, as with the Christian expectation of the Second Coming of Christ which involved the beliefs that the Biblical verses regarding 'stars' falling from heaven would be literally fulfilled and that the promised one would descend in the 'clouds of heaven' (Matthew 24: 29–31) (Bahá'u'lláh's use of a Christian example is of note), but such verses were to be understood metaphorically. Again, God was not bound by human expectations: he had chosen Moses, a murderer, and Jesus, with no known father, as messengers, and had directed Muhammad to change the direction of prayer from Jerusalem to Mecca to the consternation of his followers. God tested the people at the coming of each new Manifestation of God, such that the faithful and faithless might be distinguished. True understanding was only possible to those who had put their trust in God and did not use human standards as a measure of God and his prophets. Those who sought the truth should 'cleanse' their hearts from worldly standards of judgement. The essential proof of any of God's messengers was the messenger's own self and the divine word revealed in the scripture which he brought. Other signs were his constancy in proclaiming his cause in the face of opposition; the transforming influence he had on his followers; the willingness of those followers to give their lives for his cause; and the fulfilment of prophecy. All these evidences, the Báb had, and it was similarly necessary to interpret the traditional beliefs regarding the coming of the Mahdí symbolically. Those Muslims who had rejected the Báb had done exactly the same as those Jews who had rejected Jesus and those Jews and Christians who had rejected Muhammad. Again, people expected the messengers to exercise worldly sovereignty (as Shi'is did of the *Qá'im*/Mahdi), but each messenger's true sovereignty was a spiritual ascendancy which he exercised over all in heaven and on Earth. During their lives, each suffered from opposition and perse-cution, and it was only later when the religions they founded had grown, that peoples bowed before their name.

Other major doctrinal concerns in these writings was the Babi-Baha'i conception of the 'Manifestations of God' – God's messengers (see Chap-ter 8), Bahá'u'lláh stressing their fundamental unity and the continuity of divine revelation. He also noted the sufferings borne by God's chosen ones, but proclaimed their ultimate victory – the power of God's cause being like an irresistible river which overcame all obstructions to its progress; identi-fied the religious leaders of each age – the stars of the heaven of knowledge – as the primary opponents of God's messengers; referred to the coming of the Babi messianic figure of He Whom God Shall Make Manifest; asserted God's bounties to the human soul and the soul's immortality; extolled for-titude and patience in the face of suffering; and interpreted particular verses of the Qur'án.

It should be noted that in a number of his writings at this time Bahá'u'lláh revealed a knowledge of parts of the Bible, which together with his defence of the Christians and Jews from the common Muslim allegation that they had intentionally falsified their scriptures, were extremely unusual amongst nineteenth century Muslim writers. Again, in choosing exemplars of forbearance, he expiated on the sufferings of the Jewish prophet Job as well as the Shi'i figure of the Imám Husayn (with whom he identified).

In many of Bahá'u'lláh's early writings, there is also reference to this being the 'Day of God'. Presumably this could easily be understood as referring to the Báb's mission, but towards the end of the 'Baghdad period', hints of the approaching unveiling of a messianic secret increased, and some of the Babis were informed that the 'nightingale of paradise' [presumably Bahá'u'lláh himself] was now about to establish a new nest. The faithful should expect their faith to be tested. Finally, on the eve of his departure for Istanbul, whilst camped outside Baghdad in a garden which he named 'Riḍván' ('Paradise') (22 April–3 May 1863), he announced to some of his immediate disciples that he was indeed the promised one foretold by the Báb.

3. THE RUMELIAN PERIOD, 1863–68

The Riḍván declaration marked the beginning of a new phase in Bahá'u'lláh's leadership of the Babi community that was to culminate in the emergence of the Baha'i Faith as a distinctive successor movement to Babism (1866). Bahá'u'lláh's journey from Baghdad to Istanbul (3 May–16 August) itself was effectively a triumphal progress. Travelling with a large entourage of family members, servants and followers, and dressed like a Sufi shaykh, he was received with respect in the towns visited en route and was welcomed as a government guest when he arrived in the Ottoman capital. Beyond moving him away from the sensitive Iranian border, Ottoman objectives in inviting him are unclear. Possibly it was hoped that as an influential person with a growing following in Iran, he might be of political use, but if this was the intention, then Bahá'u'lláh's own refusal to try to ingratiate himself with Ottoman grandees negated it. For whatever reason, after three-and-a-half months in Istanbul, perhaps in response to pressure from the Iranian ambassador, orders were given for Bahá'u'lláh to depart for Edirne (Adrianople) in Ottoman Rumelia. Unlike the march from Baghdad, this second journey (1–12 December 1863) was clearly in the nature of an exile – and like Bahá'u'lláh's departure from Iran was made in difficult winter conditions.

The four-and-a-half years spent in Edirne (12 December 1863–12 August 1868) marked a crucial period in the development of Babism. Bahá'u'lláh was now the clear leader of the newly established Babi colony in the city and through the journeys of Babi couriers to Iran was able to maintain communications with the Babis there, an increasing number of whom were to some degree his followers. In this context, a definite breach between Bahá'u'lláh and Azal was perhaps inevitable – Bahá'u'lláh's publicly acknowledged and growing preeminence meant the final end to any hopes

Azal may have maintained of leadership. Again, we are confronted by later rival Azali and Baha'i accounts of events, but the Baha'i account of Azal's growing jealousy (egged on it would seem by one of his supporters, a Sayyid Muḥammad Iṣfahání) appears credible, with Azal being accused of plotting to kill Bahá'u'lláh – culminating in a poisoning attempt (c. 1865) which made Bahá'u'lláh gravely ill for a while and left him with a tremor in his hand. This incident was followed by Bahá'u'lláh making a formal written announcement to Azal to be He Whom God Shall Make Manifest in the *Súri-yi Amr* (the 'Chapter of Command'), and for the first time referring to his followers as being 'the people of *Bahá*' (i.e. Baha'is). Bahá'u'lláh then secluded himself in one of the Babi houses in the city and instructed the Babis to chose between himself and Azal (10 March 1866). This 'Most Great Separation' continued for two months, during which most of the Edirne Babis identified themselves as Baha'is. Baha'i missionaries were then sent to Iran, quickly winning the allegiance of most of the Babi remnant to Bahá'u'lláh. An active minority (Azali Babis as we might now term them) rejected Bahá'u'lláh's claims in favour of Azal's, and in some instances there were confrontations between the two factions. In 1867, Azal challenged Bahá'u'lláh to let God judge between them (the Shi'i practice of mutual cursing [*mubáhala*], in which each party to a dispute called down the wrath of God on the wrongdoer in the expectation that God would indicate who was speaking truly), but did not attend the projected meeting, seriously weakening his credibility.

4. THE RUMELIAN WRITINGS

This period was marked by a great outpouring of writings from Bahá'u'lláh, most addressed to various of his followers as well as to Azali Babis. The major theme of these works was the proclamation of Bahá'u'lláh's own mission. He was the 'Celestial Youth', the messianic figure of He Whom God Shall Make Manifest foretold by the Báb; the return of the Imám Ḥusayn expected by Shi'is; the 'Ancient Beauty' through whose command the whole of creation had first come into being. As with the Prophet Muḥammad and the Báb, the proof of his mission was his revelation of divine verses. The value of the believer's faith in God was now dependant upon recognizing him. If the peoples of the world wished to hear the voice of God, they should listen to his verses. This was the day of tests on which the deeds of all human beings would be weighed with justice. He also complained of his own sufferings at the hands of Azal and his followers, stigmatizing them as the hosts of Satan, accusing them of treachery, and warning that those Babis who rejected his call would be found wanting by God.

During this time, Bahá'u'lláh also instructed certain of his followers to present his claims to the Babis in Iran and Iraq who had not yet heard his call; appealed to the Baha'is to be united and detached from worldly things; predicted the future triumph of his cause; and began to outline some aspects of what would become distinctive Baha'i ritual practices, with the composition of specific prayers for fasting and the designation of the House of the Báb in Shíráz and the House of Bahá'u'lláh in Baghdad as pilgrimage sites at which particular rites of visitation were to be observed.

This period also marks the beginning of Bahá'u'lláh's 'proclamation to the kings', a series of letters addressed to the world's rulers, and followed the pattern set by the Prophet Muḥammad, who is supposed to have dispatched a similar series of messages to the rulers of his day.[7] This was initiated with a lengthy letter sent to the Ottoman Sultan Abdulaziz (reg. 1861–76) and his chief ministers, apparently condemning the ministers for ordering Bahá'u'lláh's banishment to Edirne. This epistle was followed by a general address to all rulers, the 'Súra of the Kings' (*Súratu'l-Mulúk*, c. 1867), which was circulated amongst the Baha'is. In it, the 'kings of the earth' were summoned to heed Bahá'u'lláh's call, cast away the things they possessed, and fear and follow God. They were reproved for having neither recognized nor aided the Báb and were warned of the divine chastisement that would befall them if they did not heed Bahá'u'lláh's counsels. The Christian monarchs were also specifically addressed, being reminded of their obligation to be faithful to Jesus's call to follow the promised 'Spirit of Truth' who had now appeared. Bahá'u'lláh also expatiated on the duties of kings to rule with justice. The reigns of government had been committed into their hands that they might safeguard the rights of the downtrodden, listening to their appeals and punishing wrong-doers. If they did not do this, they had no right to vaunt themselves amongst men. Again, the poor were their trust for whom they would answer to God. The rulers should become reconciled among themselves, so that they would no longer need armaments except for defence, and thus lessen their outlays: by increasing their expenditures, they were laying an unjust burden on their subjects. Only by adhering to and enforcing God's laws would they gain glory. In terms of worldly possessions, the Earth itself was richer than them. Passages were also addressed to the Sultan, deploring the extremes of wealth and poverty

---

[7] Bahá'u'lláh, *Summons.*

which Bahá'u'lláh had witnessed in Istanbul, and calling upon him to rule with justice as God's 'shadow on earth', ensure the well-being of his subjects, and cease to entrust the affairs of state into the hands of corrupt and godless ministers.

5. THE SYRIAN PERIOD, 1868–92

After the split between Bahá'u'lláh and Azal, the Azali group sought to discredit Bahá'u'lláh with the Ottoman authorities, accusing him of sedition. The resultant investigation cleared Bahá'u'lláh of these charges, but alerted the authorities that both Bahá'u'lláh and Azal were making and propagating religious claims. This, it was decided, represented a potential source of disorder and merited the further exile of the 'Babi' leaders. Accordingly, a royal command was issued (26 July 1868) condemning them to perpetual banishment, imprisonment and isolation. Bahá'u'lláh's property in Baghdad was also confiscated at this time and the leading Babis/Baha'is of Baghdad arrested and exiled to Mosul.

The Ottomans determined to exile Bahá'u'lláh and his entourage to Akka (the ancient port city of St. Jean d'Acre, now Acco in Israel) in Ottoman Syria, a walled city then used as a place of exile and imprisonment. Azal and a few others were to be sent on to Famagusta in Cyprus. The whole group departed from Edirne on 12 August 1868 under armed escort, and was taken first to Gallipoli and thence by sea to their respective destinations, the ship going by way of Egypt. The Akka group arrived in the city on 31 August, and were confined in the barracks-citadel. They were 67 in number: Bahá'u'lláh, two faithful brothers and their families and servants, other Baha'is who would not be parted from Bahá'u'lláh, and two Azalis, the latter no doubt intended to serve as spies on the rest. Living conditions were at first appalling, everyone becoming sick, and three of the exiles dying. One of Bahá'u'lláh's sons, Mírzá Mihdí, also died, following a fall (23 June 1870). Living conditions eased significantly after the Baha'is were moved out of the barracks (4 November 1870), although the exiles were still confined to the city. A major crisis occurred in 1872, when a few Baha'i hotheads finally murdered the resident Azalis who had been making endless difficulties for them. This action was strongly condemned by Bahá'u'lláh. Thereafter, however, relations between the Baha'is and the local authorities and inhabitants eased, Bahá'u'lláh's eldest son, the future 'Abdu'l-Bahá, in particular acting as an effective go-between. Finally, following the overthrow of Sultan Abdulaziz (1876), the order of imprisonment became null-and-void and it became possible for Bahá'u'lláh to leave Akka (June 1877) after almost nine years in the city, moving first to a villa and then a mansion in the surrounding countryside. With 'Abdu'l-Bahá taking care of organizational work, he was able to devote himself to the 'revelation of verses' and the enjoyment of nature. He died at the mansion of Bahjí on 29 May 1892 following a slight fever, and was buried in a room in an adjoining house (the abode of his daughter by his third wife). He was then aged seventy-four.

The English orientalist E. G. Browne, who had an audience with Bahá'u'lláh in 1890, some two years before his death, has left us a pen-portrait of the Baha'i Prophet, describing him as 'a wondrous and venerable figure', whose face he could neither describe nor forget, and whose piercing eyes 'seemed to read one's very soul'. Though his face was deeply lined with age, his 'ample brow' emanated power and authority. Browne noted that Bahá'u'lláh wore both his hair and beard long (the beard almost to his waist) and dyed them jet-black. In addition to his robes, he wore a tall dervish hat round the base of which was wound a small white turban.[8] Pen-portraits of Bahá'u'lláh by his followers and companions are not available, their great devotion and love for him preventing them from describing him, other than to emphasize his overwhelming and ineffable presence, one writer stating that it was almost impossible for anyone to look into his eyes or utter a complete sentence when near him.[9]

6. THE SYRIAN WRITINGS

During this period, Bahá'u'lláh continued to write extensively. As throughout his ministry, he wrote in both Persian and Arabic, and even on some occasions when writing to Zoroastrians, in a form of 'pure' Persian without any Arabic admixture.[10] Everything that he wrote or dictated to his chief secretary was now regarded by his followers as divine revelation. His previous writings prior to his declaration of mission were also retrospectively incorporated within this body of revealed writings (with over fifteen thousand letters and books identified so far). As with the Báb's revelations, Baha'is regarded Bahá'u'lláh's compositions as distinctive from human inspiration. Bahá'u'lláh himself seemed transformed at such times, surrounded by an aura of great vibrancy and power, his body in a very energized state, which would continue for some time afterwards such that he would be unable to

---

[8] Browne, *Traveller's Narrative*, pp. xxxix–xl.

[9] Taherzadeh, *Revelation*, vol. 2, p. 9. A passport photograph of Bahá'u'lláh was made in Edirne and may be viewed by Baha'is during their pilgrimages to Haifa. Baha'is consider it extremely disrespectful to display this portrait in any less exalted setting.

[10] For translations of some of these, see Bahá'u'lláh, *Tabernacle of Unity*.

eat. The verses themselves would be uttered without apparent forethought and with great rapidity, with perhaps a thousand verses being revealed in the space of a single hour. Indeed, Mírzá Áqá Ján, his amanuensis, had to develop a special form of speed-writing ('revelation writing') in order to take them down.[11] During the early period of his mission (presumably up to the time he was poisoned in Edirne), Bahá'u'lláh might continue in this fashion for lengthy periods, day and night, but later he was only able to continue for an hour or so. In several instances, the revelations involved visionary experiences (as with Bahá'u'lláh's visions of the 'Maid of Heaven' and other angelic figures), and on a number of occasions he also chanted in what was regarded as a special heavenly language which was not comprehensible to his hearers.[12]

Bahá'u'lláh's writings during this period include his proclamatory letters to the rulers; his book of laws, the *Kitáb-i Aqdas* (c. 1873); and a series of letters in which he outlined his vision for a united and just world.[13] Themes from his earlier writings were also continued, notably his references to the immediacy of the relationship he felt with the Godhead; his emphasis on the need for piety and ethical action on the part of his followers, and his announcement that this was the 'day of God'. He also continued to compose many prayers.[14]

'Proclamation'

One of the most important themes of the early part of the Akka period was Bahá'u'lláh's continuing proclamation to the world's leaders. Whilst still in Edirne, he had sent a letter to Napoleon III of France, and before leaving Gallipoli, he sent a verbal message to the Sultan asking for a ten minute audience at which he could prove his claims. In Akka, the letter he had already written in Edirne to Náṣiri'd-dín Sháh of Iran was dispatched, a second letter was sent to Napoleon III, and letters were sent to Queen Victoria of Britain, Alexander II of Russia, and Pope Pius IX (all c. 1869).[15] Other world leaders – Wilhelm I of Germany, Franz-Joseph of Austria-Hungary and the rulers of the American states – were subsequently referred to in the *Kitáb-i Aqdas*.

---

[11] For an illustration of Mírzá Áqá Ján's 'revelation writing', see CEBF, p. 295.
[12] See CEBF, 'revelation', loc. cit.
[13] See Bahá'u'lláh, *Kitáb-i-Aqdas*; and idem, *Tablets of Bahá'u'lláh*.
[14] For a selection, see Bahá'u'lláh, *Prayers and Meditations by Bahá'u'lláh*.
[15] See Bahá'u'lláh, *Summons*. CEBF, 'Alexander II'; 'Napoleon III'; 'Náṣiru'd-dín Sháh'; 'Pius IX'; 'Victoria', loc. cit.

Also of interest are three 'tablets', written in 1868 and 1869, two named after Âli Paşa ('Alí Páshá) (1815–71) and one for Fuat Paşa (Fu'ád Páshá) (1815–69), the two Ottoman ministers whom Bahá'u'lláh held to be primarily responsible for his exile from Edirne and the resultant sufferings of his family and followers.[16] These recount the sufferings of the Baha'is in Edirne and the Akka prison, proclaiming their innocence of any wrong-doing and censuring the ministers for their role in the treatment meted out to them; announce the greatness of Bahá'u'lláh's cause, reminding the reader that opposition to God's messengers in every age was unavailing; warn that the ministers' actions would merit God's wrath; and predict upheavals in the Ottoman domains, including the downfall of Abdulaziz and the loss of Edirne. The early deaths of the two ministers (in 1869 and 1871, when the two men were both in their fifties), followed by the deposition and suicide or murder of Abdulaziz (1876), and a disastrous war with Russia (1877–8) – during which the Russians occupied Edirne, and subsequent major Ottoman losses of territory, were all seen by the Baha'is as evidences of divine judgement and Bahá'u'lláh's prophetic prowess.

The lengthiest and perhaps most important of the letters sent to the rulers was Bahá'u'lláh's epistle to Náṣiri'd-dín Sháh, the *Lawḥ-i Sulṭán* ('Tablet of the King'). The messenger was a Áqá Buzurg Khurásání (c. 1852–69), the teenage son of one of the early Babis who was one of the few to be able to meet Bahá'u'lláh whilst he was still in the Akka prison. Warned that the mission might lead to his death, Áqá Buzurg returned to Iran with the letter and approached the Shah whilst the latter was on a hunting trip, delivering the letter to members of the entourage. Taken into custody, he was then tortured and killed.[17] The letter included an appeal to the Shah to grant religious toleration to the Baha'is as they were loyal and obedient subjects, and stated that Bahá'u'lláh himself had not only consistently opposed violence, but had summoned the Babis to lay down the sword and eschew sedition. The clerics were those who were primarily to blame for the persecution of the Babis, and if the Shah wished, Bahá'u'lláh would return to Iran to confront the *'ulamá* and establish the truth of his cause (presumably by argument or in *mubáhala*). If the Shah would respond to Bahá'u'lláh's call, he would attain a great spiritual station. He was reminded that kingship was itself transitory. The physical remains of a

---

[16] These are the *Súratu'l-Ra'ís* (the 'Chapter of the Chief' – 'Chief' here referring to Âli Paşa); The *Lawḥ-i Ra'ís* (the 'Tablet of the Chief'); and the *Lawḥ-i Fu'ád*. See Bahá'u'lláh, *Summons*, pp. 141–81.

[17] He was named *Badí'* (wondrous, unique, new) by Bahá'u'lláh. See Balyuzi, *Bahá'u'lláh*, pp. 294–309; Taherzadeh, *Revelation*, vol. 3, pp. 176–91.

king and a pauper in their graves were the same, and numerous rulers and countless great men had come and gone without leaving a trace of their existence.

Bahá'u'lláh's letters to the European monarchs proclaimed his mission and summoned them to God. The first to be addressed was Napoleon III, but the exact message contained in the initial letter to the emperor is uncertain: Bahá'u'lláh apparently praised him for his claims to be the avenger of the oppressed and a succourer of the helpless and complained of his own sufferings, which Napoleon seems to have interpreted as a request for assistance. The emperor is also reported to have flung down Bahá'u'lláh's letter dismissively, however, an action for which he was reproved in the second letter, Bahá'u'lláh stating that the emperor's sincerity had been found wanting, and that as a consequence his kingdom would be thrown into confusion and his empire pass from his hands. Only if he made amends for his actions, would France be spared the commotions that would otherwise seize it. Abasement was hastening after him, and his pomp would not endure. He was reminded that earthly treasure and dominion would perish – it was pointless to make them a cause of exultation. Instead, he should arise to serve God and help his cause. As with the Ottoman Sultan and his ministers, Napoleon's subsequent downfall (the collapse of the Second Empire during the Franco-Prussian War of 1870–1) was seen by Baha'is as evidence of divine wrath.

Both the British and Russian monarchs were summoned to accept Bahá'u'lláh's claims, but were also praised, in Victoria's case for Britain's prohibition of the slave trade (1807) and the system of parliamentary government (the Second Reform Act had been passed in 1867, greatly extending the franchise), and Alexander for the offer of refuge which the Russian minister in Iran had given to Bahá'u'lláh on his release from his imprisonment in the Black Pit (1852), by dint of which the Tsar now occupied a 'sublime station' which he should be careful to preserve. Alexander's prayer – according to one account to make his forces victorious against the Ottomans – had been heard and answered, and he was now summoned to listen to the voice of God and himself call the nations unto God, ensuring that nothing deter him from this mission. The letters to the Western monarchs all contained asides: including an address to Christian monks in the second letter to Napoleon, summoning them to abandon their seclusion, marry and work to benefit the people of the world, and an appeal to parliamentarians throughout the world to work for the betterment of the world and its peoples in the letter to Victoria, together with an appeal to the world's rulers to work for peace.

In his letter to the Pope, Bahá'u'lláh announced that 'the Lord of Lords' had come down from heaven with grace and justice, and that Christ's promises had been fulfilled. The Pope should not let himself be debarred from God, nor dispute with Bahá'u'lláh as the Pharisees had disputed with Jesus. He should leave his palaces to such as desired them, abandon his kingdom to the kings, and arise to promote God's cause, summoning the kings to justice and selling all his embellished ornaments so as to expend them in the path of God.[18]

Although no letters were sent to the rulers of Austria-Hungary and the newly established German Empire, both monarchs were addressed by Bahá'u'lláh in the *Kitáb-i Aqdas*, the Hapsburg Emperor Franz-Joseph being reproved for not having enquired about Bahá'u'lláh during a visit which the Emperor had made to Jerusalem in 1869, whilst Wilhelm I was warned not to let pride debar him from recognizing Bahá'u'lláh and bidden to remember the fate of Napoleon III, whose power had surpassed his own but who had been overthrown. God brought down conquerors and rulers 'from their palaces to their graves'. In what Baha'is came to see as a significant prophecy after the twentieth century's world wars, Bahá'u'lláh also addressed the 'banks of the Rhine', envisioned them 'covered with gore' when 'the swords of retribution' were drawn against them, and predicting that they would have 'another turn', and that the lamentations of Berlin would be heard, though for now the city was in 'conspicuous glory'. As for the rulers of the American republics, Bahá'u'lláh counselled them to 'adorn the temple of dominion' with the ornament of justice, God-fearingness, and divine remembrance. They should bind 'the broken' with 'the hands of justice', and 'crush the oppressor' with the rod of divine commandments.[19]

Bahá'u'lláh also wrote to and of several of the most prominent Iranian clerics, castigating several for their tyranny and injustice in persecuting and causing the killing of Baha'is; accusing them of having subverted Islam; and comparing at least one of them to those Jewish leaders who had been responsible for the crucifixion of Christ.[20]

---

[18] Again, the occupation of the Papal States in September 1870 by the army of the new Italian state in the immediate aftermath of the defeat of Napoleon III which finally ended the temporal sovereignty of the Papacy is regarded by Baha'is as further evidence of divine judgement.

[19] Bahá'u'lláh, *Kitáb-i-Aqdas*, pp. 50–53.

[20] Those rebuked included three leading Isfahani clerics: Shaykh Muḥammad-Báqir – stigmatized by Bahá'u'lláh as the 'wolf'; his son, Shaykh Muḥammad-Taqí Isfahání (Áqá Najafí), named as the 'son of the wolf'; and Muḥammad-Báqir's associate, Mírzá Muḥammad-Ḥusayn, the 'she-serpent'. See CEBF, '*Burhán, Lawḥ-i*'; '*Epistle to the Son of the Wolf*'; and 'Wolf' and 'the Son of the Wolf', loc. cit.

Law

A second theme in Bahá'u'lláh's writings at this time was divine law, most particularly the composition of his own book of holy law, the *Kitáb-i Aqdas* ('The Most Holy Book'). Composed in Arabic, the book was completed in c. 1873 whilst Bahá'u'lláh was still in the city of Akka. It was supplemented by various later writings, and by Bahá'u'lláh's replies to a series of questions to explicate legal points posed by one of his secretaries, Zaynu'l-Muqarrabín (1818–1903), an eminent Iranian Baha'i cleric and an expert in Islamic law.[21] Quite apart from its literary importance as part of Bahá'u'lláh's oeuvre, the *Aqdas* and its supplementary texts also had major symbolic significance, of course, underlining Bahá'u'lláh's prophetic role by indicating that he was also a lawgiver as Muḥammad and Moses had been before him. The details of these laws are discussed elsewhere (see Chapter 13). It is of note that as stated by Bahá'u'lláh himself, the *Aqdas* was revealed *in response* to repeated requests from his followers for laws to follow.[22]

Social Reconstruction

The third major theme in Bahá'u'lláh's writings during the 'Syrian period' was his vision of the future and his delineation of the elements of social reconstruction that were needed to accomplish it. As he repeatedly stated, his message was for the whole human race, and his teachings were intended to guide the reconstruction of the world and promote the advancement of humanity as a whole. Specifically, he proclaimed the unity of the human race, and enjoined that the world's rulers should gather together to establish and uphold peace between their countries, converting weapons of war into instruments of reconstruction; exercise their divinely ordained responsibilities towards their citizens by promoting and upholding justice; choose a common universal language and script to be taught to all the world's children; and promote education and agriculture. He also expatiated on the importance of religion and the fear of God as means of preventing human wrong-doing and maintaining social order; praised constitutional monarchy as the ideal form of government (as it combined democracy with kingship); and stressed the importance of parenthood (see Chapter 11).

[21] On Zayn, see H. M. Balyuzi, *Eminent Bahá'ís in the Time of Bahá'u'lláh* (Oxford: George Ronald, 1985), pp. 274–6.
[22] Bahá'u'lláh, *Kitáb-i-Aqdas*, pp. 55–56.

Other Themes

In his final years, Bahá'u'lláh continued to proclaim his mission as the revealer of God's cause. Were anyone to judge Bahá'u'lláh fairly then they would recognize him as the Manifestation of God for the present age. He had fulfilled the prophecies regarding the promised one; he was the 'All-Knowing Physician' who had his finger on the pulse of mankind. The peoples of the world should drink from the springs of his knowledge and aid his Cause. In this day, knowledge of God could only be attained through recognition of him and attainment of the divine presence could only be reached through him. Through his potency, all hidden truths were now unveiled. He was the guiding light that illumined the way, and all should seek him and none other, lest they be bereft of all things. Invested with divine sovereignty, power, and glory, he was the lawgiver and redeemer of the entire human race, the 'Lord of all men'; the river of life; God's lamp, light, voice, testimony, and proof.[23] The blessedness of those who had accepted him contrasted with the utter loss of those who had rejected him. Opposition to God's cause would be unavailing.

He also continued to call upon the remaining Babis and their leaders to recognize him and to sorrow over the behaviour of Azal and his followers. The Babis should not to be misled by their prejudices and 'vain imaginings'. Those who had failed to recognize him had known the Báb only by name, and not through his own self or revelation.

Again, he counselled the Baha'is. They should promote the Baha'i Cause, both by teaching about the Faith to others and, most importantly, by trying to live praiseworthy lives. They should be tolerant of others, associating with the followers of other religions 'in a spirit of friendliness and fellowship'. All forms of religious violence – specifically the Islamic-Babi concept of holy war – were forbidden to them. They should also be exemplary subjects of the states in which they lived: loyal, honest and truthful in their behaviour towards their government and serving any king who protected their community. More generally, they should never allow themselves to become the cause of strife; flee from anything which caused strife or mischief – in a tumultuous world, they should be prudent in their conduct; and seek to serve the human race. If they truly recognized him, they would follow his law.

---

[23] Taherzadeh, *Revelation*, vol. 3, pp. 270–71; Bahá'u'lláh, *Tablets*, pp. 50, 169; Ruhiyyih Rabbani, *The Desire of the World: Material for the Contemplation of God and His Manifestation for this Day* (Oxford: George Ronald, 1982), pp. 175–86.

He also expounded on various religious and philosophical concepts as well as on practical topics such as health and medicine; addressed the London *Times* (the 'dawning place of news'), calling for the paper, and newspapers throughout the world, to concern themselves with the plight of the persecuted Baha'is in Iran; and stated that there would be no further Manifestation of God after him for at least a thousand years. More immediately, after his own demise, the Baha'is were directed to follow the one 'Whom God hath purposed' from amongst his sons.

Taking Bahá'u'lláh's writings as a whole, together with those of the various Baha'i authors who were working to elaborate them during his own lifetime (notably the recently converted cleric Abu'l-Faḍl Gulpáygání and Bahá'u'lláh's eldest son, 'Abbás ['Abdu'l-Bahá], see later and next chapter), it is evident that a profound transformation had been effected. Babi thought provided the main matrix for the developing ideas of the Baha'i Faith, but it was also changed into something new. The Babis had never transcended the world of sectarian Shi'ism, and many of their ideas are quite difficult of access to the modern reader. By contrast, from the Baghdad period onwards, Bahá'u'lláh was clearly intent to address a much wider audience, utilizing Sufi and Judeo-Christian themes, and presenting Babi beliefs in a style which could appeal directly to literate Iranian Muslims and which did not need to be mediated through clerical leaders. Later, particularly from the 1870s onwards, he presented a wide-ranging program of societal transformation on semi-Western lines (Western ideas of constitutionalism, a new international world order, etc.) whilst retaining important traditional cultural values, a combination which was to prove appealing to some of those who were concerned with the modernization of Iran.

7. THE FAMILY OF BAHÁ'U'LLÁH

As Bahá'u'lláh's sons came of age, they began to assist their father as auxiliary secretaries and in other tasks. Of particular importance was the role of the two eldest sons: 'Abbás – eventually better known by his self-selected title *'Abdu'l-Bahá* (the 'Servant of Bahá') (1844–1921), the son of Bahá'u'lláh's first wife, Ásíyih, and Muḥammad-'Alí (1853/4–1937), the son of the second wife, Fáṭimih. Bahá'u'lláh referred to his sons collectively as the *Aghṣán* (Ar. 'Branches'; sing. *ghuṣn*), 'Abbás being the 'Most Great [or Mighty] Branch' (*ghuṣn-i a'zam*), whilst Muḥammad-'Alí was the 'Greater [or Greatest] Branch' (*ghuṣn-i akbar*).

At the time of the family's departure from Baghdad (1863), 'Abbás was eighteen years old and taking increasing responsibility for the practical affairs of the family as well as acting as one of his father's secretaries. His organizational role increased with the move to Akka (1868) when he become effectively responsible for the day-to-day care of the whole exile community of Bahá'u'lláh's family and disciples and for its relations with Ottoman officialdom. As conditions stabilized in Akka, he was also able to engage in intellectual pursuits, and whilst he had never attended any school, he evidently read widely and now became well known and respected amongst Ottoman officials and reformers, including several of the provincial governors in their various places of exile and prominent figures such as Midhat Pasha and the Egyptian Shaykh Muhammad 'Abduh. He also found time to write two books, a 'Treatise on Civilization' (the *Risáli-yi madaniyyih*, 1875) and an historical narrative of early Babi and Baha'i history, '*A Traveller's Narrative*' (*Maqáli-yi shakhsí sayyáh*, c. 1886), both of which were published anonymously during his father's lifetime and became significant additions to the corpus of early Baha'i literature. During his lifetime, Bahá'u'lláh hinted that 'Abbás would be his successor as head of the Baha'i movement.

Muhammad-'Alí, who was about ten years younger than his brother, meanwhile kept close to his father, acting as a secretary, until sent briefly to India (in c. 1884 and c. 1891) to oversee the production of some of the early Baha'i literature that was published there. As a teenager in Edirne, he incurred Bahá'u'lláh's anger after apparently 'playing' at revealing verses and claiming an exalted spiritual station, an incident that later Baha'i apologists saw as evidence of pride and as prefiguring his subsequent rebellion against 'Abbás after their father's death.

After Bahá'u'lláh moved out of the city of Akka in 1877, his large family lived in two separate domiciles, with 'Abbás continuing to live in Akka, together with his mother, sister, wife, and daughters, whilst Bahá'u'lláh took his second and third wives and their children and spouses with him to Bahjí. In Akka, 'Abbás gained increasing acceptance as a local notable despite his origins as a political prisoner. Giving alms to the poor and regularly attending the local mosque, he came to be seen by the local population as a pious, albeit heterodox Muslim leader rather than as the son of the founder of a new religion. Significantly, despite considerable encouragement from male Baha'is of the time, 'Abbás refused to take a second wife (he had married a girl from a prominent Isfahani Baha'i merchant family in 1873),[24] and later disallowed Baha'is from contracting polygynous marriages.[25]

---

[24] This was Munírih Nahrí (1847–1938). The couple had four daughters who survived to adulthood as well as two sons and three daughters who died in childhood.

[25] Modern Baha'is understand the present Baha'i insistence on monogamy as being evolutionary in nature, 'Abbás ['Abdu'l-Bahá] leading the Baha'is away from what had hitherto been a deeply rooted cultural practice, and his early refusal to take a second wife subsequently denying later would-be

8. THE EMERGENCE OF THE BAHA'I FAITH, C. 1866–92

Following the split between Bahá'u'lláh and Ṣubḥ-i Azal in Edirne in 1866, the great majority of Babis seem to have quickly sided with Bahá'u'lláh, becoming his followers as Baha'is. A small but active group of Azali Babis also emerged and there were also some Babis who refused to join either faction. It is impossible to say with any certainly how large the developing Baha'i community was (perhaps fifty thousand to one hundred thousand persons by the end of the century), but as early as the 1870s, Western observers were beginning to comment on its activity and growth.[26] By the 1880s, the community was widespread and strongly established in most of Iran's cities and there were large local groups in several rural areas. New converts were being gained, including a number of clerics such as Mírzá Muhammad 'Abu'l-Faḍl' Gulpáygání (1844–1914) and Mírzá Muhammad-Hasan 'Adíb' (1848–1919), both of whom became prominent and influential Baha'i teachers.[27] Unlike the Babis, the Baha'is were also able to attract a significant numbers of new believers from two of Iran's religious minorities – the Jews and Zoroastrians (but significantly not amongst the Christians), thus decisively broadening the religious base of the Baha'i community.[28] Only the nomadic and semi-nomadic tribal populations (comprising at this point perhaps a third of the total population) remained largely outside the Baha'i orbit.

One indicator of the growth of the Baha'i community during this period was the recrudescence of persecution. At least forty-four Baha'is were killed for their beliefs between 1867 and 1892, sometimes in legal executions by

Baha'i polygynists any legitimation for multiple marriages. Given the Baha'i commitment to gender equality (see Chapter 11), some Western writers have expressed surprise at examples of early Baha'i polygyny, in particular Bahá'u'lláh himself having three wives. Baha'i apologists note that Bahá'u'lláh's marriages all took place early in his life before he had declared his mission and women's rights became part of Baha'i teachings; were in conformity with Islamic law; and reflected the social mores of the time (it was normal for upper-class Iranian men to have several wives, as with Bahá'u'lláh's father, Mírzá 'Abbás, who had four wives and three concubines), as well as the expectations of his own family.

[26] For a discussion, see Smith, 'A note on Babi and Baha'i numbers in Iran'. *Iranian Studies* 17 (1984): 295–301.

[27] On these two men, see Balyuzi, *Eminent Bahá'ís*, pp. 263–65; 272–3; and Barron Deems Harper, *Lights of Fortitude: Glimpses into the Lives of the Hands of the Cause of God* (Oxford: George Ronald, 1997), pp. 17–18. Several of Abu'l-Faḍl's books have been translated into English, see Abu'l-Faḍl Gulpáygání, *The Bahá'í Proofs*. Trans. Ali-Kuli Khan. 3rd ed. (Wilmette, IL: Baha'i Publishing Trust, 1983); *Letters and Essays, 1886–1913*. Trans. Juan R. I. Cole (Los Angeles, CA: Kalimát Press, 1985); and *Miracles and Metaphors*. Trans. Juan R. Cole (Los Angeles, CA: Kalimát Press, 1981).

[28] On the Zoroastrians, see Susan Stiles. 'Early Zoroastrian conversions to the Baha'i Faith in Yazd, Iran'. In *From Iran East and West*, ed. J .R. Cole and M. Momen (Los Angeles, CA: Kalimát Press, 1984), pp. 67–93.

city governors (for refusing to deny their faith), at others by mob action.[29] A mixture of motives seems to have been involved: Islamic clerics sometimes whipped up hatred for local Baha'is, but cupidity and the desire to seize the Baha'is' possessions or renege on debts was certainly involved in a number of cases. There were also numerous arrests and beatings of Baha'is, as well as the looting of property. Unlike their Babi predecessors, the Baha'is strictly avoided conflict and militancy (in obedience to Bahá'u'lláh's commands). Persecution stemmed from reactions to the Baha'is' rising prominence and not from any other provocation by the Baha'is. It was not general or systematic, many local governors clearly appreciating that the Baha'is were no threat to society and seeking to protect them from persecution.

It is likely that several different factors were responsible for the Baha'is' success. For the former Babis who made up the core of the movement, Bahá'u'lláh's refashioning of Babism may have been seen as a powerful reanimation of their original beliefs, enabling them to recover emotionally and intellectually from the shock of Babism's destruction by the state, but other elements of appeal can also be suggested, including the authority and spiritual power which many Iranians saw in Bahá'u'lláh writings; the details of his message, perhaps particularly the Baha'i reformist vision with its wide-ranging program of societal transformation on semi-Western lines combined with its retention of important traditional cultural values; and for some, the Baha'is' social acceptance of the members of minority groups and people of lower social rank in a society that was strongly hierarchical and had pervasive beliefs in the religious impurity and inferiority of religious minorities.[30]

Another aspect of Baha'i success was effective organization. Faced with the challenge of coordinating a widely spread movement in Iran from various places of exile in the Ottoman Empire, Bahá'u'lláh and his immediate assistants constructed a transnational courier system which enabled them to communicate on a fairly regular basis with the Baha'is in Iran and subsequently elsewhere. The Baha'is also arranged for the large-scale transcription of some of Bahá'u'lláh's writings so that they could be widely distributed across the local communities. From the early 1880s onwards, some Baha'i books also began to be printed in India enabling even readier access to key texts. As the conditions of Bahá'u'lláh's exile eased, carefully organized pilgrimages by Baha'is from Iran provided a further means of contact and

---

[29] Calculated from Moojan Momen (comp.), 'A chronology of some of the persecutions of the Bábís and Bahá'ís in Írán, 1844–1978'. *Bahá'í World, Vol. 18*, pp. 380–91.

[30] For a discussion of these questions, see Smith, *Babi and Baha'i Religions*, pp. 93–97.

direction, with Baha'i 'agents' in Beirut and other staging posts assisting them in their journeys. With the introduction of *Ḥuqúqu'lláh* payments in 1878, a certain regularization of funds available to support Baha'i activities occurred, the appointed trustees of the *Ḥuqúq* making regular journeys to visit Bahá'u'lláh and deliver contributions from the Baha'is.[31]

Again, within Iran itself, Baha'i organizational structures began to be developed, with Bahá'u'lláh recognized a number of prominent Baha'is (mostly former Islamic clerics) as the 'teachers' (*mubalighín*) of his Faith, according them particular respect and giving them an effective local leadership position on his behalf – effectively they were full-time employees of the Faith and were able to devote considerable energies to its propagation. In Tehran, a council of leading Baha'is was also established to act as an organizational hub.[32]

9. WIDER DIFFUSION

The Baha'i movement also began to be diffused more widely during this period, with Iranian Baha'is establishing themselves in various parts of the Ottoman Empire and Egypt and sometimes gaining a few local converts (including Sunni Muslim Turks, Arabs and Kurds and some Levantine Christians). An increasing number of Baha'is also joined the northern migration of their countrymen into Asiatic Russia (Turkestan and the Caucasus), a large and flourishing Baha'i community eventually forming in Ashkhabad (modern Ashgabat, the capital of Turkmenistan) just across the Iranian border. To their delight, the Baha'is in Russia found themselves protected from persecution by the authorities from the Shi'is amongst their fellow migrants (with the murder of a Baha'i by Shi'i fanatics in 1889 being dealt with harshly by the Russians, something that would have never happened in Iran).[33]

Groups were also established in British India and Burma, primarily as a result of the missionary journeys of the Iranian Baha'i teacher Jamál Effendi in the 1870s, who utilized his own Sufistic manner and interests to attract

---

[31] The *Ḥuqúqu'lláh* ('Right of God') is a voluntary tithe payable by adult Baha'is on a certain level of wealth. See CEBF, '*Ḥuqúqu'lláh*', loc. cit.

[32] See Juan R. I. Cole, 'The evolution of charismatic authority in the Bahá'í faith (1863–1921)'. In *Religion and Society in Qajar Iran*, Robert Gleave (ed.), (London and New York: RoutledgeCurzon, 2005).

[33] On Ashkhabad, see Anthony A. Lee, 'The rise of the Baha'i community of 'Ishqábád'. *Bahá'í Studies*, vol. 5 (January 1979), pp. 1–13; and Moojan Momen, 'The Baha'i community of Ashkhabad: Its social basis and historical importance'. In *Cultural Change and Continuity in Central Asia*, ed. Shirin Akiner (London: Kegan Paul, 1991), pp. 278–305.

a wide circle of sympathizers amongst Indian Muslims. Members of the Afnán trading clan resident in Bombay provided a focus for activities and a strong local community emerged there, including an increasing number of Iranian Zoroastrian immigrants. A strong local community also emerged in Burma (initially amongst Muslim traders), where Jamál's associate, Siyyid Mustafa Rumi, established himself. The inhabitants of one village also converted en masse.[34] Further east, Iranian Baha'i merchants (Afnáns) also settled in Shanghai, but no Baha'i group seems to have developed there at this time.

10. SOCIAL REFORMIST IDEAS WITHIN THE MOVEMENT

The social ideals which became such a prominent aspect of the Baha'i message also had an impact on the Baha'i community itself, particularly with the emphasis on the high value of education; the importance of working honestly and diligently; and the relatively equalitarian attitude towards women. No proper study has ever been made of the consequences, but it seems likely that these ideals had a cumulative effect within the Iranian Baha'i community, leading to a progressive process of internal socio-economic development which firmly linked the Baha'is with developing ideas of 'modernization' and as such became an important new element in attracting interest to the Faith.

A major contribution to this developing Baha'i vision of their mission was 'Abbás Effendi's ['Abdu'l-Bahá's] 'Treatise on Civilization' – now commonly known by its English title, *The Secret of Divine Civilization*, essentially a provocative essay on Iranian 'modernization'.[35] Composed in 1875, the work was lithographed in Bombay in 1882, thereafter gaining wide circulation in Iran. Published anonymously, it was not identified as a specifically Baha'i work – presumably so as to avoid prejudicing readers against its contents, but it is unlikely that its Baha'i origin was unknown.

The main thrust of 'Abdu'l-Bahá's argument was the urgent need for Iran to adopt reform measures on Western models. Ancient Iran had been a powerful empire, honoured for its culture and civilization. By contrast, the country was now in a wretched and degenerate state, pitied by others for its backwardness. Injustice and misgovernment had led to its decline. The Iranians should arise out of their torpor and resolve to transform their

---

[34] See Moojan Momen, 'Jamál Effendi and the early spread of the Bahá'í Faith in South Asia'. *Bahá'í Studies Review*, vol. 9 (1999–2000), pp. 47–80.
[35] 'Abdu'l-Bahá, *Secret of Divine Civilization.*

country and its institutions: promoting education, industry, commerce, technology, and the arts and sciences; establishing just laws and protecting the rights of individuals equally before the law; ending corruption and the absolute powers of local governors; strengthening relations with other countries, including the great powers and friendly governments; increasing trade linkages and developing national resources and infrastructure; and strengthening the army – such that its soldiers were well housed and fed, its officers well trained, and its armaments up-to-date. Other nations had once been as Iran was now, but through adopting such measures they had progressed. The rapid progress of Japan and the continuing backwardness and weakness of China indicated the contrast between those nations which modernized and those which did not.

In the context of nineteenth-century Iranian reformism, the book was unusual in that whilst forcefully advocating borrowing from the West, ʿAbduʾl-Bahá also emphasized the fundamental role of religion and spirituality in development: rejecting Western secularism as well as the religious bigotry he saw as so prevalent in Iran. He also provided a critique of religious resistance to reform. Thus, those Iranians who objected that such reforms involved copying the practices of non-Muslims and were hence un-Islamic ignored the fact that there were many Islamic precedents for the adoption of foreign practices and that many elements of European civilization were in any case derived from Islamic roots during the medieval period. Again, reforms such as the introduction of assemblies of consultation could be given Qurʾánic justification. For ʿAbduʾl-Bahá, as for his father, political, social, and economic reform and development were religious questions, and those who opposed reform would be answerable to God. Apart from its specifically Iranian context, the treatise can be seen as a general Bahaʾi prescription for developmental reform in any society.

In terms of practice, we know frustrating little. Evidently, at least some Iranian Bahaʾis had began to promote what we would now term socio-economic development projects during Baháʾuʾlláhʾs lifetime, but in the absence of any proper studies of these activities, we can not judge their extent or success. There was, for example, one northern village (Máhfurúzak in the province of Mázandarán), where the local Bahaʾi leaders established schools both for boys and for girls perhaps as early as the late 1870s, as well as forming a village cooperative and encouraging craft production.[36]

---

[36] Moojan Momen. ʿThe role of women in the Iranian Baháʾí community during the Qajar periodʾ. In *Religion and Society in Qajar Iran*, Robert Gleave (ed.), (London and New York: RoutledgeCurzon, 2005), pp. 346–69 (see pp. 357, 360).

This was probably exceptional, but it undoubtedly reflected an emerging consciousness within the Baha'i community, which was soon to see a variety of initiatives, most particularly in education.

The changing role of women in this emerging Baha'i community is also of interest, although again, it has as yet received little scholarly attention.[37] Given that Iran was a strongly patriarchal society – and remains so to the present day, Bahá'u'lláh's teachings represented a strong advocacy of female emancipation, and as early as the 1870s, European accounts referred to the greater freedom enjoyed by Iranian Baha'i women compared to their Muslim counterparts. We also know that many of Bahá'u'lláh's extensive circle of correspondents were women, and that there were several women who were prominent within the Baha'i community, at least one as a village leader and several as teachers of the Faith – primarily to other women.

[37] Both Cole (*Modernity*, pp. 163–87) and Momen ('The role of women') provide brief accounts, Cole's in the context of developing ideas on women's social role in the late-nineteenth-century Middle East.

Figure 1 ʿAbdu'l-Bahá. Copyright 2006, Baháʾí International Community.
http://media.bahai.org/.

CHAPTER 3

The Ministry of 'Abdu'l-Bahá, 1892–1921

I. THE SUCCESSION

Immediately following his father's death, 'Abbás – 'Abdu'l-Bahá – assumed leadership of the Baha'i religion. Bahá'u'lláh had made a formal and explicit appointment of 'Abdu'l-Bahá as his successor in a final testament, a document, written in Arabic in his own handwriting, which has come to be known as the *Book of the Covenant* (*Kitáb-i 'Ahd*). This testament was read to witnesses and to a large gathering of Baha'is shortly after Bahá'u'lláh's passing. In addition to naming 'Abdu'l-Bahá (by his title, the 'Most Great Branch') as his successor and directing that his family and the Afnán relatives of the Báb now turn to him, Bahá'u'lláh stated that his second surviving son, Mírzá Muhammad-'Alí was subordinate (and implicitly second in rank) to 'Abdu'l-Bahá; that whilst the Baha'is should love Bahá'u'lláh's sons (the *Aghṣán*) and respect the Afnán, the sons had no rights over the property of others;[1] and that the Aghṣán, the Afnán, and other members of Bahá'u'lláh's family were to fear God and perform praiseworthy deeds. He also stated that his purpose in revealing verses had been to establish concord and tranquillity, so that God's religion should not be made a cause of enmity; that rulership was entrusted to the kings, themselves the manifestations of divine power, whilst God's domain was the hearts of men; and that the rulers (*umará*) and learned (*'ulamá*) among the Baha'is were Bahá'u'lláh's trustees.

'Abdu'l-Bahá's succession elicited no surprise and was readily accepted by almost all Baha'is. Not only was it a written and unambiguous appointment, but it followed traditional custom in favouring the eldest son and reflected a widespread perception of 'Abdu'l-Bahá as a worthy successor who had already proved himself as a devoted and capable assistant to his father.

---

[1] This is in contrast to Islam, where descendants of Muhammad, the *sayyids*, may still be accorded special privileges.

Nevertheless, a family rebellion was soon in train, led by 'Abdu'l-Bahá's half-brother, Muḥammad-'Alí, who, whilst accepting the validity of his brother's appointment charged that he was exceeding his authorized powers and was claiming the right to amend their father's teachings. Focussed on the Baha'is in the Akka area, this rebellion was important in that it occurred within Bahá'u'lláh's own 'holy family', with his surviving wives and their families and some other followers conducting an at first covert and then open campaign to try to discredit 'Abdu'l-Bahá, whilst within the extended family, 'Abdu'l-Bahá himself retained the support of only his immediate relatives (his sister, wife and daughters), together with a surviving uncle and his family.

The rebellious family members were able to gain the support of two notable Baha'i leaders – Jamál Burújirdí in Iran and Ibrahim Kheiralla, the pioneer Baha'i teacher in the United States, but both men were soon rejected by the majority of the Baha'is.[2] The family also created severe problems for 'Abdu'l-Bahá with the Ottoman authorities, including the reimposition of close surveillance and semi-confinement in Akka (1901) and the appointment of two official commissions of enquiry, the second of which (1907–8), was expected to cause his further exile to the deserts of North Africa – an eventuality only prevented by the Young Turk revolution (1908), which led to the freeing of Ottoman political prisoners and the ending of the dangers which had faced 'Abdu'l-Bahá in Akka (a timely change which Baha'is would see as further evidence of divine intervention).

During these initial years of persistent difficulty and danger, 'Abdu'l-Bahá underlined his appeals to the mass of the Baha'is to remain united with his elaboration of the doctrine that there was a sacred covenant which ensured the preservation of Baha'i unity through obedience to the properly appointed leaders of the Faith. Those who broke this covenant, such as Muḥammad-'Ali and his associates, were denounced as 'Covenant-breakers'. 'Abdu'l-Bahá came to liken them to the carriers of a spiritual disease, eventually excommunicating them from the Faith and instructing the mass of the Baha'is to avoid associating with such people because of the danger of spiritual infection. It was also during this period that 'Abdu'l-Bahá made arrangements to try to ensure that the Faith would remain coordinated and protected from his opponents even if something were to happen to him, encouraging the formation of locally elected Baha'i councils in the various parts of the Baha'i world to superintend Baha'i activities as well as of several 'national' bodies to provide regional coordination, and

[2] CEBF, 'Jamál Burújirdí'; 'Kheiralla, Ibrahim George', loc. cit.

writing a will (kept secret until after his death), in which he appointed his eldest grandson, Shoghi Effendi – then still a child – to be his successor as 'Guardian' of the Faith; outlined the system to be employed for the election of the Universal House of Justice referred to by Bahá'u'lláh; and excluded Muḥammad-'Alí from the succession on account of his Covenant-breaking.

2. 'ABDU'L-BAHÁ'S WORK AND LEGACY

The 1908 Turkish revolution marked the beginning of an important new stage in 'Abdu'l-Bahá's life, giving him a freedom which he had not enjoyed since leaving Baghdad. Whilst still under surveillance in Akka, he had evidently determined to try to leave the old walled city as soon as it proved possible to do so, buying land across the bay on the flank of Mount Carmel above the developing port of Haifa and close to the German Temple Society colony. Here he had a house built, and from February 1907 began to transfer members of his family to this new abode. Higher up the mountain, at a site indicated by Bahá'u'lláh during one of several visits to the mountain, he also had constructed a shrine to house the remains of the Báb (1899–1907).[3] Now that he was free, he formally interred the Báb's remains (21 March 1909) and then transferred his own residence to Haifa (August 1910). Henceforth, Haifa became the administrative centre of the Faith as well as the site of the second holiest shrine in the Baha'i world (after the shrine of Bahá'u'lláh at Bahjí).

Taking further advantage of his new freedom of movement, 'Abdu'l-Bahá next determined to leave Palestine altogether for a while, moving suddenly and without warning to Egypt in about August 1910, and then, from September to December 1911, embarking on a three-month journey to visit the newly emergent Baha'i groups in England and France.[4] 'Abdu'l-Bahá was now in his late sixties and far from well, but after resting for the winter in Egypt, he made a longer and very arduous second journey to visit the Western Baha'is (March 1912–June 1913). After eight months of extensive travelling in the United States and Canada, during which he visited thirty-eight cities, he returned to Europe, where he visited Britain, France, Germany, and Austria-Hungary. He returned to Egypt (June 1913) and to Haifa (December) in a state of exhaustion.

---

[3] After the Báb's execution, his remains were taken by his followers and kept in a succession of hiding places in Iran until 'Abdu'l-Bahá instructed for them to be secretly transported to Akka.

[4] For the itinerary of 'Abdu'l-Bahá's journeys to Europe and North America, see CEBF, p. 17.

Less than a year after 'Abdu'l-Bahá's return to Haifa, World War I began (August 1914) preventing any further travel and leading to new threats against 'Abdu'l-Bahá's life from the new governor of Syria, Jamal Pasha. This danger ended with the collapse of Ottoman rule in Palestine in 1918. The war years and their immediate aftermath also brought famine to the region, 'Abdu'l-Bahá averting local catastrophe through the supply of grain stocks from Baha'i farms in the Jordan valley. He also gained the respect of the newly established British authorities who secured him the award of a knighthood (1920). The post-war years were spent attending to the work of directing the affairs of the Faith. In addition to being a prominent and widely respected local notable, 'Abdu'l-Bahá was now clearly recognized as the head of an international religious movement. He died peacefully on 28 November 1921, his funeral being marked by the great number and religious diversity of its mourners. He was interred beneath one of the rooms in the shrine of the Báb. 'Abdu'l-Bahá was survived by his sister, wife and daughters and their families, Shoghi Effendi succeeding him as head of the Faith.

'Abdu'l-Bahá's legacy for the Baha'i faith is multi-faceted. A strong and effective leader, he shepherded the Baha'is through the potentially difficult period following the death of Bahá'u'lláh. All new religious movements are likely to be challenged by the loss of their original prophet and founder and the consequent danger of schism and doctrinal drift. In this context, 'Abdu'l-Bahá was able to maintain the movement's unity and doctrinal focus despite the very real threats posed by his half-brother's attacks. This achievement is all the more remarkable because the period of 'Abdu'l-Bahá's leadership was also one of significant Baha'i expansion beyond its original geographical and cultural home. For both old and new Baha'is, 'Abdu'l-Bahá represented a powerful charismatic focus for their faith, an emotional bond reinforced by the doctrine of the divine Covenant and (for a tiny minority), the reality of expulsion from the Faith as 'Covenant-breakers'.

Organizationally, 'Abdu'l-Bahá both encouraged and honoured individual Baha'is of capacity in their work to promote the Faith whilst simultaneously working for the development of systems of locally elected councils and various 'national' bodies to provide the Baha'is with a means of coordinating their activities and dealing with their problems without having to refer everything to him. Given that the Faith was now developing into a genuinely international religion with followers scattered across the world, this was a crucial step.

Doctrinally, 'Abdu'l-Bahá's role was both largely conservative and significantly innovative. Accepted by the Baha'is as the authoritative interpreter of his father's writings, he was able to both reinforce Bahá'u'lláh's teachings, whilst also addressing issues which had not been central or not been addressed in his father's writings. This innovative aspect was particularly important in terms of the expansion of the Faith to the West and its response to Christian and social questions of the day.

In matters of practice, 'Abdu'l-Bahá also spoke authoritatively on matters of Baha'i law, as in his effective banning of Baha'i polygyny. More significantly, perhaps, he provided the Baha'is with what they saw as an exemplary pattern of life. However Baha'is might understand his spiritual 'station', 'Abdu'l-Bahá was not Bahá'u'lláh. If many Baha'is had seen Bahá'u'lláh in unapproachable, God-like terms, barely daring to look at him because of the awe they felt, 'Abdu'l-Bahá by contrast was an approachable and more human figure who yet still embodied something of the divine, and as such showed the Baha'is how they should try to live.

Finally, in addition to effectively coordinating the Baha'i movement during its first real moment of international expansion, 'Abdu'l-Bahá was able to guide the Iranian Baha'is through the difficult and politically disturbed period marking what proved to be the approaching end of the Qájár era.

3. 'ABDU'L-BAHÁ AND THE BAHA'IS OF THE EAST

In the Middle East, 'Abdu'l-Bahá's period of leadership coincided with a period of general political unrest, including the assassination of Násiri'd-dín Sháh by a radical reformist (1896) – initially, and erroneously, blamed on the 'Babis' – and constitutionalist revolutions in both Iran (1905–9) and the Ottoman Empire (1908). Iran, the home of most of the world's Baha'is at this time, remained weak, unstable and violent.

In these troubled times, the Iranian Baha'is remained active, and may well have attracted new followers, with the Baha'i combination of social reformist ideas and religious devotion representing a form of 'modernization' which sought to reshape traditional religious concerns. Certainly, many Baha'is were increasingly confident that they were on the verge of achieving a major breakthrough in gaining wider support at this time, and Baha'i activity continued to elicit persecution, with a total of at least 164 Baha'is killed for their faith between 1893 and 1921 (compared to perhaps only 44 in the 1867–92 period), in addition to numerous beatings, arrests and instances of torture and looting. Baha'i graves were also desecrated and corpses mutilated. Baha'is of Jewish and Zoroastrian background were amongst those attacked. The disorder of the Constitutionalist period was indicated by the heavy incidence of Baha'i martyrdoms in that period, with eighty-six killed in a nationwide series of attacks in 1903 and another twenty-eight killed in 1909.[5]

Within the Iranian Baha'i community, ideas of socio-economic development and female emancipation were now becoming stronger and were encouraged by 'Abdu'l-Bahá – furthering the process of internal socio-economic development within the community as well as firmly linking the Baha'is with the concept of 'modernization'. The details of these socio-economic trends have not yet been properly studied, but it is evident that existing moves towards female emancipation within the Baha'i community now increased, most obviously with the major efforts that began to be made towards the education of girls – a development of massive importance in a society in which most women were illiterate – with education classes and schools for girls being started by Baha'is in various parts of Iran, such that an increasing number of Baha'i women of all social classes gained at least a basic education.[6] Of particular significance was the establishment of the increasingly prestigious Tarbíyat School for girls in Tehran in 1911, which whilst run by the Baha'is was open to pupils of all religions and became a key institution in training the first generation of Iranian professional women. Also significant was the formation of a Baha'i committee for the advancement of women in Tehran (1909) and the arrival in Tehran of a small number of American Baha'i women to promote Baha'i education and health care in the capital (from 1909).[7]

We know less about changes in family and social life. Significantly, 'Abdu'l-Bahá forbade polygamy, and we also know that on occasion some Baha'i women had now started symbolically discarding their veils at Baha'i meetings, even allowing themselves to be photographed unveiled, albeit that 'Abdu'l-Bahá and later Shoghi Effendi advised caution on this matter, not wanting the Baha'is to attract unnecessary criticism.[8]

The need for caution was underlined by the increased persecution of the period, and it is clear that the identification of the Baha'is with aspects of

[5] Calculated from Momen, 'A chronology of some of the persecutions'.
[6] By the 1970s, when the majority of Iranian women were still illiterate, most Baha'i women could read and write, and literacy amongst those under forty was almost universal (*Bahá'í World*, vol. 15, p. 248).
[7] See R. Jackson Armstrong-Ingram, 'American Bahá'í women and the education of girls in Tehran, 1909–1934'. In *In Iran*, Peter Smith (ed.), (Los Angeles CA: Kalimát Press, 1986), pp. 181–210.
[8] Momen, 'The role of women', pp. 349–50.

social reform – particularly the emancipation of women – did have political consequences, in that it enabled traditionalists to charge that all reformists were 'Babis' (i.e. Baha'is), as during the Royalist siege of Tabriz in 1908–9, when the troops were told that the Constitutionalists were all Babis whom it was their religious duty to kill.[9]

The other major 'Eastern' communities also continued to develop at this time. In the Russian Caucasus and Turkestan, the Baha'i communities rapidly became some of the most important centres of Baha'i activity in the world, with that of Ashkhabad with several thousand Baha'is achieving particular prominence, as expressed by it being the site for the construction of the first Baha'i House of Worship in the world (1902–07).[10] In addition to their temple, the Ashkhabad Baha'is also established kindergartens, elementary schools, a clinic, libraries, a meeting hall, public reading-rooms, a printing press and a magazine – the fullest realization of the Baha'i ideal of combining religious and social institutions ever accomplished. Good relations were maintained with the Russian authorities, and after the first ('February') revolution of 1917, the Baha'is became free to teach their religion amongst the local Russian populations – with some success until the Soviet anti-religious policies of the 1920s took effect.

Again, the Baha'i groups in India and Burma remained active, with a continuing stream of Baha'i visitors from the Middle East, the beginning of production of Baha'i literature in Urdu, English, and Burmese, and the conversion of a few individuals from outside the Indian Muslim and Bombay Zoroastrian constituencies (notably Pritam Singh, a Sikh, and Narayanrao Vakil, a high-caste Hindu, both of whom were to become prominent leaders of the Indian Baha'i community).[11] A 'national' Baha'i teaching plan for India and Burma was launched in 1910, and in 1911, a national teaching council formed to coordinate activities. The first All-India Baha'i Convention was held in Bombay in 1920.

4. THE INTERNATIONALIZATION OF THE BAHA'I FAITH

During the lifetime of Bahá'u'lláh, the Baha'i movement had transcended its Babi origins, but despite the powerful universalistic vision of its founder, was still largely confined to the environing culture and society of the Islamic Middle East. This situation changed significantly under 'Abdu'l-Bahá's

---

[9] Momen, *Bábí and Bahá'í Religions*, p. 368.
[10] See Lee, 'Rise'; and Momen. 'The Baha'i community of Ashkhabad'.
[11] CEBF, 'Singh, Pritam'; Vakil. Narayanrao', loc. cit.

leadership, with Baha'i missionary endeavour leading to the formation
of Baha'i groups outside of the Middle East, notably in the United States of
America, but also in Europe and East Asia. This marked the emergence
of the Baha'i Faith as an international religious movement able to attract
followers from a wide range of religious and cultural backgrounds. Although
these new Baha'is, mostly Westerners, were not numerous, they were often
intensely active and had a major impact on the future development of the
religion.

Baha'i expansion in the West began in Chicago in 1894 through the
activities of Ibrahim G. Kheiralla (1849–1929), a recently converted Syrian
Christian who had just migrated to the United States.[12] Kheiralla developed his own eclectic mix of Baha'i and Christian ideas which, combined
with his energetic enthusiasm, attracted a sizable following of Americans in
several cities, including Phoebe Hearst, the millionaire philanthropist, who
financed the first group pilgrimage of Western Baha'is to visit 'Abdu'l-Bahá
in Akka (1898–9). After returning to the United States, Kheiralla became
disaffected, however, mostly, it would seem, because 'Abdu'l-Bahá refused
to give him the status of supreme leader of the American Baha'is. Kheiralla
then transferred his allegiance to Muḥammad-'Alí and a temporary schism
resulted. Whilst a small and dwindling minority of American Baha'is –
termed 'Behaists' – supported Kheiralla, the majority, some fifteen hundred or so, remained loyal to 'Abdu'l-Bahá, establishing close links to him
through the interchange of letters, more pilgrimage journeys to Akka, and
the dispatch of Baha'i teachers from the East to teach the new believers
proper Baha'i doctrine.

With the emergence of an indigenous leadership, the American Baha'is
became a forceful element in the world Baha'i movement, producing their
own Baha'i literature and in 1909, initiating the mammoth project of
constructing their own Baha'i temple (in the Chicago suburb of Wilmette).
They also developed the earliest Western Baha'i administrative bodies

---

[12] On early American Baha'i history, see Stockman. See also William P. Collins, 'Kenosha, 1893–1912:
History of an early Bahá'í community in the United States'. In *Studies in Bábí and Bahá'í History,
Vol. 1*, Moojan Momen (ed.), (Los Angeles CA: Kalimát Press, 1982), pp. 225–53; Richard Hollinger,
'Ibrahim George Kheiralla and the Bahá'í Faith in America'. In *From Iran East and West*, J. R.
Cole and M. Momen (ed.), (Los Angeles, CA: Kalimát Press, 1984), pp. 94–133; Peter Smith, 'The
American Baha'i community, 1894–1917: A preliminary survey'. In *Studies in Bábí and Bahá'í History,
Vol. 1*, Moojan Momen (ed.), (Los Angeles, CA: Kalimát Press, 1982), pp. 85–223. On developments
in Canada, see Will van den Hoonaard, *Origins*, and idem, 'The development and decline of an
early Bahá'í community: Saint John, New Brunswick, Canada, 1910–1925'. In *Community Histories*,
Richard Hollinger (ed.), (Los Angeles, CA: Kalimát Press, 1992), pp. 217–39.

and played the major role in the early introduction of the Faith to other countries. The Hearst pilgrimage had already led to the formation of small Baha'i groups in Paris and London, and more groups were now established in Hawaii, Canada, and Germany, and later in Brazil, Japan, and South Africa.[13]

In 1911–13, 'Abdu'l-Bahá visited the Baha'is of Europe and North America.[14] His journeys both enthused the Baha'is, giving them a wider vision of their faith and encouraging them to greater action, and attracted considerable public attention – including extensive sympathetic newspaper coverage; many meetings with eminent people (including churchmen such as Archdeacon Wilberforce and T. K. Cheyne in England; academics such as the comparative religionist J. Estlin Carpenter, David Starr Jordan of Stanford University, the orientalist Arminius Vambery, and the philosophers John Dewey and Henri Bergson; the suffragette leader Emmeline Pankhurst; Annie Besant, the president of the Theosophical Society; and the author Khalil Gibran); and addresses to members of sympathetic organizations such as peace societies and the Esperantists. Given his status as an Iranian exile and former Ottoman prisoner, the warm reception he received also had an impact in the East, particularly the respect he was accorded by both the Turkish Ambassador and the Iranian *chargé d'affaires* (at that time Ali-Kuli Khan, a Baha'i) in Washington, DC.

The new American and European Baha'is played a major role in reformulating the Baha'i teachings in Western and Christian terms: composing their own introductions to the Faith (often quoting extensively from the

[13] There is as yet little published material on early European Baha'i history. On Britain, see Philip R. Smith, 'The development and influence of the Bahá'í Administrative Order in Great Britain, 1914–50'. In *Community Histories*, R. Hollinger (ed.), (Los Angeles, CA: Kalimát Press, 1992), pp. 153–215; idem, 'What was a Bahá'í? Concerns of British Bahá'ís, 1900–1920'. In M. Momen (ed.), *Studies in Honor of the Late Hasan M. Balyuzi* (Los Angeles, CA: Kalimát Press, 1988), pp. 219–51; and Robert Weinberg, *Ethel Jenner Rosenberg: The Life and Times of England's Pioneer Worker* (Oxford: George Ronald, 1995). For the Pacific region, see Agnes B. Alexander, *Personal Recollections of a Baha'i Life in the Hawaiian Islands: Forty Years of the Baha'i Cause in Hawaii, 1902–1942* (Honolulu, HI: NSA of the Hawaiian Islands, 1974); idem, *History of the Baha'i Faith in Japan, 1914–1936* ([Tokyo:] Baha'i Publishing Trust, 1977); Barbara R. Sims (comp.), *Japan Will Turn Ablaze! Tablets of 'Abdu'l-Bahá, Letters of Shoghi Effendi, and Historical Notes About Japan* ([Tokyo:] Baha'i Publishing Trust, Japan, 1974); and idem (comp.), *Traces That Remain: A Pictorial History of the Early Days of the Baha'i Faith Among the Japanese* ([Tokyo:] Baha'i Publishing Trust, 1989).

[14] See Eric Hammond (comp.), *'Abdu'l-Bahá in London*. Rev. ed. (London: Bahá'í Publishing Trust, 1982); National Spiritual Assembly of the Baha'is of Canada (comp.), *'Abdu'l-Bahá in Canada* (Forest, Ontario: Forest Free Press, 1962); Agnes Parsons, *'Abdu'l-Bahá in America: Agnes Parson's Diary, April 11, 1912–November 11, 1912*. Ed. Richard Hollinger (Los Angeles, CA: Kalimát Press, 1996); and Allan L. Ward, *239 Days: 'Abdu'l-Bahá's Journey in America* (Wilmette, IL: Bahá'í Publishing Trust, 1979).

Bible), and for a while also continuing to use Christian devotional styles in some of their meetings.[15] In much of this they were supported by 'Abdu'l-Bahá, who took an active role in the process of reformulation: addressing Western religious and social concerns in Baha'i terms in his conversations with Western pilgrims, his letters to the Western Baha'is, and his public talks during his tours of Europe and America.[16] Given the ease with which Baha'i literature could be produced and distributed in the West, this led to a significant mass of publications, many of which dealt with Christian subjects and a range of metaphysical, social and economic issues. These included *Some Answered Questions* (1908), a compilation of talks delivered by 'Abdu'l-Bahá in Akka in response to questions posed by one of the American Baha'is,[17] and the establishment of a Baha'i magazine, *The Star of the West* (1910), which printed translations of many of 'Abdu'l-Bahá letters and talks. Separate volumes of compiled letters and talks were also published as well as 'pilgrim's notes' recording the conversations and experiences of Western Baha'is who were able to visit 'Abdu'l-Bahá in Akka and Haifa. A number of translations were also made of Bahá'u'lláh's writings.

In his public talks in the West, 'Abdu'l-Bahá frequently summarized the main points of Baha'i belief in a set of principles (9,10,11,12,14, the number varied), included the following: (i) Each individual should independently investigate truth, putting aside historic prejudices; (ii) All divine religions are one: expressions of a single reality, best expressed today by the 'universal' teachings of Bahá'u'lláh; (iii) Genuine religion is a powerful support for social stability, and without it crime and irreligion flourish; (iv) For all its present fruits, material civilization by itself is not sufficient to promote human progress: only when combined with 'divine civilization' and empowered by the holy spirit will it be the cause of genuine advance; (v) Religion should be the cause of love and unity. If a particular religion only produces hatred and division then it is no longer an expression of true religion and should be abandoned; (vi) Religion must be in conformity with science and reason, if it is not then it is only ignorant superstition; (vii) Bahá'u'lláh had come to establish the Most Great Peace; (viii) An international tribunal should be instituted to adjudicate disputes between nations; (ix) The whole human race is one, all human beings equally being

---

[15] R. Jackson Armstrong-Ingram, *Music, Devotions, and Mashriqu'l-Adhkár.*

[16] See 'Abdu'l-Bahá, *Paris Talks; Promulgation of Universal Peace;* and idem, *Tablets of Abdul Baha Abbas.* Comp. Albert R. Windust. 3 vols. (Chicago, IL: Bahai Publishing Society, 1909–16). See also Soraya Chamberlain (comp.), *Abdul Baha on Divine Philosophy* (Boston, MA: The Tudor Press, 1916).

[17] 'Abdu'l-Bahá, *Some Answered Questions.*

the children of God, differentiated only in terms of levels of education
and spiritual health; (x) Religious, racial, political, national and class prejudices are destructive and based on ignorance, they cause strife and impede
moral progress; (xi) Human progress can not occur as long as people are
still forced to struggle for their daily existence; (xii) Extremes of wealth
and more especially of poverty must be abolished so that all have access to
the necessities of life; (xiii) All individuals must be equal before the law,
and justice must be securely established in society; (xiv) Women are the
equals of men and should have equality of rights, particularly of educational
opportunity. Without such equality the progress of both sexes is impeded;
(xv) All children must receive an education; and (xvi) There should be an
international auxiliary language.[18]

During his Western tours, 'Abdu'l-Bahá also devoted much attention to
the subject of peace, warning that the unrest in the Balkans could easily
spark a trans-European war and making pubic appeals in the United States
for American action (as an 'honest broker') to try to calm the situation.
Later, critical of the Versailles peace settlement – which he predicted would
lead to a further war, he wrote a ' *Tablet to the Hague*' (1919), a letter to the
executive committee of the Central Organization for a Durable Peace, in
which he provided an overview of Baha'i social teachings and placed the
attainment of international peace within the context of the need for wider
political, economic, and cultural change, and stated that the newly created
League of Nations was too restricted to realize such an objective.[19]

Again, in the United States, 'Abdu'l-Bahá gave considerable attention
to the question of race relations, warning that, if not checked, American
racism would lead to bloodshed, and appealing to the races to seek the
points of partnership and agreement that existed between them. He also
sought to promote racial harmony amongst the Baha'is (most of the early
American Baha'is were white but there was also a significant minority of
African-American Baha'is from an early date), making what were then
extremely radical gestures by encouraging inter-racial marriage and placed
the leading black Baha'i in the seat-of-honour at a formal luncheon held
in Washington, DC.[20] In Europe and America, he also made a point of
visiting the poor, emphasizing what he saw as the social responsibilities of
the rich.

[18] CEBF, 'Baha'i principles', loc. cit.
[19] 'Abdu'l-Bahá, *Selections from the Writings of 'Abdu'l-Bahá*, pp. 296–308.
[20] See Gayle Morrison, *To Move the World: Louis G. Gregory and the Advancement of Racial Unity in America* (Wilmette, IL: Bahá'í Publishing Trust, 1982).

'Abdu'l-Bahá believed that the Americas had a special destiny as the place where God's light would be revealed. To this end, during the war years, he wrote the *Tablets of the Divine Plan* (1916–17), a series of fourteen letters addressed to the American and Canadian Baha'is in which he instructed them to teach the Faith systematically in those American states and Canadian provinces in which there were as yet few or no Baha'is; establish it throughout Latin America; and propagate it throughout the rest of the world 'as far as the islands of the Pacific'.[21] Long lists of territories and islands where the Baha'is should go were given, and particular significance was attached to teaching the Eskimos and other indigenous Americans, and to establishing the Faith in Alaska, Greenland, Mexico, Panama, and the Brazilian city of Bahia (Salvador) – this last because of its similarity to the name 'Baha'i'. In a war-weary world, people yearned for peace and would be receptive to the Baha'i message. Baha'i teachers should learn the various languages of the world so that they could teach its peoples and provide them with Baha'i literature which they could read. Firm in the Covenant and united amongst themselves, the Baha'i teachers should be completely dedicated and sanctified in pursuing their global mission.

Although ceremonially 'unveiled' at a special convention in New York in April 1919, at first only a few Baha'is responded to 'Abdu'l-Bahá vision of the 'Divine Plan', with Baha'is from the United States settling in Australia (1920) and Brazil (1921), and one Baha'i – Martha Root (1872–39) – embarking on an extended missionary journey around Latin America (1919) and devoting most of the rest of her life to a series of worldwide teaching trips.[22]

---

[21] 'Abdu'l-Bahá, *Tablets of the Divine Plan.*
[22] See Mabel R. Garis, *Martha Root: Lioness at the Threshold* (Wilmette, IL: Bahá'í Publishing Trust, 1983).

CHAPTER 4

The Guardianship of Shoghi Effendi, 1922–57

I. 'ABDU'L-BAHÁ'S WILL AND THE ESTABLISHMENT OF THE GUARDIANSHIP

Following the death of 'Abdu'l-Bahá, leadership of the Faith passed to his eldest grandson, Shoghi Effendi Rabbání (1897–1957), the eldest son of 'Abdu'l-Bahá's daughter, Ḍíyá'iyyih (Ziaiyyih) Khánum (d. 1951) and Mírzá Hádí Shírází Afnán (d. 1955), a great nephew of the Báb's first wife. Shoghi's appointment was made in his grandfather's will, and was only made public at the first reading of the will on 3 January 1922 – over a month after 'Abdu'l-Bahá's death. It evidently came as a surprise both to a number of eminent Baha'is and to Shoghi Effendi himself, who had no knowledge of his appointment until a few days before the reading of the will and had anticipated that 'Abdu'l-Bahá might instead have called for the election of the Universal House of Justice, a grand council referred to in the Baha'i writings. It will be noted that the *Will* implicitly set aside the original successorship established by Bahá'u'lláh in his *Book of the Covenant*, 'Abdu'l-Bahá specifically stating that Muḥammad-'Alí (the 'Centre of Sedition' and 'the focal Centre of Hate') had, by dint of his own actions, 'passed out from under the shadow of the Cause' and been 'cut off from the Holy Tree'.[1]

Although unexpected, Shoghi Effendi's appointment as 'Guardian of the Cause of God' (*Valí amru'lláh*, a title immediately reminiscent of the Shi'i Imáms) was readily accepted by the great majority of Baha'is. 'Abdu'l-Bahá's *Will* was quite explicit, Shoghi was the 'primal' and 'chosen' branch of the family of Bahá'u'lláh, and as Guardian, was to be the Centre of the Cause, the 'sign of God' on earth, and the 'expounder of the words of God'. All Baha'is should to turn to him and take the greatest care of him, showing 'their obedience, submissiveness and subordination' unto him.

---

[1] 'Abdu'l-Bahá, *Will and Testament*.

Rebellion against him would be rebellion against God. Given the force of this language, there was little direct challenge to Shoghi's leadership, other than from Muḥammad-ʿAlí and his partisans. Having been schooled by ʿAbduʾl-Bahá to regard 'firmness in the Covenant' as a fundamental requirement of faith, the mass of the Baha'is obediently acknowledged the appointment and rallied round Shoghi as a new focal centre.

In addition to appointing Shoghi Effendi as his immediate successor, ʿAbduʾl-Bahá's *Will* outlined a new system of Baha'i leadership that was to comprise a projected line of guardians of the Cause aided by a group of leading Baha'is (the 'Hands of the Cause'),[2] and the then as yet unelected Universal House of Justice. The line of guardians would follow on after Shoghi Effendi amongst the male descendants of Bahá'u'lláh (the *Aghsán*), ideally according to the principle of primogeniture. It was incumbent upon each guardian to appoint his successor during his own lifetime so that differences amongst the Baha'is would not arise after his death. In this, he should ensure that his successor had the necessary goodly character (that the child was the 'secret essence' of its sire). The qualities required of the appointed Guardians were: detachment from worldly things, purity, the fear of God, knowledge, wisdom and learning. All Baha'is were to be submissive and subordinate to them. The guardians would be aided by a body of eminent Baha'is whom they would appoint as Hands of the Cause, the Hands being charged with teaching and protecting the Faith and promoting learning. The Hands as a body were also to elect nine of their own number to work directly for the guardians and to approve each guardian's choice of successor.

As to the 'Universal' or 'Supreme' House of Justice, this had been referred to in the writings of Bahá'u'lláh as a body that would eventually assume authority within the Faith, in part to adjudicate on matters which had not already been determined by Bahá'u'lláh in his writings, its members ('Trustees') being assured of divine inspiration, and being empowered to enforce 'that which is agreeable to them'.[3] ʿAbduʾl-Bahá specified that the Supreme House of Justice should be elected by representatives of the various

---

[2] Bahá'u'lláh named four eminent Iranian Baha'is as 'Hands of the Cause of God' (*Ayádí amru'lláh*) (1887–c. 1890) and this group came to play a key role in the development of a national Baha'i organization in Iran as well as consolidating support for the succession of ʿAbduʾl-Bahá. ʿAbduʾl-Bahá himself only used the term as an honorific, posthumously designating a number of prominent Baha'is as Hands, but not appointing any further individuals to this rank, and it was not until the 1950s that further Hands were appointed in a functional role. Only one of the original Hands was still alive in 1921 (Ibn-i Aṣdaq (c. 1850–1928). See CEBF, 'Hands of the Cause of God', loc. cit.

[3] Bahá'u'lláh, *Tablets*, p. 68.

'national' Baha'i communities through their 'secondary Houses of Justice'. Protected by Bahá'u'lláh, it would be inspired by the Holy Spirit. It would be 'the source of all good and freed from all error', and whatever it decided would be 'of God'. In addition to their own duties, the successive guardians would be lifelong members and serve as head of the House. They were also authorized to expel any of its members who committed a sin 'injurious to the common weal'.

2. SHOGHI EFFENDI'S LEADERSHIP

At the time of his succession, Shoghi Effendi was still a young man of twenty-four (he had been named in the *Will* as 'Abdu'l-Bahá's successor when he was still a child). Born in Akka, Shoghi had been initially educated at home with siblings and maternal cousins, but was later sent to Catholic schools in Haifa and Beirut (which he disliked), and then to the Syrian Protestant College (the predecessor of the American University) in Beirut, gaining an Arts degree from the College in 1918. Having spent his previous Summer holidays as one of his grandfather's assistants, he then briefly became 'Abdu'l-Bahá's chief secretary, until in 1920, he went to England to study at Oxford University (Balliol College), taking courses in political science and economics, and seeking to perfect his English with the objective of being better able to translate Baha'i literature into that language. He was still in the midst of his studies when told of his grandfather's death, returning to Haifa on 29 December 1921.

Shoghi Effendi evidently found the first few years of his guardianship extremely difficult to bear. Shocked by his grandfather's death (to whom he seems to have been particularly attached – more so perhaps than to his parents), he was initially traumatized by the responsibilities of office and the enormous work load that went with it. Thus, several times during the 1920s he felt himself unable to cope with the burdens of office and took sudden and lengthy breaks to recuperate, often spending long periods of time walking in the Swiss Alps. Despite this, he had from the outset a clear vision of the future progress of the Cause, and was successfully able to communicate this to the Baha'is of the world, crucially defining many salient aspects of the Faith.

Shoghi Effendi's personal life was generally uneventful, and was largely subordinated to his work as guardian. The problem of securing capable and sufficient secretarial support to help with the ever-growing mass of correspondence was only really resolved in the 1950s, by which time Shoghi had long since adjusted to a pattern of unremitting hard work when in Haifa interspersed with Summer breaks in Europe (continuing his love of walking in the mountains) – or on two occasions lengthy journeys traversing Africa from south to north (1929, 1940). In 1937, he married Mary Maxwell (1910–2000), the only daughter of two North American Baha'is.[4] The couple had no children, but Rúḥiyyih Khánum, as Shoghi Effendi titled her, became his helpmate and constant companion until his passing. He died unexpectedly during a visit to London on 4 November 1957 following a bout of influenza and was buried there.

Western-educated and, apart from a black fez which he normally wore, Western in dress, Shoghi Effendi had a very different style of leadership from the venerable, patriarchal figure of 'Abdu'l-Bahá (leading to criticism from some members of his family). To the Baha'is, he signed his letters, 'your true brother', and referred to the institution of the guardianship rather than to his own personal role. Whilst 'Abdu'l-Bahá had acted as a local notable, even attending the mosque, Shoghi distanced himself from the local Palestinian notability and concentrated his energies on the worldwide direction of the Faith. Unlike 'Abdu'l-Bahá, he never journeyed to visit the Baha'is overseas after he became guardian, his primary contacts with the Baha'i world being through his extensive correspondence. He also met with all visiting Baha'is during their pilgrimages to Haifa, sharing his ideas with them, and in many instances using them as emissaries to reinforce his instructions to the Baha'is in the various national communities.

Shoghi Effendi wrote extensively in both Persian and English. For the most part, these writings were letters (over 17,500 letters by him or written on his behalf by a secretary collected so far), ranging from routine correspondence dealing with the activities of the Baha'is in various parts of the world to lengthy monographs addressing specific themes. He also wrote one book in English, *God Passes by* (1944), an interpretive history of the first century of Babi-Baha'i history, as well as a shorter Persian-language version, the *Lawḥ-i Qawn*; published a number of major translations of Baha'i texts and other works in English; prepared several compilations of Baha'i statistics and reference materials and a number of historical maps, and was extensively involved in editorial work for the *Bahá'í World* reference volumes recounting contemporary developments in the Faith.

Shoghi Effendi's major work as guardian can be summarized in terms of five areas of development: administration; definition and inspiration; history and 'metahistory'; 'planification' as an expansion strategy; and the 'Baha'i World Centre'. He also had to respond to specific situations which

---

[4] Harper, *Lights of Fortitude*, pp. 168–82.

affected the Baha'i Faith, including persecution in several parts of the world, limited opposition to his leadership from some of the Baha'is, and the creation of the state of Israel.

3. ADMINISTRATION

One of the major tasks which Shoghi Effendi set himself almost as soon as he became guardian was to build up what he came to term the 'Administrative Order'. Shortly after his own accession, he called together a group of prominent Baha'is from various countries to discuss the situation of the Faith, apparently considering the possibilities of calling for the election of the Universal House of Justice. With deliberation, however, he decided that the level of administrative development and maturity in the Baha'i world as a whole was as yet insufficient to take this step. Instead, he regularized and extended the system of Baha'i councils which under various names had already formed in some parts of the world. The basic elements were laid out in 1922–3.[5] All Baha'i groups in which there were at least nine adult (twenty-one years old and above) Baha'is were called upon to form their own '*local spiritual assemblies*', each assembly superintending all Baha'i activities in its locality. In all 'national' communities in which there were a sufficient number of Baha'is, '*national spiritual assemblies*' ('Abdu'l-Bahá's 'secondary Houses of Justice') were to be elected by a convention of locally elected delegates, and would have authority over national Baha'i activities, including the local assemblies under their jurisdiction.[6] The national assemblies were also to keep in regular contact with the Shoghi Effendi. Both local and national assemblies would have nine members and be reelected annually. They were to elect their own officers (chairman or president, vice-chairman, secretary, treasurer) and establish their own funds and the necessary committees to help them in their work of promoting Baha'i teaching endeavour; publishing; and organizing the community life of the Baha'is. There were subsequent elaborations of detail, but in its key aspects, the assembly system has not changed to the present day.

Other administrative developments from the 1920s included the delineation of specific requirements for voting membership of the Baha'i

---

[5] Key texts are two general letters to the Western Baha'is, dated 5 March 1922 and 12 March 1923 (Shoghi Effendi, *Bahá'í Administration*, pp. 17–25, 34–43).

[6] Seven national spiritual assemblies were initially established: Britain (with Ireland), Germany (with Austria), and India and Burma in 1923; Egypt (with the Sudan) in 1924; and Turkistan, the Caucasus, and the United States of America and Canada (transformed from the old executive committee of the Bahai Temple Unity) in 1925.

community; the establishment of national administrative centres, each overseen by the elected secretary of the relevant national spiritual assembly, the secretaryship in some cases becoming a full-time occupation; and the introduction of membership rolls, of enrolment cards to record professions of faith, and of credential cards or letters to validate membership. Certain regular community meetings (the Nineteen Day Feasts, see Chapter 15) were also strongly emphasized and came to include a period of consultation on local Baha'i activities and assembly directives. Wherever possible, the national and local assemblies secured some form of legal identity, enabling them to own property. The overall effects of these developments were to create a far more tightly organized network of Baha'i communities. Organization came to be a central element in Baha'i community life and was invested with spiritual and moral importance. Levels of administrative functioning varied of course, but by the 1930s, a generally efficient system was in place, the establishment of local and national spiritual assemblies coming to provide one of the major goals of Baha'i activity as well as a significant measure of Baha'i expansion plans from the 1930s onwards (see later).

There were no further significant administrative developments until the 1950s, by which time there had been a marked increase in the distribution and numbers of Baha'is worldwide, and the overall work of promoting and coordinating Baha'i activities had become correspondingly more complex. In this new context, Shoghi Effendi made important changes in administrative structure, creating two new major institutions and reanimating another.

The first of the new institutions was the International Bahá'í Council (1950–63).[7] Eventually consisting of nine members, the Council served to assist Shoghi Effendi with such tasks as Baha'i building work in Haifa, forging links with the Israeli authorities (Israel was established in 1948 and the Haifa-Akka area was incorporated into the new state) and functioning as an international Baha'i secretariat. It also investigated the possibilities of establishing a state-recognized Baha'i religious court to oversee matters of personal status (e.g. marriage and divorce).

Closely following on from the establishment of the International Council was the reanimation of the institution of the Hands of the Cause of God. The last of the Hands appointed by Bahá'u'lláh had died in 1928, and although empowered to appoint Hands of the Cause by the provisions of 'Abdu'l-Bahá's *Will*, Shoghi Effendi had not done so during the early years of his ministry, although he did name several individuals as Hands

---

[7] See CEBF, 'International Bahá'í Council', loc. cit.

(mostly posthumously) as a mark of respect.[8] This situation changed in 1951, with his first appointment of functioning Hands: an initial group of twelve (24 December 1951) being soon raised to nineteen (29 February 1952), and finally to twenty-seven in October 1957, shortly before Shoghi Effendi's death. Another five individuals were appointed between 1952 and 1957 to replace Hands who had died – in two cases, replacing parents (see Appendix). Five of the Hands also were or became members of the International Council, the remainder being assigned responsibilities in the continents in which they resided, notably to assist in the achievement of teaching plan goals, and later to protect the Faith by exercising vigilance for attacks from its external and internal enemies.

The third institution – a new one – was that of the Auxiliary Boards, whose members were to act as the 'deputies, assistants and advisors' to the Hands. These were to be appointed by the Hands on a continental level, with five Boards with a total of thirty-six members being authorized in April 1954 and a second set of Boards being authorized in October 1957 to deal specifically with issues relating to the protection of the Faith (i.e. safe-guarding the unity of the Baha'i community and responding to attacks by Covenant-breakers and non-Baha'i opponents), whilst the original Boards were assigned to focus on its propagation and expansion. Continental funds were established to support their work, and individual members became responsible for specific geographical areas, each area coming under the purview of both a member of the propagation and protection Boards.

4. INSPIRATION AND DEFINITION

Again from the beginning of his ministry, Shoghi Effendi clearly saw inspiration of the Baha'is as an important part of his work. This can be seen both in the frequent and repeated words of encouragement which are a characteristic feature of his correspondence, and in his translation work, whereby he sought to share important parts of the corpus of Baha'i writings with the Baha'is outside the Middle East.

Shoghi Effendi's primary objective in going to Oxford had been to perfect his English so as to be better able to translate Baha'i scriptures, but to his evident regret, he found that he had only limited time for this work after becoming guardian. Even so, he was still able to make a major contribution to the availability of good quality translations of some of Bahá'u'lláh's

---

[8] See CEBF, 'Hands of the Cause of God'. For short biographies of the Hands of the Cause, see Harper, *Lights of Fortitude*.

writings into English, including the *Hidden Words* (1929); *Kitáb-i-Íqán* (1931); and *Epistle to the Son of the Wolf* (1941), as well as two large compilations of shorter pieces: *Gleanings from the Writings of Bahá'u'lláh* (1935), and *Prayers and Meditations by Bahá'u'lláh* (1938). He also translated 'Abdu'l-Bahá's *Will and Testament* (in 1922, but only published in full in 1944 – it had initially circulated in typescript); and an important inspirational narrative of the Babis by Nabíl Zarandí, which appeared in English under the title *Dawn-breakers* (1932). Many other translated passages from Baha'i scripture peppered his letters.

The scriptural translations also had a wider impact, setting the style of modern English-language Baha'i writings with the use of a cultured 'elevated' language clearly modelled on that of older 'biblical' English. Several Anglophone Baha'is, most notably the Irishman George Townshend, served as Shoghi's literary advisors, reading and commenting on a number of his manuscripts.[9]

Beyond translation, Shoghi Effendi also played a major role in defining Baha'i doctrine. As he himself emphasized, 'Abdu'l-Bahá had conferred upon the guardians the function of interpreters of scripture so that they could 'reveal the purport and disclose the implications of the utterances of Bahá'u'lláh and of 'Abdu'l-Bahá'.[10] As Shoghi Effendi's interpretations were to be regarded as authoritative and binding they have been a primary element in the shaping of modern Baha'i belief, as in his lengthy letter, *The Dispensation of Bahá'u'lláh* (1934), in which he delineated the religious 'stations' of Bahá'u'lláh, the Báb, and 'Abdu'l-Bahá.[11]

Of necessity, Shoghi Effendi also had to make numerous decisions about matters of Baha'i practice, although in these instances, he often qualified his decisions by saying that they were provisional in nature, and that final statements on these matter would be made by the Universal House of Justice after it had been formed – that is, he had a strong sense of the limits of his own authority.

5. HISTORY AND 'METAHISTORY'

Another major aspect of Shoghi Effendi's work was to give the Baha'is a keener sense of their own history as a religious community and to develop

---

[9] Diana Lorice Malouf, *Unveiling the Hidden Words: The Norms Used by Shoghi Effendi in His Translation of the Hidden Words* (Oxford: George Ronald, 1997). On Townshend, see David Hofman, *George Townshend* (Oxford: George Ronald, 1983).

[10] Shoghi Effendi, *World Order*, p. 151.

[11] Shoghi Effendi, *World Order*, pp. 97–157; Smith, *The Babi and Baha'i Religions*, pp. 136–7.

a particular vision of the significance of that history, most notably in his own book *God Passes By* (1944), and in his translation of *The Dawn-Breakers* (1932). Both books were quite lengthy – over four hundred and over seven hundred pages respectively, and both were packed full of information and inspirational in intent, the later giving the Western Baha'is – who hitherto had been largely ignorant about their Babi predecessors – a vivid portrayal of the heroic acts and martyrdoms of the Babis, whilst the former provided them with an overall vision of the Babi and Baha'i religions as a single evolutionary development and of the Faith's onward progress in the face of opposition and tribulation.

In various of his writings, Shoghi Effendi also outlined the future 'World Order of Bahá'u'lláh' as a millennial vision of a unified and peaceful world; described the present as an age of 'Frustration' and 'Transition'; and referred to the processes of change that were tearing down the existing Old World Order and building up the new order that would replace it. In his *The Promised Day is Come* (1941), he focussed on the response of the rulers addressed by Bahá'u'lláh in his 'proclamation to the kings', and the sufferings and general decline of monarchical power which Shoghi Effendi attributed to their largely negative or non-committal responses.

6. 'PLANIFICATION'

Building on 'Abdu'l-Bahá's appeal to the Baha'is to develop a systematic and worldwide campaign of organized teaching in his *Tablets of the Divine Plan* (1916–17), Shoghi Effendi initially encouraged the North American Baha'is to achieve particular local goals in two 'Plans of Unified Action' (1926–8; 1931–c. 1933), before seeking to make expansion planning a regular part of Baha'i activity worldwide with a series of national plans (1937–53), which set each of the national Baha'i communities domestic expansion goals and began the process of establishing Baha'i groups and local assemblies in those countries and territories in Europe, Southeast Asia, and Africa in which there were few or no Baha'is.[12] The two-year 'Africa campaign' (1951–3) was of special note, in that it involved collaboration between several national assemblies, and was thus the forerunner of the international plans

---

[12] The first of the national plans was the first North American Seven Year Plan (1937–44). This was followed by plans for India and Burma (1938–44; January 1946–June 1950; September 1951–April 1953; the British Isles (1944–50; 1951–3); the United States and Canada (a second Seven Year Plan, 1946–53); Iran (October 1946–July 1950); Australia and New Zealand (1947–53); Iraq (1947–50); Egypt and the Sudan (1948–53); Germany and Austria (1948–53); Canada (1948–53); and Central America (1952–3).

to come. Also of particular significance was a four year plan specifically for Iranian Baha'i women, aiming for them to further their education and attain equality with men in Baha'i administrative work.[13]

The culmination of these national endeavours was the 'Ten Year Crusade' (1953–63), an elaborate and ambitious project which aimed to settle Baha'is in every significant territory and island group throughout the world and to enormously increase the total number of national and local assemblies, Baha'i centres, and the range of languages in which there was Baha'i literature. All twelve national spiritual assemblies formed by 1953 participated. The results surpassed expectations, with the beginning of massive growth in a number of communities (see Chapter 6).

These plans included continued work on the Wilmette House of Worship near Chicago (completion was delayed by financial problems, and it was not until May 1953 that the temple was finally dedicated for worship) and the initiation of work on three new Houses of Worship: Kampala, Uganda as the 'Mother Temple' for Africa; Sydney, Australia for the Pacific; and Frankfurt, Germany for Europe, the first two of which were both opened for worship during the Crusade (in 1961). The first temple dependency outside of Ashkhabad was also constructed – a home for the aged at Wilmette (1959).

Shoghi Effendi also organized a series of international Baha'i conferences to bring together Baha'is on different continents to discuss the needs of the Faith and to help create a common vision for activity. The first of these were held in 1953 under his overall direction in Kampala (for Africa); Chicago (for the Americas); New Delhi (for Asia and Australasia); and Stockholm (for Europe). Each conference was attended by Hands of the Cause (one of whom acted as Shoghi Effendi's representative at the conference) and brought together Baha'is and national spiritual assembly members for its region and beyond. Beyond discussing plan objectives, the conferences functioned to inspire and encourage participants and to stimulate a wider and more-global sense of Baha'i identity. In accordance with Shoghi Effendi's plans, a further set of five conferences were held in 1958 after his death (at Kampala; Wilmette; Singapore (as replacement for a proposed conference in Jakarta); Sydney, Australia; and Frankfurt, Germany), and in 1963, the Baha'is held their first World Congress (in London, as Shoghi Effendi's original chosen venue of Baghdad proved impractical).

[13] *Bahá'í World*, vol. 12, p. 65.

7. THE 'BAHA'I WORLD CENTRE'

There was considerable development of the Faith's spiritual-administrative centres during Shoghi Effendi's ministry, involving a number of separate projects. Thus, in the Akka area, he obtained possession of the mansion of Bahá'u'lláh at Bahjí in 1929 (hitherto it had been in the hands of Muḥammad-'Alí and his supporters), and began an extensive renovation,

Figure 2 Shrine of the Báb, Haifa, Israel. Copyright 2006, Bahá'í International Community. http://media.bahai.org/

furnishing it as a Baha'i museum and place of pilgrimage (by 1932). Later, during the 1950s, he secured legal possession of the surrounding lands and created a number of gardens and installed ornamental lighting. He also renovated the house in which Bahá'u'lláh had spent most of his years in Akka and obtained possession of other sites associated with Bahá'u'lláh. In Haifa, he extended the shrine complex in which the Báb and 'Abdu'l-Bahá were interred (1929), and had an elaborate golden-domed superstructure constructed to envelop the shrine (1948–53). He also purchased the surrounding lands and created gardens, again with ornamental lighting. Above the shrine, he constructed a series of monuments to the various members of 'Abdu'l-Bahá's family (the graves of 'Abdu'l-Bahá's sister [1932] and wife [1938], and later the remains of his mother and brother, which Shoghi Effendi had moved from Akka [1939]), as well as a Parthenon-like International Archives Building to house and display Baha'i relics and scriptures (1955–57), which together with the Shrine of the Báb and the gardens became a major Haifa landmark.[14]

8. OPPOSITION AND COVENANT

Like 'Abdu'l-Bahá before him, Shoghi Effendi emphasized the importance of the Covenant doctrine. Instances of opposition to his leadership were relatively limited in extent, however: 'Abdu'l-Bahá's insistence on firmness in the Covenant had become a firmly-rooted part of Baha'i belief and his appointment of Shoghi Effendi as guardian had been strong and unambiguous.

Thus, the only initial challenge to Shoghi's succession came from his great-uncle, Muḥammad-'Alí, who argued that by the terms of Bahá'u'lláh's will, he should be the successor, an argument which seems to have been unconvincing to everyone apart from his existing partisans. Nevertheless, Muḥammad-'Alí and his associates created a succession of problems for Shoghi Effendi in relationship to disputed legal claims to Baha'i property in Palestine during the early years of the British Mandate.

As Shoghi Effendi's policies and leadership style became established, there was some limited movement of opposition. This was most evident in the West, where some Baha'is were unhappy with the increasing emphasis that was being given to the system of Baha'i administration. In the mid-1920s, this discontent was given voice by Ruth White, an American Baha'i, who

---

[14] These developments are described in Ugo Giachery, *Shoghi Effendi*, and David S. Ruhe, *Door of Hope: A Century of the Bahá'í Faith in the Holy Land* (Oxford: George Ronald, 1983).

insisted that 'Abdu'l-Bahá had said that the Baha'i religion was an inclusive movement that could never be organized, and subsequently (from 1927) that 'Abdu'l-Bahá's *Will* was a forgery – a claim rejected even by opponents of Shoghi Effendi who were familiar with 'Abdu'l-Bahá's writings. Few Baha'is followed White into outright opposition, however, apart from in Germany, where Wilhelm Herrigal (d. 1932), one of the earliest and most prominent of the believers, established a 'Bahai World Union' inspired by her ideas. The group remained small, but reorganized after World War II, forming a 'World Union for Universal Religion and Universal Peace' for a while.[15]

A more subtle challenge came from Ahmad Sohrab (c.1893–1958), one of 'Abdu'l-Bahá's former secretaries and English-language interpreters who had settled in the United States after World War I. Whilst accepting the legitimacy of Shoghi Effendi's appointment as Guardian, Sohrab did not agree with his policy of putting all Baha'i activities under the overall control of the spiritual assemblies, and in 1929, with the help of Julie (Lewis Stuyvesant) Chanler (1882–1961), established the New History Society in New York City to propagate the Baha'i teachings. A confrontation with the American National Spiritual Assembly ensued when Sohrab refused to place this venture under the control of the local assembly, and Sohrab and Chanler were excommunicated (1930), Sohrab subsequently penning a series of books highly critical of Shoghi's leadership. Sohrab and Chanler also started a youth organization, the Caravan of East and West (1930), which developed into a worldwide pen-pal club (both organizations are now defunct).[16]

Amongst Eastern Baha'is, challenges mostly came from a few disaffected individuals, most prominently the eminent Iranian Baha'i teacher and historian, Ávárih (Mírzá 'Abdu'l-Husayn Taftí, 1873–1953). Frustrated in his apparent desire for a position of leadership (1924), he withdrew from the Faith and later wrote extensively to try to discredit it.[17] Although damaging to the Baha'is' public image in Iran, such attacks seem to have had little effect within the Baha'i community. Far more serious was a conflict which

---

[15] A polemical attack on '*Political Shoghism*' by Hermann Zimmer, one of these 'Free Bahais', was translated and published in English in 1973 and widely distributed to libraries throughout the world. White herself eventually became a follower of Meher Baba. Shoghi Effendi's first two *World Order* letters are partly a response to her attacks. See Loni Bramson-Lerche, 'Some aspects of the establishment of the Guardianship'. In *Studies in Honor of the Late Hasan M. Balyuzi*, Moojan Momen (ed.), (Los Angeles, CA: Kalimát Press, 1988), pp. 253–93; and Adib Taherzadeh, *The Covenant of Bahá'u'lláh* (Oxford: George Ronald, 1992), pp. 347–49.

[16] Smith, *Babi and Baha'i Religions*, pp. 124–5.

[17] See CEBF, 'Ávárih', loc. cit.

developed during the 1940s between Shoghi Effendi and members of his family (his siblings, cousins, and aunts), in large part because of their contacts, including marriage, with Covenant-breaking members of Bahá'u'lláh's extended family.[18] Unlike many of his relatives, Shoghi took the view that Abdu'l-Bahá's instructions regarding the shunning of Covenant-breakers should be followed without any compromise and consequently excommunicated most of his immediate relatives when they refused to cut their ties with the earlier families of Covenant-breakers. As those expelled included his surviving brother and male cousins, the eventual consequence was that there were no eligible descendants of Bahá'u'lláh who could succeed Shoghi as guardian.

9. 'INTERREGNUM': THE CUSTODIANSHIP OF THE HANDS OF THE CAUSE, 1957–63

Shoghi Effendi's death (4 November 1957) was entirely unexpected and came as a terrible shock to the Baha'is. After his funeral in London, the Hands gathered together in Haifa (18–25 November). To their distress, they discovered that Shoghi had not left a will nor left any instructions as to what to do regarding the future leadership of the Faith. What was to be done? After considerable discussion, they decided that they themselves had no choice but to assume headship, there being neither an appointed successor nor any possible candidate (Shoghi having declared all of his immediate family to be Covenant-breakers). The Hands' decision was taken on the basis of a reference to them as the 'Chief Stewards' of the Faith in Shoghi Effendi's last general letter to the Baha'is (October 1957).[19] Accordingly, the Hands appointed nine of their number to serve as 'Custodians' in Haifa to coordinate activities and oversee the continued progress of Shoghi Effendi's plans. Power was assumed on a temporary basis until such time as the 'Universal House of Justice' (*baytu'l-'adl-ia'zam*) referred to in Baha'i scripture could be elected. All twenty-six Hands in Haifa signed a declaration to this effect (25 November), the one missing Hand – the American Corinne True, then aged 96 and the eldest of the group, who had been unable to attend – sending an affidavit notifying her consent.[20]

---

[18] Following the norms of many upper-class Middle Eastern families, six out of Shoghi Effendi's twelve siblings and maternal cousins married relatives – four of these marriages being with descendants of Bahá'u'lláh's daughter Furúghiyyih who had been declared Covenant-breakers. See CEBF, 'Núrí family'; 'Rúhí Afnán', loc. cit.

[19] Shoghi Effendi, *Messages to the Bahá'í World*, p. 127.

[20] For the major documents for this period, see Universal House of Justice, *Ministry of the Custodians*, pp. 28–31.

The Hands' move received the support of the Baha'is worldwide. Meeting in annual conclave, the Hands determined that the best response to the absence of a guardian was the rapid establishment of the Universal House of Justice, a body guaranteed divine guidance and protection by 'Abdu'l-Bahá in his *Will.* To this end, in November 1959, they called for the International Council to become an elected body in 1961, and for the House itself to be elected in April 1963. Other than this, the Hands main concern was to oversee the completion of Shoghi Effendi's Global Crusade.

For the most part, this policy attracted the enthusiastic support of the Baha'is, despite the growing opposition of the veteran American believer, Charles Mason Remey (1874–1974), one of the first Hands to be appointed and President of the existing International Council.[21] Remey, who had signed the original statement by the Hands in 1957, refused to sign the 1959 announcement, and a few months later began to circulate the claim that he himself should be recognized as the second guardian (1960).

Remey's argument was that because the International Council was the precursor of the Universal House of Justice – over which successive guardians were expected to preside – his own appointment as president of the Council meant that he had been covertly designated as Shoghi Effendi's successor. This view was immediately rejected by the other Hands, who noted both that there was no letter of appointment, and that Remey could not have been eligible anyway as he was not a descendant of Bahá'u'lláh. As Remey persisted in his claims and began to gather a small following (including members of the French Baha'i national assembly), his status as a Hand of the Cause was suspended, and in July 1960, he was declared a Covenant-breaker and expelled from the Faith, as were those of his followers who continued to follow him. These 'Baha'is under the Hereditary Guardianship', as they came to call themselves, were few in number, however, and as Remey himself noted 'almost the entire Baha'i world' rejected his claim.[22]

---

[21] CEBF, 'Remey, Charles Mason', loc. cit.; Harper, *Lights of Fortitude*, pp. 287–306.

[22] Vernon Elvin Johnson, 'An Historical Analysis of Critical Transformations in the Evolution of the Baha'i World Faith', Ph.D. dissertation (Baylor University, Texas, 1974), p. 353.

Figure 3 The Seat of the Universal House of Justice, Haifa, Israel. Copyright 2006, Bahá'í
International Community. http://media.bahai.org/

CHAPTER 5

The Universal House of Justice, 1963–

I. THE ESTABLISHMENT OF THE UNIVERSAL HOUSE OF JUSTICE

Bahá'u'lláh had referred to the future establishment of a House of Justice (*bayu'l-'adl*) which would assume authority over his religion, its members taking counsel regarding matters which had not already been determined by Bahá'u'lláh in his writings, and enforcing 'that which is agreeable to them'. Its members ('Trustees') were assured of divine inspiration. Again, 'Abdu'l-Bahá had emphasized the authority of the future 'Universal' or 'Supreme' House of Justice, stating that it would be under Bahá'u'lláh's protection, and inspired by the Holy Spirit. Whatever it decided would be 'of God'. It would be 'the source of all good and freed from all error', and obedience to it would be obligatory. Opposition to it would be opposition to God.[1]

The Hands decision to call for the election of the Universal House of Justice thus provided a direct way of rapidly ending the crisis caused by Shoghi Effendi's death and the absence of a directly appointed successor. Its formation would provide the Baha'is with a new divinely guided centre. The election of the Universal House of Justice on 21 April 1963 by the members of the 56 Baha'i national assemblies then extant, in response to the summons of the Hands of the Cause and in accordance with the provisions of 'Abdu'l-Bahá's *Will and Testament* was therefore met with such great delight and relief throughout the Baha'i world that the continued activities of Mason Remey and his followers soon faded into insignificance for most Baha'is.[2]

Since then, the Universal House of Justice has acted as the supreme Baha'i administrative body. In the absence of a living guardian, it has also assumed

---

[1] CEBF, 'Universal House of Justice', loc. cit.
[2] Remey's followers soon split into a number of rival groups. See CEBF, 'Remeyite groups and orga-nizations', loc. cit. Most of the key members were Americans.

permanent headship of the Faith (in October 1963, it declared that it would be impossible to appoint further guardians). As with Shoghi Effendi, the House's guidance has taken the form of letters to Baha'i communities, institutions and individuals, and sometimes to the entire Baha'i world. Several volumes of these letters are now available, and many other letters are found in Baha'i periodicals. The letters are regarded as divinely empowered.

Various aspects of the House's functioning were outlined in its Constitution (adopted on 26 November 1972): its membership was to consist of nine men[3] elected from the Baha'i community by secret ballot by the members of all national spiritual assemblies in the world, normally at an international convention.[4] The election is held every five years. The House has no officers, but otherwise conducts its affairs much as spiritual assemblies do. To date, a total of twenty-one men have served as members of the House (see Appendix). The membership has been highly stable, the only changes of membership having occurred as a result of death or retirement. The last of the original nine members elected in 1963 retired in 2005. Although greatly respected, the members of the House do not have any special status or authority within the Faith as individuals. It is as a collectivity that the House exercises its leadership. The members clearly cultivate a public ethos of individual self-effacement.

2. ADMINISTRATION

The main developments in Baha'i administration since 1963 have been the House's ruling that there was no longer a way to appoint further Hands of the Cause (November 1964) and its creation of two new 'institutions of the learned' to continue the Hands' functions into the future – the Continental Boards of Counsellors (1968) and an International Teaching Centre (1973), respectively parallelling many of the responsibilities of the Hands in the various continents and those working at the Baha'i World Centre (Chapter 14). The Hands were actively involved in the establishment of both institutions, the creation of which freed them from many routine

---

[3] The guardianship and the Universal House of Justice are the only two Baha'i institutions which are 'gender-specific', being confined only to men. All other Baha'i institutions (local and national spiritual assemblies, Continental Counsellors, Auxiliary Board members, etc.) may include people of either sex.

[4] The Constitution of the Universal House of Justice allows for the election to be held by postal ballot in emergency situations. So far, this provision has only been utilized once – for the election of 2003, when conditions in the Middle East were deemed to be dangerously unstable. See Universal House of Justice, *Constitution*.

responsibilities so that they were able to concentrate their energies on more general tasks.

Other developments have included enormous increases in the number of Auxiliary Board members (now to almost one thousand), and the creation of a new institution of assistants to the Board members; of sub-national regional Baha'i councils in several countries to take over some of the functions of the national spiritual assemblies – effectively decentralizing aspects of the national assemblies' work; and of various specialist committees and agencies, notably Continental Pioneer Committees (1965) to organize the movement of pioneers, the various bodies linked to the Baha'i International Community, and a network of *Ḥuqúqu'lláh* deputies and representatives.

3. EXPANSION AND DEVELOPMENT PLANS

Since its establishment, the Universal House of Justice has continued the pattern set by the Ten Year Crusade, with a total of nine international plans to date: the Nine (1964–73), [first] Five (1974–9), Seven (1979–86), Six (1986–92), Three (1993–6), and Four (1996–2000) Year Plans, a Twelve Month Plan (2000–01), and then two more Five Year Plans (2001–06, 2006–11). There was also a subsidiary two-year plan (1990–92) to coordinate Baha'i activity in Eastern Europe and the former Soviet Union under the new conditions of religious freedom which followed the collapse of the Communist regimes there.

As with the Ten Year Crusade, a major part of the House of Justice's plans has consisted of various 'expansion goals', calling for increases in the numbers of local spiritual assemblies, localities in which Baha'is reside, Baha'i publishing trusts and properties, and the like. In addition there have been calls for the despatch of pioneers and travel teachers; major construction projects (temples and Baha'i World Centre projects); the organization of conferences, as well as more qualitative goals (below).

Of the temples, the House of Justice first oversaw the final completion of the Baha'i House of Worship at Frankfurt that was begun during the Ten Year Crusade (dedicated for worship in 1964), and then the construction of three new temples – in Panama City (1972); Apia, Samoa (1984); and New Delhi, India (1986) – raising the world total to seven. An eighth temple is presently under construction in Santiago, Chile. Hopes that the Baha'is might eventually recover the Ashkhabad temple ended in 1963, when it was finally demolished by the Soviet authorities (it had been severely damaged by an earthquake in 1948 and had thereafter deteriorated). A home for the aged was also built as the first dependency of the Frankfurt temple. Like the Wilmette temple, the Indian House of Worship is relatively large (seating capacity twelve hundred, compared to four to six hundred in the smaller temples), and with its unusual design – it appears as a giant opening lotus flower – has attracted considerable public interest.[5]

Following the example of Shoghi Effendi, the Universal House of Justice also organized several sets of international conferences (a total of twenty-nine between 1967 and 1982) to further focus attention on plan goals, galvanize activity and increase the sense of global solidarity amongst the Baha'is.[6] The House also organized a second World Congress in New York in 1992 – with twenty-seven thousand participants; the first mass pilgrimage to the Baha'i World Centre in 1968 following a conference in Palermo; and what were effectively the second and third mass pilgrimages in 1992 and 2001, each with some three thousand Baha'is gathered in Haifa to respectively commemorate the centenary of Bahá'u'lláh's passing and mark the opening of the terraces of the Shrine of the Báb.

4. BAHA'I WORLD CENTRE

Like Shoghi Effendi, the House of Justice has worked to secure ownership of sites associated with the central figures of the Faith and to extend and beautify the gardens surrounding the shrines at the Baha'i World Centre. More dramatically, the House has overseen a series of extensive building projects in Haifa. Three of these were constructed along an 'Arc' traced out on the mountainside above the Shrine of the Báb by Shoghi Effendi: a large, colonnaded building, topped by a low dome to serve as the House's own seat (1975–83), and flanking it, the 'Centre for the Study of the Texts' – the base for the House of Justice's Research Department, and the seat of the International Teaching Centre (completed in 1999 and 2000, respectively).[7] A large underground extension to the International Archives Building has

---

[5] Julie Badiee, *An Earthly Paradise: Bahá'í Houses of Worship Around the World* (Oxford: George Ronald, 1992).

[6] Sixteen conferences were held during the Nine Year Plan, six in 1967 (Kampala; Chicago/Wilmette; Panama City, Panama; New Delhi; Sydney; and Frankfurt); and a series of ten in 1968–72 (Palermo, Italy; Rose Hill, Mauritius; La Paz, Bolivia; Monrovia, Liberia; Kingston, Jamaica; Singapore; Sapporo, Japan; Suva, Fiji; Reykjavik, Iceland; and Panama City); eight during the first Five Year Plan in 1976–7 (Nairobi, Kenya; Anchorage, Alaska; Hong Kong; Helsinki, Finland; Paris, France; Bahia, Brazil; Merida, Mexico; and Auckland, New Zealand); and five during the Seven Year Plan in 1982 (Lagos, Nigeria; Montreal, Canada; Quito, Ecuador; Canberra, Australia; and Dublin, Ireland).

[7] The western end of the Arc is marked by Shoghi Effendi's International Archives Building, which established the stately classical style followed by the rest. It is planned to eventually complete the Arc with an International Baha'i Library at its eastern end.

also been built. The fourth major project has been the construction of a series of eighteen terraced gardens linked by steps above and below the Shrine of the Báb which stretch for about a kilometre up Mount Carmel, and at their greatest extent span some four hundred metres across the mountain (completed in 2001).[8]

The House has also greatly expanded the number of support staff in Haifa, responding both to the international growth of the Baha'i community and the increasing range of work which it itself directs or initiates (by 2001, there were about six hundred staff members from sixty countries). These include the staffs of the House of Justice's own specialized departments (secretariat, finance, research, archives, statistics, maintenance of gardens and buildings, etc.), and those of other Baha'i bodies, such as the International Teaching Centre and the Office for Socio-Economic Development.

5. 'DEEPENING', COMMUNITY DEVELOPMENT AND LAW

One major goal of the House of Justice has been to encourage the Baha'is worldwide to deepen in their knowledge of the Faith, increase their commitment, and enhance their experience of Baha'i community life. To this end, in addition to its own letters to the Baha'is on such topics, the House has arranged for the production of compilations of Baha'i writings on a wide range of subjects, including various aspects of Baha'i administration, consultation, teaching the Faith, moral behaviour, family life, marriage and divorce, prayer, music, the arts, education, peace, and conservation of the environment.[9] Translations of writings by the Báb, Bahá'u'lláh, and 'Abdu'l-Bahá have also been commissioned, including Bahá'u'lláh's book of laws, the *Kitáb-i Aqdas* (1992). The House has also sought to collect and properly preserve, classify and index all extant letters of Bahá'u'lláh, 'Abdu'l-Bahá, and Shoghi Effendi (with over sixty thousand items already collected by 1983), establishing research and archival departments in Haifa for this purpose.

The House has also greatly emphasized qualitative change within the Baha'i community, encouraging increased literacy; concern with education; and the enhancement of the role of women and youth in the community; as well as fostering family life, children's classes, socio-economic development, and communal dawn prayer.

[8] See Ruhe, *Door of Hope*, and the successive volumes of *Bahá'í World*.
[9] For an extensive selection of these, see Universal House of Justice, *Compilation of Compilations*.

Although empowered to supplement the provisions of the *Aqdas* in matters of Baha'i law, the House has made very few legal pronouncements since
it was first established, one rare exception being its decision to make the
Baha'i law of *Ḥuqúqu'lláh* applicable throughout the Baha'i world (1992).
We may note that the ongoing work of indexing all Baha'i writings also
provides the House with a massive data base on which to base its deliberations.

6. EXTERNAL AFFAIRS

The Universal House of Justice has placed great emphasis on various aspects
of the Faith's 'external affairs'. A major part of this has been concerned with
the 'proclamation' of the Faith – that is, the endeavour to acquaint as many
people as possible with its existence, aims and teachings, and the attempt to
secure greater public recognition for Baha'i institutions and religious practices (e.g. gaining state recognition for Baha'i marriage registration and
having the Faith included in educational courses on world religions). The
House's first global proclamation campaign was launched in October 1967,
to follow the centenary celebrations of Bahá'u'lláh's composition of the
Súra of the Kings, and continued to the end of the Nine Year Plan in 1973.
Following the example of Bahá'u'lláh's own proclamation of his message,
one element of the campaign was directed at the world's leaders, a specially
prepared compilation of Bahá'u'lláh's addresses to the rulers (*The Proclamation of Bahá'u'lláh*) being presented to contemporary heads of state (142
in all). At the same time, the House called on Baha'is around the world
to launch proclamation and teaching programmes designed to reach 'every
stratum of human society' and acquaint them with Bahá'u'lláh's 'healing
message'. Proclamation has since become a regular part of Baha'i activities in those countries in which there is religious freedom, with systematic
publicity campaigns, and wide-spread use of the mass media. The House
made a second proclamation to world leaders with the presentation of its
statement, *The Promise of World Peace* (October 1985), again with accompanying programmes of teaching and proclamation by the generality of the
Baha'is.[10] An Office of Public Information was established in Haifa in 1985
so as to better promote public knowledge of the Faith, and at the direction
of the House, a number of national spiritual assemblies now have their own
external relations offices.

[10] Bahá'u'lláh, *Proclamation of Bahá'u'lláh*; Universal House of Justice, *Promise of World Peace*.

A second major element of Baha'i external affairs has been the Faith's growing involvement with the United Nations and its agencies, particularly through the work of the 'Baha'i International Community' (BIC) as a body representing the Baha'is of the world at the United Nations. Although first established in 1948, the BIC only became fully active in 1967 with the appointment of a full-time Baha'i representative and a permanent office at the UN in New York. It gained consultative status with the UN Economic and Social Council (ECOSOC) in 1970, and with the UN Children's Fund (UNICEF) in 1976, and now has offices in Haifa, New York and Geneva, as well as representation at the various regional UN offices and specialist Offices of the Environment (1989) and for the Advancement of Women (1992) in New York. It is directly responsible to the Universal House of Justice.

BIC activities include extensive involvement in UN commissions, committees, conferences, and working groups, often with the presentation of Baha'i statements on issues of concern such as human rights, the status of women, education, literacy, racial discrimination, narcotic drugs, environment, and social development. It has also produced special statements such as *The Prosperity of Mankind* (1995),[11] dealing with the concept of global prosperity in the context of the Baha'i teachings, and since 1989 has published a quarterly newsletter, *One Country* (1country@bic.org), which reports on Baha'i activities and issues of global concern – with French, Chinese, Russian, Spanish and German editions now augmenting the original English-language version.

The BIC has also been a major channel for making appeal to the international community for support in instances of persecution of Baha'is, most notably of those in Iran, both under the royal and present Islamic republican regimes: criticism in the UN or in the UN Commission on Human Rights seemingly acting as a brake on action against the Baha'is. It may be noted that the severe and extensive persecutions suffered by the Iranian Baha'is since the Islamic Revolution of 1979 (Chapter 6) has also served to gain the Baha'is unprecedented and sympathetic attention from governments, organizations and the media worldwide.

---

[11] Baha'i International Community, *The Prosperity of Humankind* ([Haifa:] Office of Public Information, 1995).

CHAPTER 6

Expansion Since 1921

Baha'i expansion since 1921 can be roughly divided into two phases: the
period up to 1953, when the Faith was clearly established as an international religious movement but growth was relatively slow and most Baha'i
communities outside of Iran and the United States were quite tiny, and
the period beginning with the Ten Year Crusade (1953–63) and continuing to the present day, during which the Faith has begun to assume the
characteristics of a genuinely global religion.

I. UP TO 1953

As a religious movement, the Baha'i Faith can be seen as passing through
a series of progressive expansions both of geographical extent and socio-
cultural milieux. Thus, one aspect of Bahá'u'lláh's transformation of Babism
was a universalization of its religious message so that Iranian Jews and
Zoroastrians together with a small number of Sunni Muslims and Levantine Christians could find identity as Baha'is. A further extension occurred
during the period of 'Abdu'l-Bahá's leadership with the Faith breaking out
of the cultural confines of its original Middle Eastern milieu to attract a
small but widespread international following. This 'stage' continued during the first thirty years of Shoghi Effendi's guardianship, albeit with two
significant changes with the adoption of: (i) a relatively uniform system
of administration whereby elected spiritual assemblies became the direc-
tive agencies for organised Baha'i activities, and (ii) systematic expansion
planning (1937–), involving an extension of Baha'i teaching activities; the
settlement of pioneers in those territories in which there were as yet few
or no Baha'is; the establishment of new local and national assemblies; the
acquisition of properties (temple sites and administrative headquarters);
the translation of Baha'i literature into an increasing range of languages;
and special local projects, such as the gradual completion of the Baha'i
House of Worship in Wilmette.

Initially, the plans were assigned individually to each national spiritual assembly (eight by the late 1930s, eleven by 1951), aiming for the expansion in the size and geographical extent of each community's 'home front', as well as following a strategy of global expansion: North American Baha'is being required to establish the Faith in Latin America and the Caribbean (1937–53), and later in those areas of post-war Western Europe in which there were few or no Baha'is (1946–53); those of India and Burma being directed to Southeast Asia (1946–53); the Iranians to Afghanistan and the Arab world (1946–50); the Egyptians to North Africa (1949–53); and the British, in concert with all the above, to Africa (1951–3). The success of this collaborative inter-assembly '*Africa project*' heralded the launching of the Ten Year Crusade (1953–63), which by the extent and magnitude of its accomplishments marked the beginning of a new stage in Baha'i growth (see later).

In terms of geographical diffusion and administrative expansion, the results of the plans were impressive. Thus, in 1935, Baha'is had resided in 1,034 places in the world, whilst by 1952, this figure had more than doubled to 2,425, with a Baha'i presence in some 116 countries and major colonial territories (including quite remote areas such as Greenland and the Bismark Archipelago of New Guinea). Administratively, the number of local spiritual assemblies had increased from 139 to 611.[1] The total number of Baha'is remained small, however (c. two hundred thousand), and the majority – over 90 percent – were still Iranian. Nevertheless, the cultural adaptability of the Faith and its potential to attract a wide diversity of peoples had been vividly demonstrated, and the basis for further more extensive global expansion established.

2. THE PERIOD OF GLOBAL EXPANSION, 1953–

It is only from the 1950s onwards, that the Baha'i Faith has begun to fulfil the vision of its founders and become a truly global religion, with a world following now of over five million people. In 1953, Baha'is resided in some twenty-seven hundred localities worldwide, but by 2006, this figure had increased to over one hundred thousand localities (101,969), spread across 191 countries and 46 dependant territories (North Korea is the only country – apart from the Vatican City State – not to have a recorded Baha'i community). Established local spiritual assemblies had meanwhile increased from 670 to almost 10,000 (9,631), whilst the number of national

[1] Smith, *Babi and Baha'i Religions*, p. 161.

spiritual assemblies had increased from 12 to 165.[2] Again, whilst in the early 1950s, the number of Baha'is in most countries was minute (Iran and the United States being the only communities of substantial size), many national Baha'i communities are now quite large, particularly some of those in Latin America, Africa and Asia, whilst even many smaller communities are quite sizable compared to the past, and in several places (notably some of the Pacific Island nations), have come to form a significant component in the wider population. More generally, most national Baha'i communities have become more widely diffused, and in many areas have put down strong local roots, with the Baha'is coming to form an integral part of the environing culture.

The social composition of many Baha'i communities has also radically changed. Outside of Iran, most Baha'is in 1950 were drawn from the educated and middle classes, even in countries such as those of Latin America where such social groups constituted a tiny minority of the total population. Now the majority of Baha'is are drawn from the rural and to a lesser extent, urban masses in the 'Third World' (i.e. Latin America, the Caribbean, sub-Saharan Africa, and monsoon Asia). Even the North American Baha'i communities now comprise people from a much wider range of social backgrounds. Again, many Baha'i communities now include a much greater diversity of people in terms of religious, ethnic, and cultural backgrounds: worldwide, over 2000 (2,112) tribes and ethnic groups were represented in the Faith by the mid-1990s.[3]

Concomitantly, there is now a much greater range of cultural expressions of 'being Baha'i' both globally and within individual national Baha'i communities. There is no longer the dominance of Iranian or Western cultural styles which characterised earlier stages in the development of the Faith. This is particularly true in terms of music and other aspects of popular culture, but can also be seen in the development of Baha'i literature and teaching styles which address local perspectives – such as Baha'is in rural India utilizing traditional Hindu-style songs to convey their teachings and the fruitful indigenization of Baha'i perspectives and practices in New Ireland.[4]

---

[2] Some of these statistics were kindly provided to me by the Office of Public Information at the Baha'i World Centre in an email communication dated 4 August 2006. See also recent volumes of *Bahá'í World*. This period is also discussed in Peter Smith and Moojan Momen, 'The Baha'i Faith 1957–1988: A survey of contemporary developments'. *Religion* 19 (1989), pp. 63–91.

[3] *Bahá'í World, 1994–1995*, p. 317.

[4] William N. Garlington, 'Baha'i *bhajans*'. *World Order*, vol. 16/2 (Winter 1982), pp. 43–49; Graeme Were. 'Thinking through images: *Kastom* and the coming of the Baha'is to northern New Ireland, Papua New Guinea'. *Journal of the Royal Anthropological Institute* (NS), vol. 11 (2005), pp. 659–76.

Aspects of Expansion

Rapid Baha'i growth over the past half-century has reflected a fundamental shift in the focus of Baha'i teaching work. Thus, whilst up to the 1950s, Baha'is commonly concentrated their attention on urban, educated audiences – which meant that in areas such as India and Latin America, they had little contact with the mass of the population, in much of the world they now endeavour to take their message and teachings to the population as a whole, whether this be rural villagers, tribal minorities, or more recently, the populations of fast-growing urban slums, immigrant groups and in some places, refugees. One aspect of Baha'i growth then has simply been a matter of abandoning a narrow social focus of whom to teach.

This shift in focus has necessitated changes in teaching styles. Whilst Baha'i teaching styles were earlier generally 'elitist' in orientation – with heavy reliance on newspaper publicity, public meetings, lecture tours, and contact with universities and sympathetic liberal religious groups, many Baha'i communities have now adopted 'mass teaching' methods, learning to teach large numbers of often illiterate people directly and making much greater use of music to attract potential audiences. They have also had to develop ways of trying to integrate large numbers of new Baha'is into the existing Baha'i communities and of deepening their knowledge and commitment to the Faith. Up until the 1950s (and in some countries until much more recently), potential new Baha'is were often asked to read extensively into the Baha'i literature before making their declaration of Faith and to discuss any questions they might have with local Baha'is – a technique assuming good basic literacy and only really practical with small numbers of people, and certainly not viable when there are large numbers of new Baha'is many of whom are poorly educated, lacking in material means, and remote from the main centres of population. In this context, successful methods of integration have included various forms of study circles and institutes, the use of Baha'i radio stations (now seven worldwide, most in Latin America), and the promotion of indigenous cultural activities.

Expansion has also been linked to changes in Baha'i community life. One of the most important of these has been the increased role played by 'youth' in the Baha'i community, a development greatly encouraged by the Universal House of Justice. Linked, perhaps, to the developing youth culture in wider society, there was increasing recognition amongst Baha'is during the 1960s that the energy and enthusiasm of young people combined with their relative lack of family and other responsibilities enabled them to become a 'driving force' in Baha'i expansion through youth teaching teams and the like – a development which led to a change in the demographics of many Baha'i communities as more young people became Baha'is and which also has had a major impact on Baha'i cultural styles, as with the much greater emphasis which now came to be given to music in Western communities.

Another change has been the increasing implementation of the principle of gender equality amongst Baha'is in more traditional societies and the resultant empowerment of women that has accompanied it, with the consequences that in many communities women have come to play a greater role in Baha'i administration, teaching work and community life. Again, particularly with the extension of the Baha'i Faith into poorer rural social milieux, Baha'i socio-economic development and educational programmes have come to constitute a significant part of Baha'i activity in recent years. Normally made available to non-Baha'is as well as to Baha'is (and therefore not tied to any requirement to convert in order to gain access to them), these have had an impact on the wider societies of which these communities form part, and although not designed as means of propagating the Faith, they have often had that effect.

Not all expansions have been successful or sustained, of course. In many countries, the momentum of Baha'i teaching campaigns has been spasmodic, with periods of growth being followed by periods of stagnation or loss, and then perhaps of renewed growth. Often, these fluctuations have been linked to the difficulties of 'deepening' the new Baha'is into the Faith and of integrating them with the local Baha'i communities, but in some instances, external factors such as warfare and civil disorder have disrupted teaching campaigns or led to the formation of Baha'is groups and communities in refugee camps (as in some areas of Southeast Asia and West Africa).

Distribution

Baha'i expansion over the past fifty years has dramatically changed the distribution of Baha'is worldwide, with Baha'i communities in the Third World coming to be the dominant Baha'i demographic. Exact figures are not available, but some indication of the changing distribution of Baha'is in the world can be gained from the estimates given in Table 1. Thus, in 1954, over 90 percent of Baha'is lived in Iran, and there were probably fewer than ten thousand Baha'is in the West and perhaps no more than three thousand in the whole of Africa, Asia (excluding the Middle East), Latin America, the Caribbean and Oceania combined. By the late 1980s, however, some 88 percent of the Baha'i population lived in the Third World, South Asia (mostly India) (42%), Sub-Saharan Africa (22%), and Latin America and

Table 1. *Estimated Baha'i populations in 1954 and 1988*

	1954 (000s)	(%)	1988 (000s)	(%)
1. The 'Islamic Heartland'	200	93.6	300	6.7
2. 'The West'	10	4.7	200	4.5
3. The Baha'i 'Third World'				
– South Asia	1	0.5	1,900	42.9
– Sub-Saharan Africa			1,000	22.3
– Latin America & the Caribbean			700	15.6
– Southeast Asia	>2	0.9	300	6.7
– East Asia			20	0.4
– Oceania (excl. the 'Anglo-Pacific')			70	1.6
TOTALS	213		4,490	

Note: The division of the world into 'cultural areas' is adapted from Smith, *Babi and Baha'i Religions*, pp. 165–71. The 'Anglo-Pacific' comprises Australia, New Zealand, and Hawaii.
Source: Adapted from Peter Smith and Moojan Momen, 'The Baha'i Faith 1957–1988: A survey of contemporary developments'. *Religion* 19 (1989), pp. 63–91.

the Caribbean (16%) now being the areas of greatest numerical strength. This predominance was achieved despite significant increases in the number of Baha'is in the West (North America, Europe and the 'Anglo-Pacific') and a modest increase in the Iranian Baha'i population (with Middle Eastern and Western Baha'is probably constituting respectively less than 7 and 5 percent of the world total).[5] This pattern appears to have continued to the present day – as reflected in recent figures (2002) for the distribution of local spiritual assemblies by continent, with the largest number being in Africa (3,412, some 33 percent of the world total of 10,344), followed by the Americas (2,920), Asia (2,322), Europe (890), and Australasia (800), respectively 28, 22, 9 and 8 percent of the world total.[6]

3. REGIONAL DEVELOPMENTS

Iran

In terms of individual Baha'i communities, that of Iran remained central in the Baha'i world until the Islamic Revolution of 1979. Indeed, up until the

[5] A similar picture emerges from distribution figures for the number of local spiritual assemblies and localities in which Baha'is reside. See CEBF, p. 143.
[6] *Bahá'í World, 2002–2003*, p. 280.

1960s, the majority of Baha'is in the world were still Iranians or of Iranian origin. Although long since overtaken by India as the largest Baha'i community in the world, the Iranian community naturally retains an enormous importance in the Faith. Iran itself, of course, remains a sacred land for the Baha'is, both as the birthplace of their Faith and as the site of numerous Baha'i holy places.

By the time of Shoghi Effendi's accession, a Baha'i community had been in existence in Iran for over half-a-century (longer if we date it back to its original Babi core). This community was widespread through most of the country (the nomadic tribes were the only major social group to remain largely untouched), and had developed a distinctive sense of communal identity, supported by the development of a variety of Baha'i social, educational, and administrative bodies and by the tendency of Iranian Baha'is to marry their co-religionists and bring up their children as Baha'is – with the resultant 'familialization' of the Faith.[7] Communal identity and a tremendous sense of sacrificial dedication on the part of the most active Baha'is had also been increased by the intermittent outbreaks of persecution and martyrdom which had befallen them.

The early years of Shoghi Effendi's ministry saw the ending of the chaotic misrule of the Qájár period and the rise to power of new military-nationalist regime headed by Reza 'Pahlaví', who proclaimed himself Shah in 1925. The establishment of a centralizing, modernizing regime initially seemed to promise a better situation for the Baha'is, with an end to the clerically inspired persecution of the past. Indeed, during the early years of Pahlavi rule, the Baha'is were able to expand their activities, and for the first time to hold large public meetings, sometimes attended by government officials. They also organized a national Baha'i elective system, culminating in the election of their first national spiritual assembly in 1934; consolidated local spiritual assembly administration throughout the country; and furthered their social development activities (including establishing modern public baths). A campaign of government repression ensued (1932–41), however, seemingly as part of an endeavour to cow all potentially independent groups in Iranian society. Baha'i schools were then closed; Baha'i meetings prohibited; a number of Baha'is dismissed from government employ; and

---

[7] Baha'is are free to marry partners of any religion, but in the Iranian context the strong religious commitment of many Baha'is combined with the hostility of many Muslim families towards Baha'is meant that intermarriage was relatively uncommon. During the twentieth century, intermarriage between Iranian Baha'is of different religious backgrounds (Muslim, Jewish, Zoroastrian) and between Iranian Baha'is and Baha'is of other nationalities has become relatively common.

Baha'is imprisoned for contracting Baha'i marriages. The official campaign ended only with the overthrow of Reza Shah by the British and Russians during World War II (1941), but was followed by a partial break-down of public order, and a recrudescence of locally inspired attacks (clerical and political) on the Baha'is. Internal development of the Baha'i community continued, with the establishment of a Baha'i-linked hospital and orphanage in 1940 and the adoption of a special plan for the advancement of Baha'i women (1946–50), women becoming eligible to serve on Baha'i assemblies for the first time in 1954. Major advances in female Baha'i literacy were also made. A new wave of attacks was mounted against the Baha'is in 1951 and 1955 (Probably as a government sop to Muslim religious extremists). Persecutions leading to the deaths of Baha'is (all through mob action or assassination) were relatively uncommon throughout the period, however, with fifteen killed in the mid-1920s; none in the 1930s; eleven in the 1940s; and eleven between 1950 and 1955, for a total of thirty-seven between 1922 and 1955.[8]

More recent Iranian Baha'i history is sharply divided into the periods before and after the Islamic Revolution of 1979. Before the revolution, under the increasingly unpopular rule of Mohammad-Reza Shah (Reza Shah's son), Iran continued on a path of state-directed modernization. After the state-sponsored anti-Baha'i campaign of 1955 (and the international criticism for Iran's human rights record which that provoked), the Baha'is were tolerated and protected from persecution (only two Baha'is were killed for their Faith between 1956 and 1977), but they were not allowed to have any kind of public voice. They were allowed to organize their own activities, but were not allowed to combat the activities of various anti-Baha'i groups which were able to freely operate and widely disseminate a distorted and intensely hate-filled propaganda against them, accusing them of political manipulation, acting as agents of foreign powers, and immorality (Theoretically, Baha'is were still not allowed to contract legal marriages by the state authorities). The development of a widely spread 'culture of hatred' against the Baha'is resulted. Whilst the Baha'i community grew gradually in size through natural increase – to perhaps 350,000 by 1979 – it was unable to gain a significant number of new converts, and as the Baha'i birth rate was probably lower than that amongst the population as a whole, the proportion of Baha'is seems to have declined from what it had been earlier in the century: to between perhaps 0.5 and 1 percent of the total Iranian

---

[8] Calculated from Momen, 'A chronology of some of the persecutions'.

population.[9] The Baha'is still constituted the largest of Iran's non- Muslim minorities, however.

The situation of the Baha'is changed dramatically as the Pahlavi regime began to collapse in the face of the rising discontent which led to the establishment of the Islamic Republic in 1979. Already under attack in the violence of 1978, the Baha'is were soon to endure a massive campaign of largely state-sponsored persecution in the early years of the Republic, including a systematic endeavour to destroy all Baha'i organizations (including the judicial murder of many Baha'i leaders), and to pressurize the rank-and-file to apostatise. Baha'is were arrested, thrown out of work, and not allowed to attend school or university. Baha'i sacred sites and burial grounds were destroyed. More than two hundred Baha'is were killed or have disappeared and are presumed dead. The Faith was officially banned in 1983, and membership of Baha'i administrative bodies made a criminal offence. (The Baha'is subsequently disbanded all their assemblies.) There was widespread international condemnation and enormous publicity, which may have contributed to some easing of the situation since the mid-1980s. Persecution continues, however, the economic plight of many Baha'is remains dire, and Baha'is continue being disbarred from higher education and many forms of employment. Baha'is may not now legally inherit property, and it is difficult for them to obtain passports or exit visas. Their marriages and divorces are not recognized, and Baha'is receive little or no protection from the law, as indicated by a case of two Muslims who had killed a Baha'i, but were subsequently released from prison because their victim was 'an unprotected infidel'. The situation apparently varies from one part of the country to another, but an official document of 1991 indicated that it was then government policy to stifle any further development of the Baha'i community, and, if possible, to uproot its cultural foundations. International condemnation of human rights abuses in Iran, specifically mentioning the Baha'is, continue.

These recent persecutions have in some ways increased the international role of the Iranian Baha'is. Already, in the late Pahlavi period, a significant worldwide diaspora of Iranian Baha'is had developed, as Baha'is left their homeland for educational and economic reasons or in order to serve as overseas pioneers for their Faith, contributing significantly to the energy and cultural life of Baha'i communities around the world and serving in

[9] Smith, 'A note on Babi and Baha'i numbers'. See also Mehri Samadari Jensen, 'Religion and family planning in contemporary Iran'. In *In Iran*, ed. P. Smith (Los Angeles, CA: Kalimát Press, 1986), pp. 213–37.

the Faith's international administration. The number of emigres naturally increased with the Revolution, many thousands of Baha'is fleeing Iran so as to escape actual or possible persecution, many of them well-educated professionals and business people. Whilst large numbers of these migrants settled in Western cities, sometimes in large 'enclave communities',[10] a significant number became pioneers, using their own hardships as a vehicle for Baha'i activity, many young Westernized Iranian professionals (doctors, engineers, etc.) coming to play an important role in the development of many Third World Baha'i communities.

Another major consequence of the recent persecutions has been the enormous amount of attention that this has generated in the rest of the world amongst governments, international organizations and the media, gaining the Baha'is widespread sympathy and support. Ironically, persecution in Iran has probably been the single most important factor in enabling the Baha'is to 'emerge from obscurity' as a global religious movement.

Central Asia, the Caucasus, the Middle East, and North Africa

The area of the Faith's wider 'Islamic Heartland' experienced various difficulties during the 1920s and 1930s. In Turkestan and the Caucasus, the brief flurry of Baha'i activity which had followed the revolutions of 1917 ended with the imposition of effective Soviet rule and the consequent restriction and persecution of all forms of religious activity. The former Baha'i central assemblies for the area (some of the earliest Baha'i administrative institutions in the world) were recast as national spiritual assemblies in 1925, but in 1928, the Ashkhabad temple was confiscated by the state and the closure of the Baha'i schools and the arrest of some of the Baha'is followed. The Ashkhabad community as a whole – now consisting of about 1,400 families – was effectively destroyed in 1938, with the arrest and exile of many of the men, and the deportation of the women and children and the remainder of the men to Iran. Only with the collapse of the Soviet Union and varying degrees of liberalization has it been possible for the Baha'is to

---

[10] In some instances, the Iranian influx initially created tensions within the receiving Baha'i communities, with linguistic and cultural barriers emerging between the Iranians and the indigenous Baha'is, but such evidence as there is (from Britain and Italy) suggests that successful integration may often have occurred quite rapidly, with the newcomers soon taking part in the Baha'i administration in their adopted homelands, and a high level of intermarriage between Iranian and Western Baha'is occurring (including a third of all Baha'i marriages in Britain in 1984–6). See Moojan Momen, 'The integration into the British Baha'i community of recent Iranian Baha'i migrants'. *Baha'i Studies Bulletin* 4/3–4 (April 1990), pp. 50–53; and Chantal Saint-Blancat, 'Nation et religion chez les immigrés iraniens en Italie'. *Archives science social des religions* 68/1 (1989), pp. 27–37.

recommence their activities and reestablish their institutions in the now newly independent republics of the region.

As for the Arab world, a modest programme of Baha'i activity was mounted in some regions after World War I, notably in Egypt and Iraq (with national assemblies being established in 1924 and 1931, respectively), but this sparked opposition from conservative Islamic groups, leading to the seizure of Bahá'u'lláh's house in Baghdad (1922) and a significant legal case in Egypt, in which the Baha'is were nationally proclaimed to be unbelievers (1925). There was an increase in the spread and numerical base of Baha'is in the Arab world during the 1940s as a result of pioneer moves by Iranian Baha'is, but the Baha'is kept a very low profile for fear of provoking persecution. Indeed, in the Arab world up to the present day, it has continued to be impossible for Baha'is to conduct an open campaign of teaching and proclamation of their Faith, or even often to defend themselves publicly against misrepresentation and abuse. In this regard, the fact that the Baha'is' world headquarters is in what has now become the state of Israel has been a particular difficulty, leading to the widespread allegation that the Baha'is are pro-Zionist, an allegation vehemently denied by the Baha'is, who insist that they do not get involved in politics and are loyal to the government of whichever country they live in. As they note, the Baha'i Faith is centred in the Haifa-Akka region for reasons of historical contingency that long predate the present political borders and tensions in the Middle East. The Baha'is have also experienced a number of major reverses, including a presidential banning order against the Baha'is in Egypt in 1960 and the imprisonment of Baha'is in several countries. Of note has been a recent enquiry in Egypt as to the legal status of Baha'is who are not able to obtain official documents because of their Faith, which has attracted considerable interest from Egyptian human rights activists and the international media.[11]

The only part of the Middle East to have a more 'Western' Baha'i history has been Turkey, established as a secular republic in the 1920s when a small Turkish Baha'i community was cautiously developed. The present-day situation of the Baha'is in Turkey resembles that in Europe, with a relatively small but active and well-organized national Baha'i community, and for purposes of international Baha'i administration, Turkey is now considered part of Europe.

---

[11] On 16 December 2006, the Egyptian Supreme Court ruled that it was not possible for Baha'is to identify themselves as Baha'is on their identity documents, effectively making them non-persons under Egyptian law (see bahai-egypt.blogspot.com).

North America

Outside of Iran, the most important centre of Baha'i activity for most of the twentieth century was North America (the United States and Canada, the two countries sharing a common Baha'i administration from 1909 to 1948), and it was here that the systems of assembly administration and planned activity were effectively pioneered.[12] Enthusiastic efforts were made to attract new believers to the Faith, particularly in the United States, but numerical expansion was slow (by 1936, the U.S. Census reported a population of 2,584 (fewer than in 1916), and by 1947, there were still only 5,000 or so Baha'is in North America as a whole. Nevertheless, the North American Baha'is were able to extend the distribution of Baha'is in both the United States and Canada; consolidate a well-organized network of local spiritual assemblies; establish a separate Canadian national assembly in 1948; dispatch pioneers to establish the Faith throughout Latin America (1937-) and to consolidate it in post-World War II Europe; and finally see the completion of the Wilmette temple (dedicated for worship in 1953). As with other Western Baha'is, the Americans and Canadians enjoyed conditions of religious freedom and material opportunity unknown to their Middle Eastern coreligionists, and were so able to work to achieve Shoghi Effendi's objectives with relative ease, although often also with much personal sacrifice.

Later, during the Ten Year Crusade, there was a marked increase in the number of North American Baha'is – to perhaps around nineteen thousand by 1963, as well as further significant internal diffusion and worldwide pioneering activity. Even more dramatic growth occurred during the late 1960s and early 1970s, with a large influx of young people, and successful 'mass teaching' amongst the rural black population in the southeastern states of the United States. Conversions of members of other minority groups were also made. In both the United States and Canada, native Amerindians have come to play a significant role in the Faith. North American Baha'is have also played a major role in the international leadership of the Faith, both as serving Hands of the Cause (thirteen out of thirty-two appointed by Shoghi Effendi) and as members of the Universal House of Justice (nine out of twenty-one). As in Europe and Australasia, there has been a large influx of Iranian Baha'is since 1979.

---

[12] Opposition to Baha'i organization in the 1920s and early 1930s was also centred in North America.

Europe and Australasia

Baha'i expansion in other parts of 'the West' has been quite limited by comparison with North America. In interwar Europe, Germany was the leading centre of activity until the Nazi accession to power in 1933, after which Baha'i activities were necessarily curtailed, the Nazis eventually banning organized Baha'i activity because of the Faith's internationalist and pacifist stance (1937). Elsewhere, there were Baha'is scattered across the rest of Europe, but their numbers were tiny, despite teaching visits from North America Baha'is; frequent participation at Esperanto conferences (Lydia Zamenhof, a daughter of the language's inventor became a Baha'i); and expressed sympathy of various prominent people – including the reported conversion of the dowager Queen Marie of Romania.[13] Baha'i literature was also translated into many of the European languages and a considerable amount of original literature produced by Baha'is in Britain, France and Germany. Organizationally, the Baha'is in Britain and Germany were amongst the first to establish their own national assemblies (in 1923) and the International Baha'i Bureau (established in Geneva in 1925) came to provide an effective focus for communication for Baha'is throughout Europe up until the outbreak of World War II (1939). Only in Britain were the Baha'is active during the war years.

After the War, much of Europe was in ruins. On the continent, the task of helping to reestablish Baha'i activity was entrusted to the American Baha'is under their Second Seven Year Plan (1946–53), strong but small Baha'i communities were soon being established throughout Western Europe. Meanwhile, Britain took a different course, consolidating and expanding its own 'home front', and from the two-year Africa Plan (1951–3) onwards, becoming increasingly involved with Baha'i expansion outside of Europe. Overall, the total number of European Baha'is remained small, with only about fourteen hundred as late as 1952. Under the new Communist governments of Eastern Europe, Baha'i activity proved virtually impossible. As late as 1963, there were still fewer than five thousand Baha'is in the whole of Europe, and even now the number of Baha'is in Western Europe has remained comparatively small, despite an influx of youth in the late 1960s and early 1970s which dynamized many communities. The various national Baha'i communities are generally extremely active and individual European Baha'is have played a major role in Baha'i administration and the

[13] CEBF, 'Esperanto'; 'Marie'; 'Zamenhof, Lidia', loc. cit.; Wendy Heller, *Lidia: The Life of Lidia Zamenhof, Daughter of Esperanto* (Oxford: George Ronald, 1985).

production of Baha'i literature. The first European House of Worship was opened in Frankfurt in 1964.

Baha'i developments in Russia (from the 1920s) and the countries of the former Soviet bloc (after World War II) were quite different, with no public Baha'i activity possible until the collapse of communism (1989–91) created conditions of unexpected religious freedom for the Baha'is and other religious groups. A special two year plan (1990–92) was then devised, and extensive expansion of the Faith in this region has since taken place, with large numbers of new Baha'is, especially in some parts of the Balkans. As in Western Europe, the Eastern European Baha'is have established their own national spiritual assemblies.

Meanwhile, a similar network of small Baha'i groups developed in Australian and New Zealand in the 1920s, and in 1934, the Baha'is in the two countries formed their own joint national spiritual assembly. The growth in numbers was extremely limited with 400 or so Baha'is in the region by the early 1950s. Since the 1960s, expansion has been somewhat more impressive than in Europe, however, albeit that the Baha'i communities in the two countries remain comparatively small. A Baha'i House of Worship was dedicated in Sydney in 1961.

Latin America and the Caribbean

Sustained activity in Latin America and the Caribbean began during the first North American Seven Year Plan (1937–44), with pioneers dispatched to all the independent republics of Latin America (1939–41); an Inter-America committee appointed to co-ordinate activities; and an Inter-America Bulletin produced to give news of activities. The results were very encouraging, the first local assembly of the Plan (Mexico City) being formed in 1938, and by 1943, all the independent republics had been opened to the Faith, as also had Jamaica and Puerto Rico. There were then a total of nineteen local assemblies in the whole region and Baha'is were living in fifty-seven localities in twenty-two countries and territories. Many of the new groups were also extremely active, sending teachers to open new localities; organizing Baha'i radio programmes; translating more Baha'i writings into Spanish and Portuguese; publishing their own newsletter and pamphlets and holding children's classes. The first Latin American Baha'i congress was held in Panama in 1945 with native Baha'is from 10 of the countries in attendance. Expansion continued during the second Seven Year Plan (1946–53), and by 1953, Baha'is were living in a total of 124 localities in the region, forty of which had local spiritual assemblies. Co-ordination of Baha'i activities was

transferred from North to Latin American hands in 1947 with the establishment of two regional teaching committees (for Central and South America,
respectively), and in 1951, these were replaced by regional national spiritual
assemblies.

During the Ten Year Crusade (1953–63), large-scale conversions of
Amerindians began in several countries, most dramatically in Bolivia and
Panama. Given the largely middle class, educated *Latino* background of
most of the early Latin American Baha'is this was a major shift in community membership. Other achievements of the Plan included the establishment of independent national spiritual assemblies; the settlement of Baha'is
on more of the islands of the Caribbean as well as outlying islands such
as Easter Island and the Falklands; the formation of assemblies in several
Caribbean territories; the translation of Baha'i literature into a number of
Amerindian languages; the establishment of institutes for the Amerindians
of Bolivia and Ecuador; and the formation of Baha'i publishing trusts in
Buenos Aires (Spanish) and Rio de Janeiro (Portuguese).

Since 1963, there has been a massive increase in the number of Baha'is
in much of the region, with the successful extension of 'mass teaching'
to many countries, involving both Amerindians and those of African and
Asian descent; the first Baha'i temple of Latin America was constructed
in Panama (dedicated in 1972; work on a second temple, in Chile, has
now begun); and six Baha'i radio stations have been established. Activities
designed to foster and promote indigenous culture have been emphasized
in many countries, including holding Baha'i conferences in Quechua for
the Andean countries; using Baha'i radio stations to promote local cultural
events; and the development of a Guaymi cultural centre in Panama. Given
the despised and disadvantaged status of the American Indians in many
countries, this promotion has considerable significance. Cultural promotion, particularly with indigenous folk singing groups, has also been used as
a means of proclaiming the Faith regionally and internationally. National
spiritual assemblies have also been established in the various independent
states of the Caribbean.

Sub-Saharan Africa

There were hardly any Baha'is in non-Arab Africa until the beginning of systematic Baha'i teaching endeavour in the 'Africa campaign' of 1951–3. Coming to involve the British, American, Egyptian, Persian and Indian national
assemblies and coordinated by the British, the campaign was intended
to lay the structural basis of the Baha'i administration in the continent.

The results far exceeded the initial goals, and by 1953, there were Baha'is in nineteen territories of sub-Saharan Africa; seventeen new local assemblies had been formed; and translations into six languages had been made, with at least another eight in progress. The area of greatest receptivity was Uganda (with almost three hundred Baha'is drawn from twenty different tribal groups by early 1953), which was selected as the venue for the first ever African Teaching Conference (February 1953), the first ever intercontinental Baha'i conference. Growth accelerated during the Ten Year Crusade, and by 1963, there were probably in excess of fifty thousand Baha'is in the continent, with Baha'is resident in 2,655 localities, some 1,076 of which had local assemblies; Baha'i literature had been translated into ninety-four African languages; and 348 African tribal groups were represented in the Faith. This was an impressive achievement for essentially twelve years of Baha'i activity. Significantly, newly converted African Baha'is were already beginning to play an important role in the further progress of the Faith and in 1957, a Ugandan, Enoch Olinga, became the first (and only) native African appointed as a Hand of the Cause. The Crusade also saw the formation of four large regional spiritual assemblies to cover the entire continent in 1956 and the construction of the Baha'i House of Worship at Kampala as the 'mother temple of Africa' (dedicated January 1961).

Since 1963 there has been further impressive growth, such that African local spiritual assemblies across the whole continent (including the Arab north) now constitute a third of the global total. National spiritual assemblies have now been established almost everywhere; large-scale enrolments of new Baha'is have occurred in many areas; the advancement of women within the Baha'i community and the promotion of literacy have become increasingly important themes; and in many countries, the Baha'i communities have been able to gain favourable public attention and government recognition, a tendency strengthened by the increasing emphasis on socio-economic development projects. In a few countries, war and civil disorder have disrupted Baha'i activity.

Asia

In Asia outside of the Faith's 'Islamic heartland', the oldest Baha'i communities were in the Indian sub-continent and neighbouring Burma dating back to the late nineteenth century.[14] Later, a national spiritual assembly for

---

[14] No detailed history of Indian Baha'i history has yet been published – a major lacunae. Two unpublished Ph.D. dissertations examine developments in the Malwa area of Madya Pradesh (William

India and Burma was established in 1923; the first Baha'i Summer school was held in 1938; a succession of teaching plans were organized (1938–53); and an increasing volume of Baha'i literature was translated into a number of the major Indian languages. Yet, although these activities served to increase the number of Baha'is, groups and assemblies, the total number of Baha'is in the sub-continent remained small until the early 1960s (less than nine hundred in India itself by 1961), and the core of the community was still largely 'Persianate', with Hindu-background Baha'is as a small minority. This situation changed dramatically in 1960–61 with the first sustained village teaching campaigns in India. Later extended to more and more areas of the country and adopted also in Pakistan and Bangladesh (amongst the non-Muslim minorities), these campaigns led to large scale influxes of mainly poor, rural, and often illiterate peoples, including many who came from scheduled castes and tribal groups. The results were impressive, with dramatic increases in the numbers of Baha'is, such that by 1973, there were close on four hundred thousand Indian Baha'is; and by 1993, India had the largest Baha'i community in the world, with more than 2.2 million members. The other countries of the sub-continent have also developed significant Baha'i communities, each forming its own national spiritual assembly (1957–72). Other major developments have included successful expression of Baha'i themes in Hindu terms; the construction of a Baha'i House of Worship in New Delhi (finished in 1986), which now attracts thousands of overseas visitors every day and has become a major tourist attraction (apparently more than the Taj Mahal); and the pioneering development of regional ('state') Baha'i councils (1986–) in order to devolve Baha'i administrative work in a country of enormous size and cultural complexity.

Apart from the long-established Baha'i community in Burma (subject to severe disruption in the chaotic conditions of World War II), there were few Baha'is in the rest of Southeast Asia before 1945, after which a basic framework began to be established with the despatch of pioneers from India. Significant expansion only began during the Ten Year Crusade, but as

N. Garlington, 'The Baha'i Faith in Malwa: A Study of a Contemporary Religious Movement' (Australian National University, 1975), and Steve L. Garrigues, 'The Baha'is of Malwa: Identity and Change Among the Urban Baha'is of Central India' (University of Lucknow, 1976), and there are a number of articles on particular aspects of Indian Baha'i history, including Moojan Momen, 'Jamál Effendi and the early spread of the Bahá'í Faith in South Asia'. *Bahá'í Studies Review* 9 (1999–2000), pp. 47–80; Peter Smith, 'Shoghi Effendi's letters to the Baha'is of India and Burma during the 1920s'. *Baha'i Studies Review* 13 (2005), pp. 15–40; and William Garlington's, 'Baha'i conversions in Malwa, central India'. In *From Iran East and West*, ed. J. R. Cole and M. Momen (Los Angeles, CA: Kalimát Press, 1984), pp. 157–85, and 'The Baha'i Faith in Malwa'. In *Religion in South Asia*, ed. G. A. Odie (London: Curzon Press, 1977), pp. 101–17.

strong local communities developed, large scale enrolments of new Baha'is occurred in several countries, including members of the various 'aboriginal' peoples of the region, as amongst the Iban of Sarawak and the Mentawai islanders of Indonesia. More recently, the Baha'i communities of the region have undergone a diversity of experiences, restrictions on religious activities being introduced in some countries, but with more or less sustained Baha'i expansion elsewhere. Administratively, separate Baha'i national spiritual assemblies were established in most of the countries of Southeast Asia by 1964, and several countries (notably Malaysia) have become sources of international pioneers.

In East Asia, where active Baha'i groups had been established in Japan and China during the 1910s, several international Baha'i teachers visited the region during the 1920s and 1930s, speaking extensively in universities and colleges, and meeting dignitaries. Some eminent people became Baha'is – notably Dr. Y. S. Tsao, the President of Tsing Hua (Xinhua) University – and translations of Baha'i literature were made, but the overall response to these efforts was extremely meagre: very few Chinese or Japanese became Baha'is, and with the outbreak of the East Asian wars (1937–45), Baha'i activities more or less ceased in the face of widespread devastation and social turmoil.

After, 1945, limited activities resumed in Japan, aided by the arrival of American and Iranian Baha'is, but in China, civil war and the anti-religious stance of the new Communist government precluded any such resumption. Then, during the Ten Year Crusade, sustained teaching began in South Korea and Taiwan. Given the strong anti-religious policies adopted in the new communist states, there were no Baha'i activities in Mongolia or the People's Republic of China until the 1990s, however, when dramatic political changes in Mongolia coincided with the settlement of the first Baha'i in the country in 1988, since when there has been some modest growth. In China meanwhile there has been some liberalization of official policies regarding religion and there are now a small number of Baha'is, but no formal Baha'i organization. As far as is known, North Korea remains the only country in the world (apart from the Vatican) in which there are no Baha'is. Separate spiritual assemblies for Korea, Taiwan, Hong Kong, Japan, Macau, and Mongolia have been established.

Oceania

Sustained and systematic Baha'i activity in Australasia outside of the 'Anglo-Pacific' (above) only began during the 1950s, during which Baha'i pioneers settled in many of the island groups, all then under colonial control. Translations of Baha'i literature into several local languages were made, but overall progress was at first slow, apart from in the Gilbert Islands (Kiribati). In some islands, opposition from the established churches was encountered, sometimes amounting to actual persecution of newly declared Baha'is, and the colonial authorities were sometimes suspicious of the friendliness towards the indigenous population displayed by white pioneers. Since 1963, there has been a marked increase in the extent and success of Baha'i activities throughout most of the region and the Baha'is generally now enjoy good relations with the various independent governments and churches of the region. Relatively large numbers of converts have been gained in relationship to the tiny populations of most of these states, and there are a number of Baha'i schools and socio-economic development projects in the region. Of particular note was the conversion of Malietoa Tanumafili II, the head of state of Western Samoa, in 1968, and the construction of the first oceanic Baha'i temple at Apia in Samoa (dedicated in 1984).

PART II

Beliefs

CHAPTER 7

Baha'i Texts: Sources of Belief and Practice

I. BAHA'I TEXTS

Before examining Baha'i belief and practice, it will be useful to describe the textual basis which underlies these beliefs and practices. Like any religious community, Baha'is in various parts of the world have their own popular understandings of their religion, and individual Baha'is undoubtedly have their own interpretations of particular Baha'i texts and teachings, but it is clear that Baha'is find it relatively easy to identify 'official' Baha'i beliefs and conduct: the major canonical texts are readily identifiable and in many cases easily accessible, and there is a strong sense of ongoing authoritative guidance based on the Baha'i doctrine of the Covenant.

To an extreme degree, the Baha'i Faith is a religion of 'the Word', and its teachings are derived from written material – often in the hand of the writer, sometimes in that of a secretary – and there is now an extensive archive of original writings which comprise the religion's 'canonical texts'. These comprise the writings of the Báb, Bahá'u'lláh, 'Abdu'l-Bahá, Shoghi Effendi, and the Universal House of Justice, together with the authenticated talks of 'Abdu'l-Bahá.[1] Of these, the writings of the Báb and Bahá'u'lláh are regarded as divine revelation – the 'Word of God'; the writings and talks of 'Abdu'l-Bahá and the writings of Shoghi Effendi as authoritative interpretation; and those of the Universal House of Justice as authoritative legislation and elucidation. In all cases, some measure of divine guidance is assumed. The authenticated writings of secretaries written on behalf of the principals are included, in so far as these were either dictated or written on specific

---

[1] See CEBF, 'Abdu'l-Bahá's writings and talks'; 'Báb, writings of'; 'Bahá'u'lláh, writings of'; 'Shoghi Effendi, writings of'; and 'Universal House of Justice, writings of', loc. cit. When 'Abdu'l-Bahá gave talks, he was frequently attended by one or more secretaries, who would write down his words verbatim and present a copy of what they had written to 'Abdu'l-Bahá for his approval and signature. Only when a certified transcript in the original language is available can the talk be regarded as fully authentic.

instructions and then read and approved by the principal. The terms 'Baha'i scriptures' and 'sacred texts' are sometimes used to refer to the writings of the Báb, Bahá'u'lláh, and 'Abdu'l-Bahá.

Explicitly excluded from the official Baha'i canon are the various '*pilgrims'* *notes*' recording the memories of individual Baha'is of the words spoken by an authoritative leader, particularly 'Abdu'l-Bahá and Shoghi Effendi.[2] Of these, notes by several of the pilgrims who visited 'Abdu'l-Bahá have been published, and are commonly read for their inspirational content, as are a smaller number of accounts of meetings with the Báb and Bahá'u'lláh, but none of these are taken as a basis for official Baha'i belief and practice.[3] Transcripts of the extempore oral translations of 'Abdu'l-Bahá's talks into Western languages (e.g. *Paris Talks*, *Promulgation of Universal Peace*) have a more ambiguous status: officially they must be excluded from the scriptural canon until they can be checked against transcripts of the original Persian where these exist, but in practice some of them seem to be popularly accorded authoritative status by most Baha'is. Various pilgrims' notes of meetings with Shoghi Effendi exist in cyclostyled form (hardly any are published), and sometime form the basis for some popular Baha'i beliefs, but they are very strictly regarded as non-canonical.[4]

The canonical texts have different levels of importance: those of Bahá'u'lláh, 'Abdu'l-Bahá, and Shoghi Effendi are normative for Baha'i practice and belief, and are sources of law and doctrine. Those of the House of Justice, by contrast, are concerned with the leadership of the Baha'i community and the supplementary legislation necessary for a particular time in its development. They are not a source of doctrine, the House explicitly refraining from interpretation – although the House is empowered to 'elucidate' matters which are uncertain or controversial. Again, whilst the writings of the Báb are important doctrinally and are seen as a source of

---

[2] See CEBF, 'pilgrims' notes', loc. cit. There is therefore no equivalent of the use of recorded traditions from the sayings and actions of the Prophet Muḥammad (the *hadíths*), which constitute such an important basis for Islamic law and lore.

[3] Accounts of visits to 'Abdu'l-Bahá include Thornton Chase, *In Galilee* (Chicago: Bahai Publishing Society, 1980; rev. ed. Los Angeles, CA: Kalimát Press, 1985); Helen S. Goodall, and Ella Goodall Cooper, *Daily Lessons Received at 'Akká, January 1908* (Rev. ed. Wilmette, IL: Bahá'í Publishing Trust, 1979 (1st publ. 1908)); Julia M. Grundy, *Ten Days in the Light of 'Akká* (Wilmette, IL: Bahá'í Publishing Trust, 1979 (1st pub. 1907)); May Maxwell, *An Early Pilgrimage* (Oxford: George Ronald, 1953); Roy Wilhelm, Stanwood Cobb and Genevieve L. Coy, *In His Presence: Visits to 'Abdu'l-Bahá* (Los Angeles, CA: Kalimát Press, 1989); and Bahiyyih Randall Winckler, *My Pilgrimage to Haifa, November 1919* (Wilmette, IL: Bahá'í Publishing Trust, 1996).

[4] Shoghi Effendi insisted that notes made of his own remarks were only for the personal use of the pilgrim who had heard them. They might be circulated if they were a source of inspiration, but they should not be printed. They were not official pronouncements, and as recorded were sometimes inaccurate and misleading (Hornby, *Lights*, pp. 438–40). On folk beliefs amongst Baha'is, see David Michael Piff, *Bahá'í Lore* (Oxford: George Ronald, 2000).

inspiration, they are not binding in terms of Baha'i practice – the laws of the *Bayán* having been superseded by those of the *Aqdas*.

Given that a very large part of the canon was originally composed in Persian, Arabic or a mixture of the two, authorized translations from the original writings are of great importance, those by Shoghi Effendi into English having the highest status because of his official position as an appointed interpreter of the teachings of the Faith (including of its writings), and it is official policy that translations into most other languages are made from Shoghi Effendi's English rather than the Persian and Arabic originals. Shoghi Effendi's translations are also important because of his adoption of a elevated form of English (partly based on the King James' version of the Bible), which has come to represent the norm for Baha'i scriptural translations into English.[5]

Given the very large number of written documents composed by the Báb and the successive Baha'i leaders, the collection, authentication and preservation of texts has been of major concern since the nineteenth century, the Universal House of Justice in particular building up archival and textual research centres. To date, the materials amount to approximately 60,000 items, including 15,000 'tablets' from Bahá'u'lláh, 27,000 letters from 'Abdu'l-Bahá and 17,500 letters from Shoghi Effendi.

Only a small portion of this enormous body of texts has been translated into English, but clearly a major resource for delineating Baha'i doctrine and practice has been accumulated. Even so, a substantial quantity of material is already published in English (see Table 2), with forty-one titles of major works, including twelve from the writings of Bahá'u'lláh, eight from those of 'Abdu'l-Bahá (excluding the extempore oral translations), fifteen from Shoghi Effendi, and five from the Universal House of Justice, but only one (a compilation of extracts) from the Báb. I have excluded statistical reports prepared by Shoghi Effendi and on behalf of the Universal House of Justice from this listing. Other material is found in various Baha'i periodicals, and the Universal House of Justice frequently includes new translations and extracts from hitherto unpublished letters in its own letters and in compilations which are prepared on its behalf by the Haifa-based Research Department.[6]

As yet, there are no scholarly editions of these texts, although translations of some Baha'i texts with accompanying scholarly apparatus can be found on the internet. Both the House of Justice's own Research Department and

---

[5] See Malouf, *Unveiling.*
[6] A compilation of these compilations has been published in Australia (3 volumes to date). See Universal House of Justice, *Compilation.*

Table 2. *Major works in the English-language Baha'i canon (by category and in chronological order of publication). Translations by Shoghi Effendi marked *TSE. Dates of earlier now superceded translations and writings in square brackets. Many of the texts exist in more recent editions but with only minor revisions.*

I. English-language texts of the Báb (1):
    1. *Selections from the Writings of the Báb* (1976).
II. English-language texts of Bahá'u'lláh (12):
    1. *The Hidden Words of Bahá'u'lláh.* *TSE ([1921] 1929).
    2. *The Kitáb-i-Iqan: The Book of Certitude.* *TSE ([1904] 1931).
    3. *Gleanings from the Writings of Bahá'u'lláh.* *TSE (1935).
    4. *Prayers and Meditations by Bahá'u'lláh.* *TSE (1938).
    5. *Epistle to the Son of the Wolf.* *TSE (1941).
    6. *The Seven Valleys and the Four Valleys* (1945).
    7. *The Proclamation of Bahá'u'lláh to the Kings and Leaders of the World* (1967).
    8. *Tablets of Bahá'u'lláh Revealed After the Kitáb-i-Aqdas* (1978).
    9. *The Kitáb-i-Aqdas: The Most Holy Book* (1992).
    10. *Gems of Divine Mysteries: Javáhiru'l-Asrár* (2002).
    11. *The Summons of the Lord of Hosts: Tablets of Bahá'u'lláh* (2002). [Incorporates most of item 7].
    12. *The Tabernacle of Unity* (2006).
III. English-language texts of 'Abdu'l-Bahá.
  A. Translated from authenticated texts (8):
    1. *A Traveller's Narrative* (1891).
    2. *Some Answered Questions* (1908).
    3. *Tablets of Abdul Baha Abbas* (1909–16).
    4. *The Tablets of the Divine Plan* ([1919]; 1959).
    5. *The Will and Testament of 'Abdu'l-Bahá.* *TSE (1935).
    6. *The Secret of Divine Civilization* ([1910] 1957).
    7. *Memorials of the Faithful* (1971).
    8. *Selections from the Writings of 'Abdu'l-Bahá* (1978).
  B. Transcriptions of extempore oral translations (2):
    1. *Paris Talks: Addresses Given by 'Abdu'l-Bahá in 1911* (1912).
    2. *Promulgation of Universal Peace* (1922–25).
IV. English-language texts of Shoghi Effendi (15):
    1. *Bahá'í Administration* ([1928] 1936).
    2. *The World Order of Bahá'u'lláh* (1938).
    3. *The Advent of Divine Justice* (1939).
    4. *The Promised Day is Come* (1941).
    5. *God Passes By* (1944).
    6. *Messages to America: Selected Letters and Cablegrams Addressed to the Bahá'ís of North America, 1932–1946* (1947).
    7. *The Faith of Bahá'u'lláh, A World Religion* (1947).
    8. *Citadel of Faith: Messages to America, 1947–1957* (1965).
    9. *Messages to Canada* (1965).
    10. *Messages to the Bahá'í World, 1950–1957* ([1958] 1971)

Table 2. *(cont.)*

11. *High Endeavours: Messages to Alaska* (1976).
12. *The Unfolding Destiny of the British Bahá'í Community* (1981).
13. *The Light of Divine Guidance: The Messages of the Guardian of the Bahá'í Faith to the Bahá'ís of Germany and Austria* (1982–85).
14. *Messages of Shoghi Effendi to the Indian Subcontinent, 1923–1957* ([1970] 1995).
15. *Messages to the Antipodes: Communications from Shoghi Effendi to the Bahá'í Communities of Australasia* (1997 [incorporates earlier works of 1970 and 1982]).
V. **English-language texts of the Universal House of Justice** (5):
  1. *The Constitution of the Universal House of Justice* (1972).
  2. *The Promise of World Peace* (1985).
  3. *Individual Rights and Freedoms in the World Order of Bahá'u'lláh* (1989).
  4. *A Wider Horizon: Selected Messages of the Universal House of Justice, 1983–1992* (1992).
  5. *Messages from the Universal House of Justice, 1963–1986: The Third Epoch of the Formative Age* (1996 [incorporates earlier works of 1969 and 1976]).
VI. **Compilations of extracts from authoritative writings** (1):
  1. *Compilation of Compilations* (3 vols., 1991–2000 [incorporates earlier publications of various dates]).

several individual scholars have begun the task of comparing sometimes variant manuscript copies of early texts, and the results of such work will presumably eventually find published form. The Baha'i World Centre also collects the original letters written to the sequent Baha'i leaders, creating a base for locating replies in their original context.

2. INTERPRETATION

All written texts have necessarily to be interpreted by the reader or hearer. Inevitably, whilst the meaning of some texts is relatively straightforward, easy to understand and generally agreed on, the meaning of others is more elusive and subject to variant understandings. In the history of religions, variations of interpretation and understanding have often underlain vehement and sometimes violent disagreements about religious 'truth' and the process of sectarian division. Baha'is believe that they will escape this condition, both through their common adherence to the Covenant doctrine (see later, Chapter 8), and because of the sharp distinction they make between authoritative and individual interpretation of the Baha'i writings.

In the Baha'i Faith, authoritative interpretation is essentially confined to 'Abdu'l-Bahá and Shoghi Effendi as the explicitly appointed and authorized interpreters of the Baha'i writings, their interpretations on matters of belief being regarded as infallible and thus as a continuing source of guidance. Although the Universal House of Justice is empowered to elucidate on obscure and controversial matters, it explicitly refrains from interpretation, so that, since the death of Shoghi Effendi in 1957 and the consequent loss of a living guardianship, there is no Baha'i institution empowered to give authoritative interpretation.[7]

Individual interpretations of the writings, by contrast, are seen as the fruits of individual human reason. In studying the writings, each individual will arrive at his or her own understanding, which may well differ from those of others. In this context, the Universal House of Justice has stressed the importance of tolerance for the views of others. It is wrong for any Baha'i to insist that his or her own understanding of the Baha'i teachings is the only correct one or to be disputatious about these teachings (and so threaten disunity within the community). Each individual should make it clear that their views are merely their own and not press them on their fellows. Again, they should learn to listen to views of others without being either overawed or shaken in their faith if these views diverge from their own. They should also remember that the meaning of the word of God can never be exhausted (which implies that different views can be simultaneously 'correct'), and that individual understanding are not fixed and may change through the process of further study. Again, Baha'is are warned against the tendency so often displayed by some religionists of trying to encompass a divine message within the framework of their own limited understanding and of defining as dogmas matters which are beyond easy simple definition.[8]

3. LANGUAGE AND UNDERSTANDING

Given the enormous importance which the Baha'i leaders have attached to the authority of the written word, and the belief that the divine word itself has an intrinsic transforming power, it is not surprising that all Baha'is are encouraged to study the Baha'i writings. More than this, the Baha'i teachings emphasize the importance of understanding more than the sanctity of the actual words themselves. Thus, unlike many religions, Baha'i has no sacred or liturgical language: Baha'is should understand their sacred writings and this can only be done if they have access to these writings in their own languages. To this end, Baha'is are strongly encouraged to become literate (and to ensure that their children become literate), and the translation of

---

[7] See CEBF, 'interpretation', loc. cit.   [8] Universal House of Justice, *Messages*, pp. 87–8.

Baha'i scriptures and other literature has formed a major part of Baha'i endeavour ever since the Faith began to spread outside of the Middle East.

This said, Arabic, Persian and English have a special status in relationship to the Baha'i 'canon', the first two because they are the languages of the original writings of the Báb, Bahá'u'lláh, and 'Abdu'l-Bahá (There are also a few writings of 'Abdu'l-Bahá in Turkish); English because it was (with Persian) the language used by Shoghi Effendi in his writings and his interpretations of the Baha'i scriptures, and by the Universal House of Justice in its pronouncements to the Baha'i world. English was also the language used by Shoghi Effendi in his authoritative translations of the Baha'i writings, and has become the predominant language of international communication among Baha'is.

4. SECONDARY LITERATURE AND REVIEW

There is a massive Baha'i secondary literature in many languages, particularly in English.[9] This includes commentaries on Baha'i texts and expositions on numerous aspects of the Baha'i belief and practice. Undoubtedly some of these works – such as the widely-read introduction to the Faith by the Scots Baha'i John Esselemont (*Bahá'u'lláh and the New Era*), first published in 1923 – have had a significant impact on popular Baha'i understandings of the Faith, but none of them have any authoritative status as guides to Baha'i belief.

Following a policy introduced by 'Abdu'l-Bahá and formalized by Shoghi Effendi in 1922,[10] all works written by Baha'is on the Faith or published under Baha'i auspices must be reviewed by an appropriate Baha'i institution (usually the reviewing committee of a national spiritual assembly) so as to guard against 'misrepresentations' of the Faith when it is still relatively unknown. For the most part, implementation of this policy has been relatively permissive, so that a diversity of views continue to appear in print.

---

[9] Collins lists 2,819 items in English on the Babi or Baha'i religions up to 1985 (*Bibliography*, pp. 41–158), including multiple editions, but excluding materials in Braille (142 items) and periodicals.

[10] Shoghi Effendi, *Bahá'í Administration*, p. 23. See CEBF, 'review', loc. cit. The procedure is regarded as only a temporary measure whilst the Baha'i Faith is 'in its infancy' and thus easily misrepresented.

CHAPTER 8

Divine Knowledge and Guidance

I. GOD AND THE MANIFESTATIONS OF GOD

God

The Baha'i Faith is strictly monotheistic: there is only one God. God in essence is unknowable, however, and is exalted above human attributes and understanding, so that it is impossible to even hint at 'His' essential nature.[1] All human conceptions of God are mere imaginations, which some individuals mistake for reality. Knowledge of God is therefore primarily to be achieved by way of the 'Manifestations of God' (below), who act as God's messengers and reflect 'His' attributes. More generally, every created thing in the whole universe is a 'sign' of God's sovereignty, and a 'door' leading to knowledge of him. All existence reflects his image, but his attributes are most particularly revealed in human beings. Thus, if a seeker turns his or her gaze to their own self they will find the signs of God within. Shoghi Effendi described God as one, personal, unknowable, inaccessible, eternal, omniscient, omnipresent and almighty, and as being 'invisible yet rational'; a supreme reality. He rejected incarnationist, pantheistic, and anthropomorphic conceptions of God.[2]

The Baha'i writings abound with the names and attributes of God, these comprising a means by which we can reach some understanding of Him. These include: Almighty; All-Knowing; All-Sufficing; All-Loving; Most Compassionate; Ever-Forgiving; Ever-Faithful; Lord of all being; Lord of grace abounding; King of the realms of justice; Shaper of all the nations; Source of all Sources; Cause of all Causes; Chastiser; Inspirer; Help in Peril; Eternal Truth; central Orb of the universe, its Essence and

---

[1] See CEBF, 'God', loc. cit. Baha'i writings in European languages follow the Western tradition of referring to God as 'Him', but God is regarded as being beyond gender, and all anthropomorphic conceptions of God are rejected.
[2] Shoghi Effendi, *God Passes By*, p. 139; idem, *World Order*, pp. 112–13.

ultimate Purpose; Fountain-Head of all Revelations; and Well-Spring of all Lights.[3]

The Manifestations of God

Given that God is in essence unknowable, Baha'is believe that the primary means by which human beings learn of God and of his purpose for humanity is through the *'Manifestations of God'* – divine messengers who are his exponents on Earth.[4] These include the Biblical-Qur'ánic figures of Adam, Abraham, Moses, Jesus, and Muḥammad, as well as Zoroaster, Krishna, and the Buddha, and for the present age, the Báb, and Bahá'u'lláh. There is no definitive list of Manifestations of God.

According to the Baha'i view, the Manifestations are theophanies: divine mirrors who reflect God's glory and reveal his attributes. They are not incarnations of God as they do not embody the divine essence. For human beings, they represent the divine presence. They are the primary means through which human beings can approach God. They are the bearers of divine revelation and law, who transmit both divine knowledge and infinite grace to humankind. They are infallible and protected from sin.[5] They exercise a spiritual sovereignty over all in heaven and Earth. Each one is himself the standard of truth which people must follow, and brings a judgement which separates the faithful (who accept the Manifestation and obey him) from the unbelievers (who reject him). They engender a transformation in the lives of their followers, bringing unity to diverse peoples, and giving them peace, courage, and certitude.

The Manifestations have a double 'station': of 'essential unity' and of individual 'distinction'. Thus, whilst they share a common role as divine revelators and proclaim the same faith, they also each have their own mission, message, and human individuality. Again, as the channels through which human beings approach the divine, they may claim to be the very voice of God, or they may refer to themselves as mere prophets and emphasize the unapproachability of the divine essence – differences in description which Baha'is believe underlie the very different understandings which adherents of the various world religions have of their founders' statuses.

---

[3] Rabbani, *Desire of the World,* pp. 164–74.
[4] CEBF, 'Manifestations of God', loc. cit. The term 'Manifestation of God' is a translations of the Persian, *'mazhar-i iláhí'*. See Juan Cole, *The Concept of Manifestation in the Bahá'í Writings. Bahá'í Studies* 9 (1982).
[5] This is the Baha'i doctrine of the *'Most Great Infallibility'*. See CEBF, 'infallibility', loc. cit.

'Lesser Prophets'

In addition to the Manifestations of God, Baha'is recognize a category of 'lesser prophets', who are followers of the Manifestations and reflect their light, but who unlike them are not independent divine intermediaries.[6] There is no definitive listing of lesser prophets in the Baha'i writings, nor is the concept discussed in detail, but it is clear that the possibilities of divine guidance and inspiration are not restricted to the recognized Manifestations of God. The contrast is most clearly seen in relationship to Judaism, with Abraham and Moses both being regarded as Manifestations, whilst Solomon, David, Isaiah, Jeremiah, Ezekiel and others are seen as lesser prophets. The Shi'i Imáms would also seem to be regarded as lesser prophets, as also perhaps the first two Shaykhi leaders. At a popular level, some Baha'is also regard figures such as the Native American prophets Viracocha (Inca), Quetzalcoátl (Toltec), and Deganawida (Iroquois) as divine messengers, albeit that such views are necessarily speculative in terms of Baha'i prophetology (which is canonically limited to the prophets mentioned in the Bible, Qur'án, and Babi-Baha'i writings, but such views express the Baha'i belief in the universality of divine guidance to humanity, as well as representing an important 'bridge' in Baha'i missionary endeavour amongst indigenous peoples.

Progressive Revelation

Baha'is see various of the world's religions as 'different stages in the eternal history and constant evolution of one religion', itself divine and indivisible, and of which the Baha'i Revelation forms an integral part.[7] The founders of these religions are linked through the Baha'i doctrine of *'progressive revelation'*, with divine revelation being seen as both recurrent and progressive, expressing both eternal truths and teachings relevant to a particular time and place. Thus, recurrence is expressed by each of the Manifestations of God proclaiming and renewing 'eternal verities' (moral and spiritual truths), in which role the appearance of the successive divine messengers was like the cycle of the year, with the coming of each new Manifestation corresponding to the coming of Spring as he brought new life to a world made spiritually cold and dead by the neglect of the teachings brought by the previous

---

[6] CEBF, 'prophets', loc. cit.
[7] CEBF, 'progressive revelation', loc. cit. The recognized religions include Hinduism, Buddhism, Zoroastrianism, Judaism, Christianity, and Islam. See Chapter 10..

Manifestation. Correspondingly, over time, each religious system declined as religionists blindly followed tradition rather than the pure teachings of the founder, necessitating the appearance of a new Manifestation. At the same time, however, the Manifestations of God brought divine teachings appropriate to the spiritual capacity of the people of their time. As such, certain aspects of 'religious truth' were relative to their recipients and not absolute, so that whilst all religions would enjoin honesty and piety and condemn murder and theft, they might have different laws concerning social institutions such as marriage and the treatment of criminals.

As a succession of interrelated figures who speak with the same divine voice, the Manifestations also foretell the coming of their successors, although in the event, their followers commonly reject the promised successor when he comes (as the Jews rejected Jesus and the Christians rejected Muḥammad), in part because they read their scriptures literally and do not understand the spiritual metaphors which are often used in prophecy; in part, because they blindly follow ancestral beliefs without thinking for themselves.

In relation to this pattern of progressive revelation, Bahá'u'lláh's revelation is held to occupy a unique role as it represents the culmination of those of the past, bringing all the world religions into unity, and establishing the basis for the future millennial age which had been prophesied in all religions. Bahá'u'lláh's message also includes the specific call for world unity based on the proclamation of the oneness of humankind – a call which could not have been made by previous divine revelators in a pre-globalized world.

As to the future, no religion – including the Baha'i Faith itself – could claim to be the final revelation of God to man, and God would continue to 'send down' his messengers to humanity until 'the end that hath no end', and they would 'unfold' an 'ever-increasing' measure of Divine guidance. Future Manifestations would arise under the 'shadow' of Bahá'u'lláh in the millennia to come, though none for at least a thousand years.

The Doctrine of the Covenant

A key Baha'i doctrine is that of two religious covenants which are believed to operate in religious history.[8] The first of these – the '*Greater Covenant*' – is that between each Manifestation of God and his followers regarding the promise of the next Manifestation. Expressed in prophecy, this is an implicit

---

[8] CEBF, 'Covenant', loc. cit.

contract which obligates the followers to respond to their own prophet's eventual successor when he comes.

The second – the '*Lesser Covenant*' – is that which a Manifestation of God makes concerning his immediate successor whom his followers should turn to and obey, as per the appointment of the apostle Peter by Jesus, the Imám 'Alí by Muḥammad, and 'Abdu'l-Bahá by Bahá'u'lláh. The Baha'i Lesser Covenant is held to be unique in that it is both explicit and in written form. By contrast, the covenants of appointment of Peter and 'Alí were neither written nor sufficiently explicit, and so did not gain universal acceptance, with the result that both Christianity and Islam soon became riven into contending sects. The strength of the Baha'i Lesser Covenant ('the most great characteristic' of the Faith according to 'Abdu'l-Bahá) assures the unity of the Baha'i religion and protects it from schism, those who reject any of the links in the chain of succession (Covenant-breakers) being deemed to have rejected Bahá'u'lláh.

Authority and Infallibility

Baha'is believe in the supreme authority of all the divine messengers, the Manifestations of God. They are sanctified from error and are in themselves the standard of truth which others are to follow. For Bahá'u'lláh, 'true belief' in God requires acceptance and observance of whatever God has revealed, whilst steadfastness in God's Cause rests upon faith that 'He doeth whatsoever He willeth', that is, a complete acceptance of God's authority as revealed through the Manifestation of God. Ultimately no one can fathom 'the manifold exigencies of God's consummate wisdom', and the Manifestations are not limited by human standards. Thus, if they were to pronounce earth to be heaven and water to be wine, then it is the truth, and no one has the right to question their authority. It is incumbent on all others to adhere to what they ordained. Whatever they said is the word of God, and no one has the right to criticize.[9]

Unsurprisingly, this claim to absolute authority is linked to a concept of infallibility, which in Baha'i belief is an intrinsic quality possessed by all the Manifestations of God, and in varying ways by certain individuals and institutions who are under the special protection of God and who thus to some degree are granted a measure of '*conferred infallibility*'.[10] These individuals and institutions mediate God's grace to humankind and act as his guides to other humans. In the present dispensation, Baha'is believe that

[9] Bahá'u'lláh, *Aqdas*, pp. 36–7; idem, *Tablets*, pp. 108–10.   [10] CEBF, 'infallibility', loc. cit.

as Manifestations of God, the Báb and Bahá'u'lláh were both intrinsically infallible, whilst 'Abdu'l-Bahá, Shoghi Effendi, and the Universal House of Justice are all believed to be acting under God's unerring guidance, and as such should be obeyed as possessors of conferred infallibility. In this context, 'Abdu'l-Bahá voiced 'the very truth', so that whatever his pen recorded was correct. By contrast, Shoghi Effendi defined his own infallibility as being confined to the interpretation and application of scripture and to the protection of the Baha'i Faith. It did not extend to economics, science, or technical matters. Unlike the Manifestations of God, he was not 'omniscient at will'. When he stated that something was for the protection of the Faith, he should be obeyed, but if he merely gave advice to an individual, then this was not binding. He also distinguished his own position from that of 'Abdu'l-Bahá, in whose person human nature and 'superhuman knowledge and perfection' had been blended. Clearly, together with the doctrine of the Covenant, the doctrine of conferred infallibility has enormously strengthened the authority of the successive heads of the Faith ('Abdu'l-Bahá, Shoghi Effendi, and the Universal House of Justice).

2. GOD AND HIS CREATION

The Baha'i leaders also utilized various conceptual frameworks drawn from Islamic philosophy to describe the relationship between God and his creation (both ultimately beyond human understanding in their view), portraying intermediate realms of existence ('worlds of God') between the unknowable, unmanifested essence of God, which even God's Prophets could not know, and the physical world familiar to human beings.[11]

A key conception here was the rejection of the idea of a purely material universe (and explicitly of Western philosophical materialism). Not only was the material universe itself pervaded by the Holy Spirit, with every created thing being a 'sign' of God's sovereignty, but human beings possessed a spiritual dimension, the soul (see Chapter 9), which enabled them to recognize and love God and to be transformed into heavenly beings if they so chose. Materialistic philosophers had their spiritual 'eyes' closed

---

[11] There is as yet no detailed study of the use of the Islamic philosophical traditions by Bahá'u'lláh, and 'Abdu'l-Bahá – a significant lacuna in Baha'i Studies. For very brief summaries of some of the issues see CEBF, 'creation'; 'materialism'; 'metaphysics'; 'philosophy', loc. cit. Both Cole, *Concept of Manifestation*, and Moojan Momen, 'Relativism: A basis for Bahá'í metaphysics'. In *Studies in Honor of the Late Hasan M. Balyuzi*, ed. M. Momen (Los Angeles, CA: Kalimát Press, 1988), pp. 185–217, make suggestive comments.

and so could not see the world of the spirit that surrounded them. A second key idea was that of the potent force of the logos (the 'Primal Will', the 'Holy Spirit', the 'Word of God') as the realm of God's command and grace by means of which God has created the heavens and the Earth, the Manifestations of God being appearances of the logos in the physical world.

The Baha'i leaders also commented on other 'philosophical' issues, maintaining views which showed their acceptance of the Islamic philosophical heritage, itself often seen as suspect by many 'orthodox' Muslims. For example, discussing the nature of creation, they rejected the 'orthodox' notion that because the material universe was created by God, it had to have a beginning and an end. Rather, they stated, whilst individual created entities – such as the planet Earth or an individual human body, originated at a particular moment in time, and subsequently might cease to exist, breaking down into their component elements, the physical universe as a totality has always existed in some form, having neither beginning nor end.

Good and Evil

According to Baha'i belief, evil has no objective reality other than in the negative and destructive behaviour of individual human beings and animals. There are no malevolent superhuman entities such as a devil or Satan.[12] God's creation is good. Human beings have free will and may either turn towards God and develop spiritual qualities, or become immersed in their own selfish desires and commit wrongdoing. If they choose the latter, then their actions are sometimes described as 'satanic' in the Baha'i writings, but this is a purely metaphorical usage.

The Baha'i leaders rejected the belief in evil spirits which can harm or exert some form of negative influence on human beings or which human beings should fear or seek to placate, dismissing such ideas as superstition. Baha'is then do not believe in such things as demons, animistic spirits, ghosts or demonic possession. Individuals who commit evil actions may have an enormous influence in this world whilst they are alive, but their own souls cease to have any influence after they die and they have no power over the living. New Testament references to people being 'possessed' by devils are symbolic descriptions of individuals who have yielded to the dark forces of their own passions and baser natures. Except when people

---

[12] CEBF, 'evil'; 'evil spirits'; and 'satan', loc. cit.

are afflicted with certain psychological disorders, they are responsible for any evil actions which they may commit.

There are references to angels in the Baha'i writings, either as spiritual beings in the mysterious realms of being between God and humans (as in traditional Jewish, Christian, and Muslim beliefs in beings who are attendant upon God and serve as his messengers or as executors of the divine will), or as individual people who have become completely selfless and endowed with spiritual qualities.[13]

3. KNOWLEDGE

All religions have their particular conceptions of the basis of true and authoritative knowledge. The Baha'i conception is multi-faceted and incorporates a certain natural tension between what we might term 'authoritarian' and 'anti-authoritarian' elements. Thus, the absolute authority and inherent infallibility accorded to the Manifestations of God, together with the doctrine of conferred infallibility of the successor leaders, seem to suggest an essentially authoritarian conception of knowledge. Yet, quite clearly, this is not the case, as the Baha'i writings also simultaneously abound with references to the importance of human reason, scientific enquiry, and what I would term a radical epistemological skepticism, all of which together have the effect of enhancing the role of individual decision making, and can be seen as intrinsically anti-authoritarian and opposed to dogmatism.

Reason and the Intellect

The Baha'i leaders placed great value on the 'rational faculty' of human beings – the 'mind' – with its capacities for imagination, conceptualization, reflection, comprehension, memory, and reasoning, and encouraged their followers to engage in the quest for knowledge and understanding. Indeed, 'Abdu'l-Bahá regarded the intellect as God's greatest gift to humanity, seeing it as distinguishing human beings from all other creatures and enabling them to be able to perceive what is true. It is an expression of the soul, born of divine light, and whilst fallible (below), is capable of potent application.[14]

Moreover, as 'Abdu'l-Bahá stressed repeatedly, according to the Baha'i view, opposition to knowledge and science is a sign of ignorance and is

---

[13] CEBF, 'angels', loc. cit.   [14] CEBF, 'intellect'; 'reason', loc. cit.

to be condemned.[15] To oppose reason in the name of religion is superstition. True religion must be in conformity with science and reason – and like science, true religion should bear the 'test' of reason. When religion was not in accordance with science, it was a human invention and should be discarded. At the present time, it was ignorance, not science, which threatened the foundations of religion. Irreligion and the growth of secularism had developed because of the dogmatism and irrationality of many religious people. The maintenance of irrational beliefs engendered vacillation and was ultimately untenable in the face of rational knowledge.

The importance of rationality extended to the basic Baha'i principle of the independent investigation of truth, again repeatedly stressed by 'Abdu'l-Bahá, and according to which everyone should investigate truth for themselves rather than following tradition and the beliefs of others. They should seek divine assistance, but also depend on their own perceptions, be guided by their own consciences, and use the power of reason. Only when religion was based on personal investigation rather than the imitation of others would it have a solid foundation. It was the blind and unthinking traditionalism and imitation which had led to the rejection of the successive Manifestations of God and stunted the mind. Independent enquiry freed society from endlessly repeating the mistakes of the past.[16]

This said, the Baha'i leaders were also insistent that there were limits to human understanding. No 'mind nor heart' could ever understand the nature of even the most insignificant of God's creatures, let alone the mystery of God himself. All the conceptions of 'the devoutest of mystics' and the most exalted of sages were the product of 'man's finite mind' and were conditioned by its limitations. They were only a reflection of what had been created within themselves. Again, whilst God had endowed the human essence with the 'rational faculty' – the mind – human beings were unable ever to comprehend this inner reality. Indeed, to acknowledge their own inability was the 'acme of human understanding'.[17] Human beings should always seek knowledge, and there was no end to how much they could learn, but they should pursue this quest with the realization that they could never transcend the inherent limitations of their own understanding.

---

[15] CEBF, 'knowledge'; 'religion and science', loc. cit.

[16] CEBF, 'independent investigation of truth', loc. cit. 'Abdu'l-Bahá's arguments are implicitly hostile to the Shi'i principle of *taqlíd* (imitation), whereby it is considered necessary for the ordinary believer to follow a learned specialist in matters of religious law (Momen, *Shi'i Islam* 175–6). By rejecting *taqlíd*, 'Abdu'l-Bahá was also rejecting the authority of certain *'ulamá* (the *mujtahids*) which rested on it.

[17] Bahá'u'lláh, *Gleanings*, pp. 62, 163–5, 316.

Epistemological Scepticism and Relativism

This limitation on human reason is linked to what I would understand to be a radical epistemological skepticism presented by 'Abdu'l-Bahá when he identified four bases for human knowledge (sense perceptions, reason, scriptural tradition, and inspiration) and asserted that each was limited and fallible.[18] Thus, he argued, sense perceptions did not necessarily represent reality, as in the case of perceptual illusions and seeing a mirage in a desert; reason could lead even the same thinker to different conclusions at different times, as with changing scientific conceptions of the cosmos; scriptural tradition could only be understood by the use of human reason, itself fallible (see earlier); and inspiration (the inner prompting of the human 'heart' or 'soul') could be good or bad.

Given this epistemological reality, what then should people do? For 'Abdu'l-Bahá, reliable knowledge was attainable through 'the bounty of the Holy Spirit', but he also advocated the combined use of the four methods to provide a system of cross-checking of ideas. This argument has two corollaries. First, the Baha'i view that human knowledge is always both limited – in the sense that our understanding is never complete or perfect, and is limitless – that is, capable of infinite progress. Second, that science/reason and religion were complementary and mutually supportive: science protected religion from becoming superstition; religion protected science from becoming a barren materialism.

The Baha'i view also allows for a relativism of understanding.[19] If ultimately, all human understanding is limited in nature, then divergent views regarding metaphysical reality are not surprising. If people hold to different views regarding the nature of God, creation, divine messengers, the soul, and the afterlife, then this merely reflects the reality that these fundamental religious concerns are beyond human understanding and definition, but also may enable the divergent views to be reconciled. Bahá'u'lláh himself regarded different understandings of the nature of creation as occurring because of divergences in thought – 'the comprehension of this matter dependeth upon the observer himself'. Similarly, 'Abdu'l-Bahá described theological differences about God as being a product of the imagination: each sect and people created a god in their own thought and worshipped that. God in essence was utterly beyond such conceptions, however. Again, Shoghi Effendi stated that a 'fundamental principle' of

---

[18] 'Abdu'l-Bahá, *Promulgation*, pp. 20–22, 253–5; idem, *Some Answered Questions*, pp. 297–9.
[19] Momen, 'Relativism'. CEBF, 'metaphysics', loc. cit.

Bahá'u'lláh's teachings was that religious truth was 'not absolute but relative', and that the [seemingly divergent] teachings of the various world
religions could thus be seen as 'facets of one truth'.[20] As a corollary of this
viewpoint, much religious disputation can be seen as at best essentially
useless, with rival protagonists arguing over matters which are essentially
beyond their understanding. Worse occurs, when such disputes are linked
to fanaticism and superstition.

[20] Bahá'u'lláh, *Gleanings*, p. 162; idem, *Tablets*, 140; 'Abdu'l-Bahá, *Selections*, p. 53; Shoghi Effendi,
    Faith 2.

CHAPTER 9

Being Human

I. THE SOUL AND ITS DEVELOPMENT

For Baha'is, human beings possess both a physical body and a non-material rational soul.[1] The soul is the essential inner reality of each human being. It is unlimited and immortal. It comes into existence at the time of conception, its light becoming reflected in the 'mirror' of the body. After death, the body decomposes, but the soul enters a new existence, freed from the constraints of its former attachment to the body. The soul is created in the 'image' of God, in that howsoever imperfectly, it can reflect God's names and attributes. It is one of God's signs; an emanation from God; a divine bounty; the 'harbinger' which proclaims the reality of all of God's worlds to human beings; an intermediary between the heavenly and lower worlds; and the medium for spiritual life. It is the first among created things to recognize and love God.

All human beings have an inherent spiritual potential. Each is like a mine 'rich in gems of inestimable value'. But the soul's treasures can only be revealed, and individuals achieve their true potential, if the human 'mirror' is cleansed 'from the dross of earthly defilements', and this ultimately depends on the individual deciding to turn to God and seek to acquire spiritual qualities. God has given human beings free will and the ability to make moral and spiritual choices during their lives. They can choose to commit good or evil actions; to be just or unjust; to praise God and practice philanthropy or the reverse. In all cases, they are responsible for their moral actions, and their decisions and actions have existential consequences.

Spiritual Education

The development of a moral sense requires both moral education and training from childhood onwards and an inculcation of an awareness and

[1] CEBF, 'soul'; 'human nature', loc. cit.

117

fear of God. Genuine religiosity motivates people to overcome their innate selfishness and express spiritual qualities in their lives. The Baha'i leaders rejected both the idea that human beings were innately evil (including the Christian doctrine of original sin) and the belief that there was 'an innate sense of human dignity' which will prevent the individual from committing evil and ensure the attainment of perfection. Babies are born sinless, but self-love is 'kneaded' into the human clay and infants display signs of aggression and lawlessness. Only through a spiritual education will the growing child learn to distinguish right from wrong, and if they lack proper instruction, their undesirable qualities will increase.

Again, if people are to realize the potential greatness of their own spiritual stations, they need to want to manifest goodly conduct. Each individual should therefore gain a knowledge of his or her own true self and of what will lead them to spiritual loftiness or abasement. The power of their moral sense will increase as they discover the purpose for which God has called them into being. Then, they will turn unto 'the treasuries latent within their own beings'. In this respect, true loss is utter ignorance of one's own self.

Because individuals are subject to temptation from their own selfishness and base desires, Baha'is are counselled to guard themselves against such influences by turning towards God, deepening themselves in the Baha'i teachings, and seeking the guidance and protection of the holy spirit through prayer. They should also be on their guard against the negative influences of others, and seek to replace that evil with good, if necessary avoiding people who are exerting an evil influence over them and cannot be influenced to the good.

'Heaven' and 'Hell'

As a consequence of their choices, individuals achieve different levels of spiritual development, some souls reaching a higher and others a lower station.[2] These differences exist both in the present and in the afterlife, and just as the soul is a non-material reality, the 'heaven' and 'hell' referred to in other religious systems are not physical places, but rather states of soul, which may be entered whilst we are still alive and in which we may exist after death. Good deeds are rewarded by God, whether in practical or spiritual terms. To come closer to God fulfils the divinely ordained purpose of human existence and raises the individual to a heavenly state, such that

[2] CEBF, 'heaven and hell'; 'sin', loc. cit.

they may attain 'eternal life' and enter the 'Kingdom of God' whilst they are still alive. The soul that is faithful to its Creator reflects the divine light and eventually returns to God. By contrast, those who are faithless and turn away from God, became victims of 'self and passion'. Immersed in worldly attachments or adopting 'satanic' qualities, they pervert the God-given purpose of their own lives, finally sinking in the depths of degradation and despair. Those who are most exalted become angelic beings; those who are most degraded become viler than the most savage beasts. After death, those who are near to God rejoice, whilst those who are distant from him lament.

From this standpoint, 'sin' is simply disobedience to God and his laws. It results from the soul's attachment to the material world, and reflects the 'animalistic' elements and demands of human nature. A sinful life separates the soul from God, hindering it from attaining its natural potential. Specific sins include anger, jealousy, disputatiousness, lust, pride, lying, hypocrisy, fraud, worldliness, self-love, covetousness, avarice, ignorance, prejudice, hatred, and tyranny. Spiritual progress requires combatting such qualities in ourselves. To do this, it is essential for people to develop a moral sense – a conscience and a concept of right and wrong, for with such a sense, people will abstain from wrong-doing of their own accord, their own inner vision acting as their guide.

Levels of Nearness

For Baha'is, 'heaven' consists of nearness to God, a condition that is both limitless and constrained by the absolute distinction between God and his creation. The relationship is asymptotic: it is always possible to come still closer to God, but complete nearness and absolute perfection are never to be obtained. Significantly as a person draws nearer to God, their understanding of what God expects of them increases, such that '(t)he good deeds of the righteous are the sins of the Near Ones [to God]'. This implies levels or a continuum of salvation, but the faithful are warned never to despise the seemingly sinful, for no one knows what their own end may be: at any time up to the hour of death, the sinner may attain the essence of faith, whilst the devout believer abandons their faith.[3] Again, God's mercy and love for his creatures are so great that with genuine repentance, all sins can be forgiven – everyone should hope and pray for God's mercy.

---

[3] 'Abdu'l-Bahá, *Some Answered Questions*, p. 126; Bahá'u'lláh, *Íqán*, p. 124.

Recognition of the Manifestation of God

In the Baha'i view, the source of the values required in moral and spiritual education is the Manifestations of God and their scriptures. Divine grace is also channelled to humanity through them. All human beings therefore are called upon to recognize the Manifestation of God for the age in which they live (at the present time, Bahá'u'lláh) and to follow his laws and teachings. This recognition is itself part of the human purpose, and, together with the acquisition of spiritual qualities, essential for spiritual progress. Thus, metaphorically, the coming of each Manifestation of God not only separates the faithful from the unbelievers, but separates the living from the dead: acceptance of God's messenger being equivalent to 'life', 'paradise', and 'resurrection', whilst rejection is equivalent to 'death' and 'hell'.

2. SUFFERING

The Baha'i leaders regarded suffering as having various causes.[4] Some is a consequence of the individual's own actions and can be avoided – for example, a person may ruin their digestion through overeating, or became poor because they gambled. In such cases, obedience to God's laws can end many of these sources of suffering. Some emotional states are also a source of suffering, and the individual should try to avoid them: anxiety and depression laying the body open to disease, whilst envy and rage are physically destructive to the body (as well as being barriers to spiritual development). Another source of suffering is the very nature of the material world and attachment to it. The world is transient and unsatisfactory, and suffering alerts people to this reality. They should learn that the only true happiness is to be found in the world of the spirit, becoming detached from material concerns and reliant upon God and the receipt of his bounties. This will also lead to contentment, itself a cause of health. Again, fear of the unknown, particularly of death, is a source of suffering, whereas if people know the nature of the afterlife, they will not fear what is a superior form of existence.

Suffering also arose in the relationship between the individual and God. God tested those who wanted to draw nearer to him, and it became a means of perfecting them: those who suffered most attained the greatest perfection. It also caused people to turn to God when in happiness they might forget him, and proved the sincerity of those who claimed to have

---

[4] CEBF, 'suffering'; 'fate', loc. cit.

dedicated their lives to him. Meanwhile, for those who had truly turned to God, separation from him was the greatest suffering.

In response to suffering, people should develop the spiritual qualities of fortitude and patience, as with those prophets and saints who had found contentment in the midst of ordeal. The fortitude displayed by the sufferer might also have a profound effect on others. Baha'is should not be fatalistic, however. Eventualities such as death could not be avoided, and should be accepted as a natural part of existence, but people should take all wise precautions against adversity. Moral and rational action could alleviate or eliminate many of the sources of human suffering and distress, such as poverty and disease, and as part of their social mission, Baha'is should work to overcome these afflictions. They should also remember that through a combination of prayer and determined and continued effort, even seemingly insuperable hindrances might be overcome.

3. DEATH AND THE AFTERLIFE

For Baha'is, the death and decomposition of the body are a natural part of human life.[5] We may lament the death of those we love, but for the individual, death represents a potential liberation whereby their eternal soul is freed from the fetters of material existence and progresses towards God's presence throughout eternity. Thus, death can be seen as a 'messenger of joy'. Again, the Baha'i leaders compared the afterlife of the soul to the birth of a child. Just as for the child the uterine existence is a preparation for its life after birth, so is the present life a period of preparation for the soul before it enters its eternal environment. In both cases, the period of preparation is of vital importance, but it does not stand by itself. Only if the soul has become purified from worldly attachment will it be able to breathe 'the sweet scents of holiness' in the afterlife. Infants who die are under the mercy and bounty of God.

The Baha'i writings do not give a clear picture of the afterlife. To the contrary, it is asserted that the actual nature of the afterlife is beyond the understanding of those who are still living, just as the present world would be incomprehensible to the unborn foetus. It is stated, however, that each soul is immortal, and that after the death of the body, it continues to progress without limit until it attains God's presence and manifests divine attributes. Again, it is believed that souls retain their individuality and consciousness after death – so that they are able to recognize and commune

[5] CEBF, 'death and the afterlife', loc. cit.

spiritually with other souls (including former marriage partners) on the basis of 'profound friendship of spirit'. The doctrine of reincarnation is rejected, as is the belief in 'earth-bound souls' or ghosts.[6]

Distinctions between souls in the afterlife are believed to exist. After death, each soul will recognize the worth of its own deeds and understand the consequences of its actions. Those who have turned to God will experience inexpressible joy and gladness. Those souls which are sanctified from the world, living in accordance with the divine will are blessed, and will converse with the prophets of God, and the dwellers of the highest heaven will circle around them. Those that have walked humbly with God will be 'invested with the honour and glory of all goodly names and stations'. By contrast, those who have lived in error will be filled with fear and consternation, whilst those who have rejected God will become aware of the good things that had escaped them and bemoan their plight, humbling themselves before him. Souls will recognize the accomplishments of other souls which had attained the same level as themselves, but they will not understand those that are higher in rank.

Prayer and Intercession

It is believed that spiritual links are possible between the living and the dead. The living may therefore pray for the spiritual progress of the dead. Specifically, children should implore pardon and forgiveness before God for their deceased parents. Again, it is acceptable to make charitable donations and perform good deeds in the name of the dead, these being helpful to the development of their souls in the afterlife. Correspondingly, the souls of those who are close to God are able to intercede on behalf of the living, and presumably may therefore be prayed to for intercession.[7] Those who are far from God are not able to exert any impact on the living, however: they have no power.

4. RATIONALISM

Baha'is view the powers of the intellect as expressions of the soul and as God's greatest gift to humanity. Human beings are distinguished from

---

[6] CEBF, 'reincarnation', loc. cit. Accounts by individuals of their 'former lives' are held not to be real memories, but merely indicate the capacity of the human mind to believe firmly in whatever it imagines.

[7] Attempts to contact the dead through occult means, such as séances, are strongly discouraged, being regarded as potentially harmful psychologically to their participants.

all other creatures by their rationality as well as their ability to recognize and worship God. Correspondingly, the Baha'i Faith generally promotes a rationalistic, 'scientific' understanding of physical and social processes, and is thus antipathetic towards the magical world view characteristic of much folk religion, albeit that there is acceptance of the concept of talismanic protection and the performance of miracles by God's chosen ones.[8]

Again, in the face of widespread interest in various forms of occultism amongst some early Western Baha'is, 'Abdu'l-Bahá and Shoghi Effendi were extremely dismissive of claims to psychic powers and esoteric knowledge, regarding most such claims as the imaginations of the subconscious mind, and sometimes as indications of psychological disturbance. Thus, no matter how real they might seem to the individual who experienced them, seemingly visionary dreams were unlikely to be true; Bahá'u'lláh and 'Abdu'l-Bahá did not send special messages to their followers in dreams; spiritualism and the belief in communications from the dead were the product of imagination and had no reality; and astrology and the occult tradition in general were derived from pseudo-science and superstition. Baha'is should avoid 'psychic dabbling' altogether.[9]

[8] See CEBF, 'magic'; 'talismans', loc. cit.
[9] See CEBF, 'astrology'; 'dreams and visions'; 'esotericism'; and 'psychic powers', loc. cit.

CHAPTER 10

The Baha'i Faith and Other Religions

For Baha'is, the mission of Bahá'u'lláh and the development of the Baha'i Faith form part of a single overarching history of religion on this planet. According to Baha'i belief, the declaration of the Báb in 1844 ended an approximately six-thousand-year-long cycle of prophecy (the 'Adamic cycle'), which began with the Prophet Adam, during which successive Manifestations of God announced the future establishment of a kingdom of God on Earth.[1] The Baha'i Faith represents the fulfilment of these expectations.

I. THE 'ADAMIC CYCLE'

This concept of the Adamic cycle provides Baha'is with their primary framework for understanding other religions. Accordingly, a series of nine divinely revealed religions are recognized within an overall pattern of progressive revelation. These encompass the ancient Near Eastern religions of Sabeanism and Zoroastrianism; the Western religions of Judaism, Christianity, and Islam; the Eastern religions of Hinduism and Buddhism; and now Babism and the Baha'i Faith. These are seen as having a 'fundamental unity': they are all the 'rays of one Light', and share a common divine origin. As God is believed to have guided all the world's peoples, the existence of other religions and revelators is assumed, though there is no official list of these.

Baha'i belief in the fundamental unity of many of the world's religions raises the problem of explaining their evident diversity. It is clear that whilst official Baha'i doctrine acknowledges the 'God-given authority' of what we might term these 'Adamic' religions, it does so very much on Baha'i terms, subsuming these various religions under a single Baha'i standard and being selective in what it accepts as valid in each of these traditions. Thus, as successive parts of the same single religion of God, their aims and basic

---

[1] CEBF, 'Adam'; 'religious diversity'; 'time', loc. cit.

principles are held to be one and the same, and their sacred books to be correlative in nature. Most are believed to have left prophetic witness of the future coming of Bahá'u'lláh. Now, in addition to restating the eternal verities of these religions, Bahá'u'lláh is believed to have reconciled and coordinated the formerly separate faiths, restoring the 'pristine purity of their teachings', and so distinguishing their essential and authentic elements from spurious and 'priest-prompted superstitions' that had become joined to them. Denying any intent to belittle the value or distort the teachings of their religions, Baha'is see Bahá'u'lláh's revelation as the basis on which these various religions' teachings and followers will be ultimately reconciled.

2. THE BAHA'I VIEW OF OTHER RELIGIONS

Islam

Baha'is uphold the divine origin and independent status of Islam and the Prophet Muḥammad as one of the Manifestations of God and the recipient of God's revelation in the Qur'án.[2] They also acknowledge that whilst the Baha'i Faith is now fully independent from Islam, it bears a particularly close relationship to it, Shoghi Effendi reminding Western Baha'is that, Islam was 'the source and background' of their own religion, and that a proper understanding of Islam was 'absolutely indispensable' if they were to gain a sound understanding of the Baha'i Faith. In particular, he encouraged them to study the Qur'án (the only scripture other than the Babi and Baha'i texts which Baha'is recognize as fully authoritative); the rise of Islamic civilization; and the particular institutions and circumstances out of which the Baha'i Faith emerged. We may also note that many elements of Baha'i belief and practice clearly have Islamic antecedents. This said, the Baha'i Faith also takes a clear and often distinctive stance on many aspects of Muslim belief and practice. Thus, Baha'is reject the belief that Islam is the

---

[2] There is as yet no detailed study of the relationship between the Baha'i Faith and Islam. CEBF includes some general references (see 'caliphate'; 'Husayn'; '*Imáms*'; 'Islam'; 'Mahdí'; 'Muḥammad'; 'Qur'án'; 'Shaykhism'; 'Shi'ism'; 'Sufism'; and "*ulamá*', loc. cit). See also James Heggie (comp.) *Bahá'í References to Judaism, Christianity and Islam, with Other Materials for the Study of Progressive Revelation* (Oxford: George Ronald, 1986), and Heshmat Moayyad (ed.) *The Bahá'í Faith and Islam* (Ottawa: Association for Bahá'í Studies, 1990). Bahá'í apologetic literature in Western languages addressed to Muslims is quite limited. For examples, see: Ṣábir Áfáqí, *Proofs from the Holy Qur'án* (*Regarding the Advent of Bahá'u'lláh*) (New Delhi: Mir'at Publications, 1993); Moojan Momen, *Islam and the Bahá'í Faith* (Oxford: George Ronald, 2000); and Muḥammad Muṣṭafá, *Bahá'u'lláh: The Great Announcement of the Qur'án*. Trans. Rowshan Muṣṭafá. Ed. Laura M. Herzog (Dhaka: Bahá'í Publishing Trust, [1993]).

final religion and follow what is an essentially Shi'i interpretation of the rightful succession following the death of the Prophet. Baha'is also have a distinctive understanding of what they see as the present decline of Islam. Again, although frequently cited in Baha'i scripture, the Islamic Traditions (reports of Muḥammad's sayings and actions, the *hadíths*) are not regarded as authoritative.

What most distinguishes the Baha'i Faith from Islam is the belief that the line of divine messengers has not ended and that Islamic messianic expectation have been fulfilled. Specifically, the Qur'ánic statement that Muhammad was the 'Seal of the Prophets' is interpreted to mean that he was the last in the cycle of Prophets preparing the way for the present Day of Resurrection, not that he was the last of God's messengers, whilst the Báb is regarded as having been the promised Mahdí (the *Qá'im* in Shi'i parlance) and Bahá'u'lláh the expected descent of Jesus (the 'Spirit of God') and the return of the Imám Ḥusayn. Moreover, contrary to traditional understandings, Baha'is do not see the present 'Resurrection' as marking the end of time, but rather as a crucial point of transition in its continuation towards a possibly far-distant millennial future. In such a context, the Báb and Bahá'u'lláh are seen as functioning as divine revelators and the initiators of the latest expression of God's eternal religion in a manner that is quite divergent from the traditional Muslim understanding of the messianic roles which they claimed to fulfill.

Regarding the succession to Muḥammad, Baha'is follow the Shi'i position and regard the rightful successors to Muhammad to have been the Shi'ite Imáms, referred to by Bahá'u'lláh as 'lights of divine guidance' and 'lamps of certitude'. Unlike orthodox Shi'is, Baha'is believe that there were only eleven Imáms in succession, seeing the existence of a Twelfth Imám as a myth. For Shoghi Effendi, the Imamate was a 'divinely-appointed institution' which had been 'the chosen recipient' of divine guidance for some 260 years after the passing of the Prophet, and was (with the Qur'án) one of the two 'most precious legacies' of Islam. Imám Ḥusayn was particularly eulogized by Bahá'u'lláh, who identified himself with him and claimed to be his spiritual return, whilst Shoghi Effendi referred to Ḥusayn's uniqueness and endowment with a special 'grace and power' amongst the Imáms. Correspondingly, the caliphate is deemed to have been illegitimate, Baha'is seeing its abolition in 1924 by the then newly created Turkish republic as fulfilling Bahá'u'lláh's promise that God would soon 'torment' those who had waged war against the Imám Ḥusayn, and Shoghi Effendi celebrating this 'catastrophic fall' of an institution which he deemed to have 'irretrievably shattered' the unity of Islam as well as opposing the Baha'i Faith.

Baha'is also have a particular understanding of what they see as the present-day decline of Islam, attributing it specifically to those amongst the Islamic learned, the *'ulamá*, who had opposed the Babi and Baha'i religions, and so opposed God and subverted Islam, abasing thereby the peoples of the Muslim world. This condemnation of the present state of Islam is combined with praise for its 'true' form. Thus, 'Abdu'l-Bahá emphasized the transforming impact of early Islam on the formerly brutish tribes of Arabia, who had thereby become the founders of a brilliant and enlightened civilization, which had in turn exerted enormous influence on the civilization of Christian Europe, and spoke of the truth and glories of Islam during his tours of the West, as well as deploring the ignorance and prejudice of many Western writers on Islam.

Whilst the Baha'i Faith spread initially in Muslim societies and most early Baha'is were originally of Shi'i Muslim background, Baha'i teaching endeavour amongst Muslims has generally been extremely circumspect given the real prospects of persecution of Baha'is in many Muslim countries up to the present day. Even in Western societies, there has been little attempt to convert Muslim minorities, and Baha'i apologetic literature addressed to Muslims in Western languages is quite limited in extent. As with Baha'i introductory works in Persian and Arabic, the focus of such literature is often on passages in the Qur'án and Traditions which Baha'is regard as prophetic of their own religion. Shoghi Effendi noted that the public acknowledgement of the validity of Islam by Baha'is of non-Muslim background represented a powerful evidence of Baha'i support for true Islam, and countered the claims of those Muslims who thought that the Baha'i Faith was anti-Islamic.

Judaism and Christianity

Baha'is share the Islamic belief that Judaism and Christianity are previous 'religions of the book', and acknowledge the various luminaries of these religions as either Manifestations of God (as in the case of Adam, Abraham, Moses, and Jesus – all Qur'ánic prophets as well as biblical figures), minor prophets (as with the prophets of Israel), or dedicated and inspired disciples.[3] Baha'is also regard the Jewish-Christian Bible as celestially inspired

---

[3] For general references, see CEBF, 'Abraham'; 'Adam'; 'Bible'; 'Christianity'; 'Jesus'; 'Judaism, Jews'; 'Moses'; and 'Noah', loc. cit. There are a number of apologetic works on the relationship between the Baha'i Faith and Christianity (of very uneven quality). Studies of general interest include those by Richard Backwell, *The Christianity of Jesus* (Portlaw, Ireland: Volturna Press, 1972); Michael Sours, *A Study of Bahá'u'lláh's Tablet to the Christians* (Oxford: Oneworld, 1990), and the same author's *The*

and authentic 'in substance' – but not necessarily in every word and detail. Within the Bible, the Torah (Pentateuch) and Gospels are regarded as of particular importance as embodying the teachings of Moses and Jesus respectively. As noted earlier (Chapter 2), Bahá'u'lláh's evident knowledge of the Bible was highly unusual in a nineteenth-century Muslim context, and he categorically rejected the common Muslim belief that the Jews and Christians had perverted their scriptures so as to expunge prophetic references to Muhammad – arguing that anyone who loved their sacred writings would never knowingly mutilate them. Instead, he held that any 'perversion' of scriptures was in the process of personal interpretation of them by religious leaders hostile to new truths, as in the case of those Jewish rabbis who had opposed Muḥammad (as well as those who had opposed Jesus) and most recently those Muslim leaders who had opposed the Báb.

In terms of prophetic fulfilment, Baha'is believe that the Báb was the spiritual return of Elijah and of John the Baptist, whilst Bahá'u'lláh was the 'Everlasting Father' and 'Prince of Peace' mentioned by Isaiah, David's 'Lord of Hosts', and Christ returned 'in the glory of the Father'. He had come to rule on 'the throne of David'. Both the Báb and Bahá'u'lláh are regarded as descendants of the Prophet Abraham (through Ishmael and Abraham's third wife, Keturah, respectively).

Baha'is have distinctive views of both Judaism and Christianity as religions. Thus, Adam is regarded as the first *known* Manifestation of God rather than as the first human, and he is assumed to have been preceded by other Manifestations of God in a preliterate world – that all human beings are regarded in the Bible and the Qur'án as descended from Adam is seen as indicating humanity's essential unity. Jesus's uniqueness and exalted station are also much stressed, 'Abdu'l-Bahá referring to him as the 'essence' of the Holy Spirit. His sacrificial death is described as having been like a ransom for the life of the world which had caused 'the whole creation' to weep, but had also infused 'a fresh capacity' and 'quickening power' into all created things. Baha'is accept the 'Sonship and Divinity' of Jesus, as well as

Prophecies of Jesus (Oxford: Oneworld, 1991), *Understanding Biblical Evidence* (Oxford: Oneworld, 1990), and *Understanding Christian Beliefs* (Oxford: Oneworld, 1991); and George Townshend's *Christ and Bahá'u'lláh* (London: George Ronald, 1957) and *The Heart of the Gospel* (Rev. ed. London: George Ronald, 1951). Works presenting the Baha'i Faith as the fulfilment of Christian prophecy include those by Ruth J. Moffett, *New Keys to the Book of Revelation*, 2nd ed. (New Delhi: Baha'i Publishing Trust, 1980); Robert F. Riggs, *The Apocalypse Unsealed* (New York: Philosophical Library, 1981); and William Sears, *Thief in the Night, or The Strange Case of the Missing Millennium* (London: George Ronald, 1961). Kenneth D. Stephens, *So Great A Cause! A Surprising New Look at the Latter Day Saints* (Healdsburg, CA: Naturegraph, 1973) presents Baha'i in relationship to the Latter-day Saints (Mormons).

the doctrine of the virgin birth, but reject the orthodox Christian view of the Resurrection, however, seeing this as a spiritual rather than a physical event.[4] They also accept the primacy of Peter as 'the Prince of the Apostles', and see Christianity as both the prophetic fulfilment of Judaism (as the promised Messiah who had abrogated Mosaic law) and the harbinger of Islam.

Ancient Middle Eastern Religions

Of the ancient Middle Eastern traditions, Baha'is include both Sabeanism and Zoroastrianism in their list of divinely revealed religions, and Bahá'u'lláh also made passing reference to the Qur'ánic prophets Húd and Ṣáliḥ. Whilst Zoroaster is accorded the status of a Manifestation of God, Zoroastrian scriptures are not accepted as completely authentic or reliable. Nevertheless, Zoroastrian prophecies are regarded as foretelling the advent of Islam, the Báb (the Zoroastrian 'Úshídar Máh'), and Bahá'u'lláh ('Sháh-Bahrám', the Zoroastrian world-saver).[5]

Given the despised and disadvantaged conditions under which the Zoroastrian minority lived in nineteenth century Iran, respectful Baha'i recognition of their religion had social significance as well as facilitating Baha'i missionary endeavour among them. The Baha'i claim that Bahá'u'lláh was descended from Zoroaster and from Yazdigird, the last Zoroastrian king of Iran was also significant.

Indian and Chinese Religions

The Baha'i Faith is the only 'Western' religion to explicitly recognize the validity of some of the 'Eastern' religions of India and China.[6] Thus,

---

[4] 'Abdu'l-Bahá taught that the Gospel account of Christ's resurrection symbolized the rebirth of faith in the hearts of his disciples after the shock of his martyrdom. His followers became animated by the Holy Spirit and they arose to promulgate his cause. It was a spiritual rather than material reality which was described, just as Christ was said to have come 'down from heaven' (though he had been born from a mother), and whilst still alive was 'in heaven' (John 3:13, 6:38). The return to life of a dead body was scientifically impossible.

[5] For brief references see CEBF (see 'Sabeanism'; and 'Zoroastrianism', loc. cit.). Little is known about Sabeanism with any great certainly. For references to Zoroastrian concerns, see Bahá'u'lláh's *Tabernacle of Unity.*

[6] For a short compilation of Baha'i writings on Eastern religions see CCI, pp. 15–23. There are brief references in CEBF (see 'Buddhism'; 'Chinese religion'; and 'Indian religions', loc. cit.). On Chinese religion, see Phyllis Chew, *The Chinese Religion and the Bahá'í Faith* (Oxford: George Ronald, 1993). On Hinduism, see P. N. Mishra, *Kalki Avatar* (New Delhi: Baha'i Publishing Trust, 1977), and Moojan Momen, *Hinduism and the Bahá'í Faith* (Oxford: George Ronald, 1990). On Buddhism, see

Hinduism and Buddhism are included in the Baha'i list of revealed religions, and both 'Abdu'l-Bahá and Shoghi Effendi included the Buddha in the succession of Manifestations of God – Shoghi Effendi later adding Krishna to the list. Of the other Indian religions – Jainism, Sikhism, and the various strands of Hinduism outside of the Krishna-centred Vaishnavite tradition – the Baha'i teachings have nothing to say. There are also very few references to the non-Buddhist elements in the traditional Chinese religious synthesis: 'Abdu'l-Bahá acknowledged Confucius as a blessed soul who had 'renewed morals and ancient virtues', and become 'the cause of civilisation, advancement and prosperity' for the Chinese, but Shoghi Effendi explicitly excluded Confucius and Lao-tse from the list of Manifestations – Confucius had been a great moral reformer but not a prophet.

Beyond acceptance of Krishna and the Buddha and praise for Confucius, Baha'i views of the Eastern religions are quite guarded, with doubt being cast on the origins and authenticity of the Hindu scriptures; the authenticity of the present Buddhist canon of scriptures being regarded as uncertain – many of the original teachings of the Buddha held to have now been lost; much of present-day Buddhist beliefs and practices being seen as not necessarily in accord with the Buddha's teachings; and present-day Confucian rites and beliefs also being described as not being in accord with Confucius' original teachings.

Given their very different origins and beliefs, incorporation of these Eastern religions into the Baha'i framework clearly raises intellectual questions that have as yet been little addressed. An obvious bridge between the Baha'i Faith and Hinduism is the Hindu belief in a succession of avatars (descents of deities in human and animal form), with Bahá'u'lláh being presented as Kalki, the prophetic 'tenth avatar' of Vishnu in succession to Krishna. Reconciling Baha'i doctrines with non-theistic Buddhist ones would appear to be more difficult, however – though parallels can certainly be drawn between Baha'i moral concepts and those of Confucianism and Buddhism, and Baha'is make appeal to Buddhist messianic traditions with the identification of Bahá'u'lláh as Maitreya, the 'Fifth Buddha'.

At a popular level, intellectual bridges are perhaps less important, and it is of note that both in India and Malaysia, large numbers of Hindus have become Baha'is, whilst there was formerly a large Baha'i community

the contrasting works of Jamshed K. Fozdar's, *Buddha Maitrya-Amitabha Has Appeared* (New Delhi: Baha'i Publishing Trust, 1976) and his *The God of Buddha*. 3rd ed. (Ariccia, Italy: Casa Editrice Baha'i Srl., 1995); and Moojan Momen, *Buddhism and the Bahá'í Faith: An Introduction to the Bahá'í Faith for Theravada Buddhists* (Oxford: George Ronald, 1995).

of mainly Buddhist background in South Vietnam until its unification with the North. Of these, only the Indian conversions have been analysed, the presentation of the Baha'i Faith in popular Hindu terms and the de-emphasis of Islamic terminology being noted as significant factors of appeal.[7]

Indigenous Religions

Although now increasingly overlain or replaced by more universal religious systems, such as Buddhism, Christianity or Islam, localized religions traditionally provided an important basis for the sense of identity for many peoples, and in some instances (notably in the Americas), Baha'is have sought to make appeal to these traditions. In this regard, whilst specific references to other religions in the Baha'i writings focus on the 'historic' world religions, it is also believed that God has communicated his will to all the world's peoples, 'Abdu'l-Bahá explicitly stating that God's call had undoubtedly been raised in the Americas in the past. Combined with the Baha'i belief in the common humanity of all peoples, this belief has provides a potential point of contact between Baha'is and indigenous groups in various parts of the world: rather than condemning traditional beliefs as 'pagan' – as has sometimes been done by the missionaries of other religions – the Baha'is have been able to accept at least elements of some traditional religious culture as compatible with Baha'i membership. Native American or Native Australian Baha'is, for example, may thus be able to regard Baha'i as a fulfilment of their own traditional beliefs. This is particularly relevant when the native tradition contains millenarian elements which can be interpreted in Baha'i terms.[8]

3. RELATIONS WITH THE MEMBERS OF OTHER RELIGIONS

The Baha'i leaders emphasized the necessity for religious tolerance and coexistence and lamented the consequences of religious hatred and fanaticism. Non-disputatious interfaith dialogue is encouraged, Baha'is offering their

---

[7] See particularly Garlington, 'Baha'i *bhajans*'.

[8] See Christopher Buck, 'Native messengers of God in Canada?: A test case for Bahá'í universalism'. *Bahá'í Studies Review* 6 (1996), pp. 97–133; Akwasi Osei, 'African traditional religion: A Bahá'í perspective'. *Herald of the South*. 23 (April–June 1990), pp. 35–39; Joseph Weixelman, 'The traditional Navajo religion and the Bahá'í Faith'. *World Order* 20/1 (Fall 1985), pp. 31–51; William Willoya and Vinson Brown, *Warriors of the Rainbow: Strange and Prophetic Dreams of the Indian Peoples* (Healdsburg, CA: Naturegraph Publishers, 1962).

support to organizations like the World Fellowship of Faiths and the World Conference on Religion and Peace, and initiating or supporting inter-religious conferences concerned with such topics as the promotion of reli-gious tolerance or the contribution of religion to peace and justice. The Baha'i celebration of 'World Religion Day' (started by the American Baha'is in 1950 and held on the third Sunday in January) is now a worldwide event, and has generated considerable interest in some countries, attracting the support of various religious leaders and other dignitaries. Its format varies, commonly featuring speakers from various religious traditions.[9]

[9] CEBF, 'interfaith dialogue', loc. cit.

CHAPTER II

Social Teachings and the Vision of a New World Order

Bahá'u'lláh and 'Abdu'l-Bahá presented their followers with a vision of a future millennial world of peace and justice whilst at the same time outlining what they saw as practical means to accomplish that objective. They also took pains to communicate their ideas to a wider audience, most notably in 'Abdu'l-Bahá's *Secret of Divine Civilization*, circulated anonymously in Iran from the 1880s. Their vision was both far-reaching and multi-faceted. Shoghi Effendi and the Universal House of Justice have subsequently provided commentary on these ideas. We may summarize these Baha'i social teachings under five main headings: world peace and unity; social order and justice; the role and advancement of women; education; and socio-economic development. First, however, we should look briefly at the Baha'i millennial vision and the processes by which Baha'is believe it will be achieved.

I. THE MILLENNIAL VISION

Bahá'u'lláh referred repeatedly to the eventual establishment of the 'Most Great Peace' as the millennial goal of his religion. This was later linked by Shoghi Effendi to a future 'Golden Age', which would be marked by the birth and efflorescence of a world civilization and the establishment of a 'Baha'i World Commonwealth'.[1] This would be a 'New World Order' that would replace the defective world order of the present. It would be established as the 'practical consequence' of the spiritualization of the world and the unification and fusion of all the world's various peoples and would represent the 'coming of age' of the entire human race. It would be characterized by the emergence of a world community, with a consciousness of world citizenship, and a world federal system with 'unchallengeable authority' which would permanently unite all nations whilst preserving

[1] CEBF, 'millenarianism'; 'time'; 'World Order', loc. cit.

their relative autonomy, as well as by the development of a world civilization and culture. There would be a world legislature, executive, police force, and adjudicatory tribunal. Force would be the servant of justice. War would be abolished. National, racial, and sectarian animosities would cease. The personal freedom and initiative of the individual in each component nation would be safeguarded. The press, would cease to be manipulated by vested interests or promote nationalist contention, and would instead give 'full scope to the expression of the diversified views and convictions of mankind'. The global economy would be unified and coordinated, with a world currency and system of weights and measures. Inordinate class distinctions would be obliterated by the abolition of the extremes of wealth and poverty. There would be a world language, script, and literature. Religion and science would be reconciled. Human energies would no longer be devoted to conflict, but instead to scientific research; the increase of productivity; the eradication of disease; the raising of physical health; the prolongation of human life; the development of the human brain; and the stimulation of the intellectual, moral, and spiritual life of the human race as a whole. The millennial hopes of past religions would be realized.[2]

2. AGENCY AND THE CREATION OF A NEW WORLD ORDER

The 'Age of Transition'

The Baha'i leaders believed that their vision of the future would ultimately be realized through the conversion of most of the world's people to the Baha'i Faith, but they also saw it both as part of a process of the societal evolution of the human race and as an objective that could be worked towards incrementally by right-thinking governments, institutions and individuals. Thus, in the present 'Age of Transition' prior to the establishment of the Most Great Peace, the Baha'is were to work to build up the bases for the future Golden Age by teaching the Faith and establishing its institutions, but at the same time they were to be conscious that they were a part of a much broader process of societal evolution. This had already seen the growth of nations and of national identity, and it would now proceed towards and eventually culminate in humanity's 'coming of age' in the achievement of the 'organic and spiritual unity of the whole body of nations'. This was a mystical process of maturation analogous to that of the individual. It might at times be 'slow and painful', but it reflected God's will. Bahá'u'lláh's message was the God-given vision for the present age, and his emphasis on

---

[2] Shoghi Effendi, *World Order*, pp. 203–6.

the unity of the human race was only possible because in the present age there was knowledge of the whole world and unification was an actual possibility. Globalization was effectively a spiritual imperative.

This process of evolution was marked by a 'titanic' spiritual struggle in which integrative and destructive societal processes coexisted. The process of integration – to which the Baha'is were one contributory element – led towards world unity, and was marked by a growing consciousness of global solidarity and an acceptance of the principle of collective security. The process of destruction tore down 'with increasing violence' the various barriers in the way of humanity's 'destined goal'. Nations and institutions could no longer isolate themselves from the wider world. They could progress when they choose to work with the forces impelling the world towards unity. Those outworn institutions which were incompatible with the new age were being swept away. Similarly, popular demands for social justice and the emancipation of women were not only idealistic objectives, but reflected powerful social forces, support for which would create a more harmonious society but opposition to which would harm society itself.

An apocalyptic element was present here, Bahá'u'lláh himself referring to an approaching 'unforseen calamity' and to calamities and commotions which would inflict the world as a consequence of its failure to heed the divine summons.[3] More generally, present worldwide suffering marked both humanity's resistance to Bahá'u'lláh's prophetic call (which alone could solve the world's ills), and more immediately, the failure of governments to adjust to the political and economic realities of a world of already interdependent parts. Ultimately, however, global integration was inevitable, and the 'fire' of ordeal would forge humanity into a single whole.

The Role of Religion

For the Baha'is, pure and revived religion is fundamental to the achievement of the new world order. The Baha'i social vision is thus ambivalent towards certain aspects of modernity, embracing what we might see as a liberal social reformism whilst at the same time strongly opposing materialism and secularism as destructive forces in the modern world. Only through a revival of 'true' religion – shorn of fanaticism, bigotry, and superstition – can the essential development of material civilization be given its necessary spiritual path.

In this regard, Baha'is believe that a central problem of the present age is the lack of spirituality in the development of its 'material

---

[3] CEBF, 'calamity', loc. cit.

civilization'.[4] Whilst praising many aspects of material development, the Baha'i leaders taught that religion was 'the light of the world' and the chief means for the establishment of social order and stability. By inculcating morality and the fear of God, religion and obedience to divine law became the source of human progress, happiness, and civilization. Religious fanatics and hypocrites brought disgrace to religion, but religion itself had to be protected by the world's rulers. The secularism which was increasingly prevalent in the world, eroded both the power of established religions and the basis for social morality and made it more difficult for individuals to cultivate their own spiritual development.

The importance of combining 'spiritual' and 'material' solutions to the world's problems is perhaps also expressed in what can be seen as a 'two track' vision of reform, the Baha'i leaders repeatedly presenting a religiously-based ideal as ultimately the only real solution, whilst accepting more secular goals as a proximate means of improving an imperfect world. This can be seen most clearly in Bahá'u'lláh's millennial vision of the 'Most Great Peace' combined with his advocacy of an imperfect 'Lesser Peace' to be developed by the world's leaders. Whilst eventually, only the 'binding force' of religion can completely unite peoples of different beliefs, creeds and temperaments and create a truly just society, the promotion of the mechanisms of international understanding and of tolerance between peoples can mark a constructive step towards that ideal. Again, whilst developing the systems of criminal justice might prevent manifest crime, only religion can inculcate the moral force to prevent covert wrong doing.

3. THE GOALS OF WORLD PEACE AND UNITY

Bahá'u'lláh taught that the human race was one indivisible whole: 'the fruits of one tree, and the leaves of one branch'. The Earth was a single homeland – one country – of which all human beings were fellow citizens. For Shoghi Effendi, this principle of the oneness of humankind was the pivotal teaching of the Baha'i Faith. It is expressed in both the Baha'i visions of world peace and of world unity.[5]

Peace

Bahá'u'lláh referred to a future 'Most Great Peace', in which all people would become as one family. This ideal would apparently be established by

[4] CEBF, 'religion'; 'civilization'; 'materialism'; 'secularism', loc. cit.
[5] CEBF, 'human race'; 'peace'; 'armaments'; 'World Order'; 'world unity', loc. cit.

the union of all the world's peoples in one common faith and could only be achieved through the power of 'an all-powerful and inspired Physician' (i.e. through universal recognition and acceptance of Bahá'u'lláh). In that true religion provided the best means for human welfare, this represented the 'sovereign remedy' for the healing of the world. However, as the world's rulers had refused the Most Great Peace (by not accepting Bahá'u'lláh), they should instead strive to establish what Baha'is have come to refer to as the 'Lesser Peace', a political peace between nations.[6] Peace was the chief means for the protection of humanity, and conflicts between the nations were the cause of calamity. Even without recognition of Bahá'u'lláh, it was imperative to end war.

For Bahá'u'lláh, the primary obligation to establish the foundations of this Lesser Peace lay with the world's political rulers. They should meet together in an 'all-embracing' assembly, whilst the great powers should become reconciled amongst themselves. After the peace was established, it should be upheld through a system of collective security, with all nations agreeing to act together in unison to oppose the attacks of any aggressor nation. 'Abdu'l-Bahá argued that the rulers' agreement should be embodied in a sacred, binding treaty that would also delimit all international frontiers, define international relations, and restrict the size of each nation's military forces. Both leaders took pains to communicate this idea beyond the confines of the Baha'i community, including in Bahá'u'lláh's letter to Queen Victoria and 'Abdu'l-Bahá's public speeches in North America, in which he called on the United States to take the lead in establishing peace.

Armaments

As part of their advocacy of peace, the Baha'i leaders noted the vital need for multilateral armament reductions. Not only did the 'crazed competition' to develop new weapons and increase the size of armed forces itself contribute to international tensions and arouse the suspicions of other nations, but armament production and development placed a vast and deplorable economic burden on the hapless masses who were required to pay for it. As part of their moves towards peace, the nations should agree to enforceable limits on the extent of each country's armaments. Indeed, even if they did not, the

---

[6] In his letters to the rulers and elsewhere, Bahá'u'lláh referred both to a 'Most Great Peace' (*ṣulḥ-i a'ẓam*) and a 'Great Peace' (*ṣulḥ-i akbar*), this later term being translated by Shoghi Effendi as the 'Lesser Peace'.

excessive costs of military expenditure would eventually force nations to seek peace. International peace would obviate the need for armaments apart from the limited quantities required for defence and to maintain internal order in each country. In such a situation, human energies and resources could instead be devoted to fostering the development and well-being of the world's peoples: war weapons being converted into 'instruments of reconstruction'.

Internationalism, the League, and the United Nations

As articulated by Shoghi Effendi and defined by the Universal House of Justice, the ultimate goal of the Most Great Peace is one which only the Baha'is can accomplish – essentially by successful evangelization, but Baha'is should also support any actions that leads towards the establishment of the Lesser Peace. In this regard, Baha'i support for the United Nations (and before that the League of Nations) is a natural corollary of these principles of internationalism articulated in the Baha'i writings. Thus, whilst 'Abdu'l-Bahá had greeted the establishment of the League of Nations (in 1920) with some scepticism because of its basis in the controversial Versailles Treaty, and Shoghi Effendi had noted that the League lacked sufficient power to enforce peace between recalcitrant nations, Baha'is nevertheless came to see it as an important step towards the realization of the Baha'i conception of collective security, and thus worthy of support.[7] From a Baha'i standpoint, the establishment of the United Nations at the end of World War II was a further step forward, albeit that the UN shares the League's weakness in being incapable of establishing peace because its powers over its constituent nations remain slight.

The Unity of Peoples

The Baha'i leaders proclaimed the unity and wholeness of the human race. All human beings have equally been created in the image of God, and God makes no distinction between people on the basis of race or colour. For the individual, glory lies in upright conduct, not in nationality or rank. On this basis, Baha'is are taught to promote the unity of the human race. Their vision should be world-embracing. They should love the whole world and

---

[7] For comments by 'Abdu'l-Bahá and Shoghi Effendi on the League of Nations, see *Selections from the Writings of 'Abdu'l-Bahá*, pp. 306–07, and *World Order of Bahá'u'lláh*, pp. 191–3.

not just their own nation. Unity does not entail uniformity, however, the Baha'i leaders also advocating the principle of unity in diversity and seeing the variety of human culture, thought, and ethnic identity as something to be valued – as in 'Abdu'l-Bahá's comparison of the human race to a flower garden, made beautiful by its diversity of colour and form. Similarly, whilst opposed to extremist nationalism and the often violent prejudices that it engenders, the Faith is not opposed to 'intelligent patriotism' and the sense of loyalty and duty towards their nations felt by individuals.

Tolerance and Freedom from Prejudice

The Baha'i Faith advocates cultural and religious tolerance, tolerance of others being seen as a means promoting unity, social order, and human progress. This includes the abolition of religious, racial, political, economic, and patriotic prejudices, such prejudices contributing to social conflict and impeding human progress. Racism, for example, is condemned not just as an 'outrageous' violation of the human dignity of its victims, but as a social evil that corrupts its perpetrators and acts as a major barrier to world peace. Both legal measures and education should be employed in combatting it.[8]

Universal Language[9]

The Baha'i leaders saw improved communication between the peoples of the world as a vital part of their goal of world unity and peace. The world's parliaments and rulers should choose one script and language (either existing or new) to be taught to school children throughout the world as an auxiliary to their own native languages. This would facilitate the spread of knowledge and lessen misunderstandings between peoples. 'Abdu'l-Bahá specifically praised the ideal of Esperanto and encouraged people to learn it, but never stated that it should become the international language.

4. SOCIAL ORDER AND JUSTICE

For Baha'is, the achievement of the Most Great Peace requires not just the cessation of war and the growth of unity between the world's peoples, but a

[8] CEBF, 'prejudice'; 'tolerance'; 'race', loc. cit.   [9] CEBF, 'language', loc. cit.

future world order characterized by social justice.[10] Ultimately, this has to be based on religious and moral motivation and principle, but the 'secular' goals of good governance; the rule of law; and the protection of the poor and downtrodden are also essential. In this regard, justice is a divine quality. Without it, tyranny, corruption and dishonesty prevail in the world. Its application secures human unity and social order and trains the world, and it is incumbent on the world's rulers to dedicate themselves to the highest interests of humanity as a whole and establish its reign. Those who neglect justice can never approach God.

Governance

Justice was of particular importance in relation to government.[11] Indeed, the essence of governance was justice. God had committed government into the hands of rulers, in order that they might rule with justice over their people, safeguarding the rights of the downtrodden, caring for the poor, and punishing wrong-doing. Those rulers who governed with justice and wisdom were blessed by God. Those who committed tyranny, injustice and oppression were answerable to God. Governments were obliged to acquaint themselves with the conditions of those whom they governed; confer office on the basis of merit; and ensure that those who were appointed were not unjust. The rulers should regard the people as their treasure, for by them they ruled, subsisted, and conquered. Yet many rulers disdained their own people, robbing them in order to build palaces and burdening them in order to pursue their own extravagances. Some rulers, holding the people at their mercy and motivated by greed, were 'so drunk with pride' that they could not even discern their own best advantage.

The Baha'i leaders emphasized that the form of government was an important element in the establishment of social justice, advocating some form of representative government in which the views of the people could be expressed through a constituent assembly, and in which there was a separation of powers between legislative and executive authorities and liberty of conscience guaranteed and safeguarded. Both Bahá'u'lláh and 'Abdu'l-Bahá praised constitutional monarchy (as in the British model) as a form of government, for whilst republican government by itself profited 'all the peoples of the world', it was better when combined with 'the majesty of kingship'

---

[10] CEBF, 'justice', loc. cit.; Charles Lerche (ed.), *Toward the Most Great Justice: Elements of Justice in the New World Order* (London: Bahá'í Publishing Trust, 1996).
[11] CEBF, 'government'; 'law', loc. cit.

(itself one of 'the signs of God'). Constitutional monarchy also gave a continuity and stability lacking in republican regimes. By contrast, 'Abdu'l-Bahá condemned the political power of Iranian clerics and hereditary aristocracies and regarded tight centralization of government as promoting despotism, predicting that federalism would become the future pattern of government.

Freedom from corruption was also essential, 'Abdu'l-Bahá arguing that not until government officials at all levels were free from corruption could Iran (and by extension any other country) be properly administered. Without good and orderly government, national development could not occur. Whilst establishing consultative assemblies elected by universal suffrage was the 'bedrock' of government, these assemblies could only be effective if ministers and the elected representatives were righteous and uncorrupt. If the elected representatives were ignorant and corrupt there would only be more people demanding bribes. In this regard, universal education was vital so that the common people could demand justice and check governmental abuse.

Again, a just society required that all should be equal before the law and that the law itself should be just. The rights of both the individual and of 'all mankind' needed to be protected. 'Abdu'l-Bahá's condemnation of the arbitrary governance of nineteenth century Iran has wider relevance here, with his calls that capital cases tried by local authorities to be contingent upon confirmation by the central government; that litigants be given the right of appeal to higher courts; and for uniform codifications of law to be made to replace the often arbitrary pronouncements of individual Islamic jurisconsults. Shoghi Effendi referred to the need for a future single code of international law with binding authority, and to the development of a world legislature and world court.

The Control of Crime

For the Baha'i leaders, every community had the right to protection from those whose violence and criminal behaviour threatened its members. In this regard, community life depended on justice, not forgiveness. Some individuals were like 'bloodthirsty wolves' and only punishment and the fear of punishment could deter them. Ultimately, however, passing penal laws and building prisons were not in themselves the solution to crime. Indeed, whilst punishment was necessary, it also served to further pervert the morality and character of the criminal – thus presumably making them more likely to commit further crimes in the future. In the long run, only moral education and the development of conscience would deter crime.

Indeed, one of the purposes of education was that children would learn to avoid wrong-doing, both as a religious duty and out of fear of divine punishment.[12]

The Abolition of the Extremes of Wealth and Poverty[13]

For the Baha'i leaders, human beings were social beings who lived together and relied upon each other for their survival. They needed to recognize this reciprocity if they were to create a just and compassionate society. 'Abdu'l-Bahá was forthright on this matter: poverty degraded and demoralized people, and the struggle for physical existence was 'the fountain-head of all calamities' and 'the supreme affliction'. The continued existence of extreme poverty was indicative of tyranny, and was against God's law. To let starvation and destitution continue whilst the rich were 'overburdened' with wealth was morally wrong. Every human being had a right to such necessities of life as food, adequate clothing, and rest from labour.

To address the problem of poverty and ensure the welfare of all, the Baha'i leaders advocated both effective institutions and the fostering of a sense of mutual social concern. Institutional means might include the traditional Islamic tax-levy (*zakát*) paid to the poor; progressive taxation; the establishment of communal village storehouses to provide for local welfare needs (including for orphans, the poor, the elderly, and the incapacitated); adequate wages or benefits to ensure that workers would not become destitute as a result of sickness or old age; and industrial profit sharing, so that workers would have a stake in the company in addition to their wages. Beyond such structures, a moral-psychological component was also vital, however: the rich should regard the voluntary sharing of their wealth with the poor as meritorious. The poor were a divine trust, who should be protected by the rich, Bahá'u'lláh warning the wealthy to heed 'the midnight sighing of the poor', so that they themselves would not follow 'the path of destruction'. The rich should be generous as this reflected the divine quality of generosity, and giving was a means whereby they could cleanse themselves from 'the defilement of riches'. Similarly, Shoghi Effendi bade the writers of wills to remember the 'social function' of wealth, and the need to avoid its 'over-accumulation and concentration in a few individuals or groups of individuals'. Issues of international inequality should also be addressed: this was a single world, and its inhabitants should be like a single family in which the existence of destitution anywhere would be unacceptable to others.

---

[12] CEBF, 'crime and punishment', loc. cit.   [13] CEBF, 'economic teachings'; 'communism', loc. cit.

We should note that whilst Bahá'u'lláh and 'Abdu'l-Bahá advocated the economic restructuring of society so as to end the scourge of poverty and abolish extreme differences of wealth, and emphasised the dignity and legal rights of all human beings regardless of their social station and the importance of social solidarity, they did not endorse a communitarian or communistic philosophy. Thus, Bahá'u'lláh legitimated individual property ownership, the right to deed property to others as one wished, and – in clear contrast to the traditional Islamic ban on usury – the charging of moderate rates of interest; 'Abdu'l-Bahá stated unambiguously that economic equality was impossible to maintain – and that even if it was ever introduced it would lead to social disorder and 'universal disappointment' and would be impossible to maintain as people created new inequalities; and Shoghi Effendi characterized communism as one of the 'false gods' of secularism which convulsed society and engendered war.

5. THE ROLE AND ADVANCEMENT OF WOMEN

The Baha'i teachings assert both gender equality and some aspects of gender distinctiveness.[14]

Gender Equality

There is no evidence for gender equality being a formal Babi teaching, but it was extremely significant in both symbolic and practical terms that the Báb appointed a woman as one of his chief disciples. In a highly patriarchal society, Ṭáhirih's preeminence was an evident challenge to the established order and she transcended the social bounds imposed on women by dint of her religious fervour and learning. It would seem anachronistic to see her explicitly as a feminist, however (as many Baha'is and others have done) – there was as yet no Iranian women's movement for her to act as spokeswoman for and her teachings were those of religious enthusiasm and not female emancipation, but in memory she was readily given the role of a proto-feminist icon and martyr.

In the case of the Baha'i Faith, a feminist message quickly became explicit, initially in limited form, but later with increasing force. Thus, Bahá'u'lláh himself stated that in the present day, God had removed the distinctions which had formerly differentiated the 'stations' of men and women. Men

---

[14] CC2, pp. 355–406; CEBF, 'women', loc. cit.; Cole, *Modernity*, pp. 163–87. Aspects of gender differentiation are discussed in relationship to Baha'i practice in Chapter 16.

and women were equal in the sight of God, and for both, it was the extent of their recognition and devotion to God's cause which determined their real status. Those women who were truly believers were recognized as being equal to the 'men' of the past, and excelled many men of the present. 'Abdu'l-Bahá was more emphatic, describing gender equality as one of the distinctive teachings of the Faith, and repeatedly emphasizing it in his talks and writings. All human beings were made in the image of God, and God did not differentiate between them on the basis of gender. Both sexes possessed the same potentialities of intelligence, virtue, and prowess. Despite this, he noted that social inequality between the sexes was general throughout the world, and even in the United States, 'the cradle of women's liberation', women remained unenfranchised (until 1920). This was wrong. Not only was it unjust, but women and men were like the two wings of a bird, and it was only if both wings were strong that the bird of humanity would be able to fly, that is, the success and prosperity of the human race as a whole depended on the advancement of women. Women were held back by their lack of education and by the conditions of oppression in which many of them lived. This had to change. Both sexes should receive equal educational opportunity (including access to the same curriculum) and be given the same political, social, and economic rights. Women should strive to achieve equality but avoid confrontation ('Abdu'l-Bahá expressed his disapproval of the militant methods employed by the British suffragettes, and counselled Iranian Baha'i women to be patient in their endeavours to attain equality and the desire of some to abandon the use of the veil). Male attitudes of superiority were baseless and had to be abandoned.

The Qualities of Gender

Both Bahá'u'lláh and 'Abdu'l-Bahá also changed what we might think of as the philosophical status of masculinity and femininity. Thus, Bahá'u'lláh's visions of the 'maid (*houri*) of heaven', described in many of his mystical writings, clearly expressed the feminine aspect of the divine in a highly unorthodox fashion. He also raised the possibility that a future Manifestation of God might be a woman. Again, 'Abdu'l-Bahá saw the achievement of gender equality as more than simply the righting of social injustices against women, but as a key factor in a wide-ranging process of societal change which would lead to a basic shift in social values and the development of a new civilization in which more 'feminine' qualities – notably tender-heartedness, intuition, and receptivity – would balance that of 'masculine' force which had hitherto been dominant. In practical terms, he also anticipated that women in their role as mothers would be a major force in opposing war and establishing peace – having raised sons to adulthood, they would oppose their slaughter.

6. EDUCATION

The Baha'i leaders strongly emphasized the importance of education in both its religious and 'secular' aspects, seeing it as a major element in the spiritual and material development of both the individual and society as a whole.[15]

Thus, from a Baha'i perspective, religious and moral education are fundamental to human well-being and dignity. God's prophets guide and educate humanity so that society may advance and each individual learn detachment and moral behaviour. Human nature is such that without spiritual education, individuals will be easily overwhelmed by their lusts and attachment to the world. Therefore, children should learn to fear God, study the sacred scripture, and be trained to distinguish right from wrong and follow the divine commandments because, beyond puberty, the individual's character is largely set. Parents, and particularly the mother as the child's first educator, had a particular duty here, but schools should also train children in the principles of religion. Religious education should not be of a manner to make the child ignorantly fanatical or bigoted, however.

The Baha'i leaders also emphasized the importance of 'secular' education. All fathers had the obligation to ensure that their children (daughters and sons) learnt how to read and write, and it was a communal responsibility to ensure that schools were established in every town and village. These schools should be well-organized and the entire community should contribute financially towards their upkeep. Baha'i children also were bound by obligations 'to exert themselves to the utmost' in becoming literate and to seek perfection in whatever they did. Education should be systematic and comprehensive, and in addition to developing their minds, children should be taught cleanliness, health education, music, kindness to animals, and such qualities as courtesy. They should also study a universal language and be trained for a profession or trade. It was not necessary for all children to achieve the same level of education, however: for some, a basic education,

---

[15] CCI, pp. 245–313; CEBF, 'education', loc. cit. For examples of Baha'i thinking on education, see Hooshang Nikjoo and Stephen Vickers, *Distinctive Aspects of Bahá'í Education* (London: Bahá'í Publishing Trust, 1993); and H. T. D. Rost, *The Brilliant Stars: The Bahá'í Faith and the Education of Children* (Oxford: George Ronald, 1979).

followed by practical skills training would be sufficient. Particular attention had to be given to the education of girls. Indeed, as the future mothers and hence the first educators of their own children, their education was more important than that of boys. As to the manner of instruction and discipline, children should be praised and encouraged: beating them perverted their characters.

Education was essential to the social, economic and political development of society itself and should focus on those subjects which were of value to society. Subjects which were of trivial importance or based on supposition should not receive undue attention. Children should study those arts and sciences which were conducive to human progress. Ignorance was the principal reason for national decline and an underlying cause of social injustice. Only if the common people were well-educated would they be able to appeal against unjust governance and secure their rights. The masses longed for happiness, but, knowing nothing of the world, were unable to attain it. Education would release the dynamic power latent in the people. Without education, the mass of the people would lack 'even the vocabulary to explain what they want'.

7. SOCIO-ECONOMIC DEVELOPMENT[16]

Baha'i concern with what is now termed socio-economic development again originates with the teachings of Bahá'u'lláh and 'Abdu'l-Bahá, finding its most systematic expression in 'Abdu'l-Bahá's *Secret of Divine Civilization*, with its appeal for the development of Iranian national resources and infrastructure; the building-up of its industry, commerce, technology, arts, and sciences; and the increase of its trade linkages. More broadly, many of the ideas already described in this chapter – the emancipation of women; the promotion of literacy and education; concern with the welfare of the poor; justice and the rule of law; opposition to corruption; and international endeavours to reduce armament expenditures and the resultant financial burdens they placed on the common people – also have obvious implications for development, are intrinsic to the Baha'i conception of development, and where possible are incorporated into contemporary Baha'i development programs (see Chapter 16).

Baha'i teachings on the importance of work are particularly relevant here, the Baha'i leaders stressing the practical and moral importance of work, effectively encouraging the development of a strong work ethic amongst

---

[16] CC3, pp. 5–17; 275–318; CEBF, 'agriculture'; 'environment'; 'socio-economic development', loc. cit.

their followers. Everyone – both rich and poor – should have an occupation, supporting themselves and their families. There was no social role for those who had no desire to work: no one should live off others 'like a parasitic plant'. Work also drew the individual closer to God, especially if it was performed in a spirit of service to others. In their work, Baha'is were admonished to be trustworthy in their dealings with others (trustworthiness being seen as a vital quality for economic success as well as a moral quality) and to strive to achieve excellence in whatever they did. They were also encouraged to try to work in occupations which were of benefit to society. Again, the importance of agricultural development in national life is greatly stressed.

PART III

Being a Baha'i: Aspects of Baha'i Life

CHAPTER 12

The Spiritual Path

I. 'THE PATH'

For Baha'is, spirituality and morality are ideally linked together in the concept of the spiritual path, whereby the individual believer strives to develop greater spirituality and acquire spiritual-moral qualities.[1] All Baha'is are confronted by the challenge to 'live the Baha'i life' presented by the successive leaders of the Faith in their writings. This is seen as an ongoing daily struggle to try to live up to the spiritual and moral demands of what is required of a 'true Baha'i'. It is a spiritual path which Baha'is believe everyone can follow, and in doing so discover the realities of their own souls and progress towards God. Socially, it is linked to a conception of the common difficulty of trying to be a good human being, and eschews both the division of the world into 'saints' and 'sinners' (or the 'saved' and the 'damned') and the moral judgementalism that often stems from that division.

In several of his Baghdad writings, Bahá'u'lláh presented behavioural injunctions in what might be thought of as a 'Sufistic' framework: as in the *Íqán*'s description of the path of the 'true seeker' after God, and more particularly in the *Seven Valleys* and the *Four Valleys* (1856), both of which were addressed to non-Babis from the Sufi milieu and employed Sufi terminology.[2] Thus, in the *Seven Valleys*, Bahá'u'lláh deliberately modelled his description of the journey of the seeker's soul towards God on a traditional framework of spiritual progress comprising seven stages ('valleys'): *search*, characterized by patient quest for the divine beloved; *love*, with its passion of pain and ecstasy; *knowledge*, with its certitude and understanding of inner truth; *unity*, in which the seeker transcended the world of limitation,

---

[1] CEBF, 'spiritual path'; 'spiritual qualities'; 'backbiting'; 'charity'; 'chastity'; 'detachment'; 'devotionalism'; 'fear of God'; 'golden rule'; 'mysticism'; 'prejudice'; 'trustworthiness'; and 'truthfulness', loc. cit.

[2] Bahá'u'lláh, *Íqán*, pp. 122–6; idem, *Seven Valleys*.

and was able to see the reality of things as they really were; *contentment*, in which the mystic saw the beauty of God in everything, and had burnt away all other veils; *wonderment*, with its bewilderment with the myriad of divine truths that could now be understood; and '*true poverty*' and '*absolute nothingness*', characterized by a dying from self and a living in God. Similarly, in the *Four Valleys*, Bahá'u'lláh referred to four 'stations' which the mystic might attain in relationship to God, each corresponding to a particular aspect of the divine: 'the self that is well pleasing to God'; attainment of the true standard of knowledge; seeing the inner reality of the divine, and 'the realm of full awareness [and] utter self-effacement', which is 'free of all the attributes of [the] earth'.

In most of his later writings, however, Bahá'u'lláh provided numerous particularistic statements of the attributes of good and pious character rather than an overarching framework of action, a pattern also followed in the extensive writings of 'Abdu'l-Bahá and Shoghi Effendi. Whilst compatible with the 'mystical path' of his Sufistic works, the effect is to present the spiritual path in far more everyday terms, with special emphasis being given to the spiritual and moral qualities which the individual should seek to acquire. Often, these qualities are presented in terms of general principles rather than as detailed instructions for behaviour, with the idea that individual Baha'is should use their own consciences and understanding to apply these principles in the particular contexts of their own lives. The consequence is that any individual who aspires to follow the path of spiritual and moral action set out in the Baha'i writings does not have a single set of rules to obey, but rather a great mass of teachings to meditate and consult on. Essentially, everyone is called upon to find their own salvation, and each individual is made responsible for his or her own spiritual life. It is also accepted that each individual will face their own spiritual challenges and difficulties in pursuing this path. Ultimately, the only source of human glory is good character. Each person must persevere in fighting their own spiritual battles and strive to become 'true servants of God'.

2. TURNING TO GOD

Fundamental to the Baha'i view of what it is to be human is the belief that the soul ('heart', 'spirit') is God's home and place of revelation. God has created human beings out of his love for them, and so that they in turn should love him. His love is their paradise and their safe stronghold. God has made human beings noble and assured them of his love. This is their natural station, but people busy themselves with the perishable world, and thus lose sight of their own true natures. Instead, they should cleanse their hearts so that they may find the divine light within themselves. The core of religious faith is the 'mystic feeling' which unites man with God.

In turning to God, Baha'is should seek to commune with him. Consciousness of God should pervade their thoughts and actions in their daily lives, so that they maintained a 'sense of spirituality' and communion with God. They should use and meditate upon the Baha'i scriptures, which as the 'word of God' for the present age, has a particular potency, capable of changing the hearts of those who hear or read them. They should immerse themselves 'in the ocean' of Bahá'u'lláh's words, and discover 'all the pearls of wisdom' that lay hidden in its depths. In addition to the requirements of daily obligatory prayer (see Chapter 13), they should recite 'the verses of God' every morning and evening, and can make such additional prayer as they wished, always remembering that the purpose of prayer was to draw the believer closer to God and to uplift the soul and not to weary it through an excess of piety – it was better to read one verse 'with joy and radiance' than to read 'all the Holy Books' with lassitude.

Beyond prayer, consciousness of God and an attitude of devotion should ideally pervade the thoughts and actions of the believer's daily life – although not to the extent that Baha'is lost contact with the everyday world. Rather, prayer should lead to action, in part through prayerful contemplation of the Baha'i scriptures, which should both deepen the individual's understanding of the Baha'i revelation and make them more open to the potentially transforming and strengthening power which these scriptures are believed to have on the human soul.[3] One of the purposes of religion was to bring about change in thought, actions and character, and prayer should have practical affect: by coming nearer to God, the believer should gain greater strength to develop his or her spiritual qualities and overcome moral weaknesses. Again, he or she should bring themselves to account each day – ere death intervened and it became necessary for them to give an account of their deeds before God.

After the 'true seeker' had begun to turn towards God with 'earnest striving' and 'passionate devotion', then divine love would be wafted over his or her soul, and 'the lights of knowledge and certitude' envelop their being, such that they could everywhere see the evidences of divine revelation and distinguish truth from falsehood as easily as the Sun from shadow. Divine love purified and transformed the human heart, preparing it for

---

[3] See CEBE, 'meditation', loc. cit. There is no formal system of Baha'i meditation, each individual being free to meditate as they see fit.

the revelation of divine grace, and empowering the individual to pursue those virtues that were conducive to human dignity and honour, and to the attainment of 'man's true station'.

True faith required detachment from the world. Baha'is should free themselves from the 'prison' of self and the 'fetters' of worldly attachments, realizing that the world, its vanities, and glories were impermanent and worthless – more contemptible than 'dust and ashes'. Worldly possessions and dominion were transient, and should not become the cause of exultation. The whole world should be seen as no more valuable than the black in the eye of a dead ant. The tombs of the proud were an object lesson for the beholder, who should flee the world and turn unto God's kingdom. The 'glamour' of the world was deceptive. What was now left of the rich and powerful of past ages, or of their treasures and palaces? The faithful believer should not let such trappings cut them off from 'God's enduring bestowals' and 'spiritual sustenance'. They should rather place their 'whole reliance' on him. Even if they passed through cities of gold and silver, they should not deign to look at them, nor be seduced by their allure. Worldly attachment caused people to follow their own covetous desires, and hindered them from entering God's 'straight and glorious path'. Detachment applied not only to earthly delights, but to the desire for paradise, pride in one's knowledge or attainments, and attachment to the self. To follow the path towards God, the seeker needed first to 'cleanse and purify' his heart from the 'obscuring dust' of 'acquired knowledge', and from those emotions that would divert him from the truth.

Equanimity was also necessary. Baha'is should trust in God, submitting themselves to him, and accepting trials for his sake, prepared to offer up their lives for God and readying themselves for martyrdom. They should be content with little, neither fearing abasement nor rejoicing in prosperity. They should be humble and patient, ever mindful of their own nothingness before God. Fearing God, they should not to be overwhelmed by earthly fears. To overcome their own fears they should rely upon God for guidance and help, trusting in him, and serving the Faith. This would give them greater strength. They should turn away from ideas which weakened the soul, such as fear of future wars and of death. No one knew what the future held in their present life, but faith in an afterlife lessened fear.

It was also necessary to control one's passions. Under all circumstances, Baha'is should try to behave in a manner that was 'seemly', acting in accordance with God's desire. This included leading a chaste and holy life. Thus, they should totally abstain from all drugs and alcohol; strive to observe modesty, purity, temperance, decency, and clean-mindedness; be moderate in their dress, language, amusements, and all artistic and literary pursuits; and be constantly vigilant in the control of their carnal desires.

Those who followed the spiritual path should never pride themselves on their piety, remembering that no individual ever knew what his or her own spiritual fate would be. Again, they should be moderate in their piety, eschewing both asceticism and excessive puritanism. God had created the bounties of the world for human beings to enjoy, and so long as the individual did not let 'the ornaments of the earth' become a barrier, then they could adorn themselves with them and partake of their benefits, and no harm would befall them. The extreme asceticism of some mystics did not bring them closer to God.

3. RELATIONS WITH OTHERS

Relationships with other people were a crucial part of the spiritual path. Love for God should be expressed both in a general love for humanity and proper behaviour towards others. The Baha'i leaders taught that their followers should strive to become the manifestations of divine love. Not only should there be love and 'spiritual communion' among the Baha'is – so that they became 'as one being and one soul' – but they should also love all human beings of whatever religion, race, or community, even including their enemies. They should have a wider vision, turning away from their own interests and cleaving 'unto that which will profit mankind'. Thus, Baha'is should engage in philanthropy and service to others; show loyalty, courage, magnanimity, generosity, compassion, forbearance, meekness, selflessness, consideration for others, courtesy and amiability; observe the Golden Rule – to 'choose . . . for thy neighbour that which thou choosest for thyself', and not wish for others 'what ye wish not for yourselves'; eschew iniquity, envy, malice, backbiting, covetousness, and bigotry; not breathe the sins of others nor exalt themselves over others; never be a cause of grief to another, or curse them, be or a cause of strife; display a sense of honour and regard for the rights of others; not vaunt themselves over the poor (who were God's trust), but rather bestow God's wealth upon them, succouring the dispossessed and the destitute; and be kind to animals. At the same time, however, whilst forgiving and praying for the sinful, they should seek companionship with those who had renounced the world and avoid fellowship with the ungodly.

Several of these 'social' virtues were particularly stressed. Thus, courtesy was described as the 'prince of virtues', and Bahá'u'lláh and 'Abdu'l-Bahá gave repeated emphasis on the need for truthfulness and trustworthiness as being foundational qualities on which other virtues depended. Truthfulness was 'the foundation of all human virtues'. It protected the individual from moral afflictions. Trustworthiness was 'the greatest portal' leading to human security and tranquillity, and 'the supreme instrument for the prosperity of the world' – upon it depended 'the stability of every affair'. Correspondingly, lying was described as the worst possible human quality – 'the destroyer of all human perfections' and 'the foundation of all evils' (Only in the case of a doctor who withheld knowledge of the patient's true condition in the belief that it would help them recover was it permissible). Piety and the performance of all good deeds were of no value without trustworthiness and honesty. Baha'is should be faithful, not promising what they did not fulfil; reliable; and act with integrity and sincerity. Their deeds should not differ from their words.

Another major goal for Baha'is is cultural and religious tolerance, Bahá'u'lláh instructing his followers to associate with all the peoples of the world with 'joy and radiance' and to 'consort with the followers of all religions in a spirit of friendliness and fellowship'. Similarly, 'Abdu'l-Bahá described fanaticism and 'unreasoning religious zeal' as repellent, and condemned the practices of shunning other people because of their religious beliefs, or regarding them as ritually unclean, or treating them with discourtesy (all common in nineteenth-century Iran). Again, Baha'is are called upon to free themselves of all prejudices in their dealings with those of a different race, class, or religion. God was not concerned with such ephemeral differences between people, but with the moral worth and spirituality of the individual.

The Baha'i leaders also condemned backbiting most severely, describing it as a practice that extinguished 'the life of the soul'. It was 'the most great sin' and the most hateful human characteristic. It was a cause of divine wrath: the backbiter was accursed. In their conversations, then, Baha'is should endeavour never to speak of the faults of others in their absence, or to gossip about them. They might speak of their praiseworthy qualities, but rather than even think of the imperfections of others, they should remember their own faults and seek to root them out. Each individual was responsible for their own life and perfecting their own character. The Baha'is should show love and patience towards others, encouraging rather than criticizing them, being understanding of human weakness, and seeking to conciliate. Love and tact could overcome jealousy and pettiness.

CHAPTER 13

Community Membership and Baha'i Law

I. COMMUNITY MEMBERSHIP

Adherence to any religious movement typically involves both personal belief and membership of a social group. In the case of the Baha'i Faith, modern-day identity as a Baha'i requires social recognition as a member of a particular Baha'i community. There are undoubtedly a wider circle of people who are sympathizers and friends of the Faith, and there are some who whilst not officially Baha'is, think of themselves as Baha'is in some sense, recognizing Bahá'u'lláh as a religious teacher and seeking to follow the Baha'i teachings, but without formal Baha'i membership, such individuals are not incorporated into full participation in Baha'i community life and not bound by Baha'i law and administration.

To become a member of a Baha'i community requires formal registration, normally on a membership list maintained by the national spiritual assembly of the country in which the believer resides. Those who are born into Baha'i families must also at some point register as full members of the community. This is often done at the age of fifteen, which Bahá'u'lláh established as the age of social and religious maturity after which Baha'is are obligated to follow the laws of prayer and fasting, and at which they can marry with parental consent if they so choose.[1] Before this age, children are considered to be under the direction of their parents – and thus need their parents' permission to attend Baha'i meetings or register as Baha'is. Further registration is required at the age of twenty-one, which is the present age of 'administrative' maturity, at which Baha'is can vote for and be elected on to spiritual assemblies.

As in any inclusive religious community, there are considerable variations in belief, commitment, and involvement amongst registered Baha'is. Baha'is

---

[1] CEBF, 'maturity, age of', loc. cit. Child marriage or engagement (i.e. before the age of fifteen) is specifically forbidden in the Baha'i Faith.

are generally fairly tolerant of this diversity, as it is assumed that there is more than one way of being a Baha'i and that religious faith is a matter of personal choice. Some individuals (not many it would seem) choose to formally withdraw from the Faith. Others become inactive or loose contact with the Baha'i administration. Unlike apostates in Islam (who theoretically, and sometimes in practice, may be punished with death) and in some Christian sects, no opprobrium is attached to this decision unless the 'ex-Baha'i' vociferously attacks the Faith. Baha'is who reject any of the recognized succession of Baha'i leaders may be expelled from the Faith, whilst those who break certain Baha'i laws may be deprived of their rights to vote in Baha'i elections and participate in some Baha'i meetings (see below).

Shoghi Effendi laid down what he considered to be the 'fundamental' aspects of membership of the Baha'i community (in 1925). These were: (i) 'Full recognition' of the station of the Báb, Bahá'u'lláh and 'Abdu'l-Bahá; (ii) 'unreserved acceptance' of their writings; (iii) 'loyal and steadfast adherence' to 'Abdu'l-Bahá's *Will*; and (iv) 'close association with the spirit as well as the form of the present day Baha'i administration throughout the world'. He also noted, however, that the question of what exactly the qualifications of a 'true believer' were was 'delicate and complex', and warned the national assembly he was writing to (that of the United States and Canada) not to be overly rigid in determining membership.[2]

2. THE CONCEPT AND PRACTICE OF HOLY LAW

Holy law is also a fundamental part of Baha'i practice.[3] In this the Baha'i Faith reflects its Islamic roots. Thus, Bahá'u'lláh, as part of his role as a Manifestation of God, acted also as a sacred law-giver, revealing his own book of sacred law, the *Kitáb-i Aqdas* (c. 1873). As with Islamic law, this is seen as providing the ideal pattern for individual human behaviour and the structuring of human society. For Bahá'u'lláh, the ordinances of the *Aqdas* were 'the highest means for the maintenance of order in the world and the security of its peoples'. They suffused the heart of the true believer with light, and should be obeyed with 'joy and gladness'. 'True liberty' consisted in obedience to these laws. Those who consciously breached the laws were heedless and were rejected by God. The book was God's 'unerring Balance', whereby all the peoples of the world were tested. True belief in God and his messenger was only complete by acceptance of what he had revealed and observance of his law. For Shoghi Effendi, the *Aqdas* was the charter of

---

[2] Shoghi Effendi, *Bahá'í Administration*, p. 90.   [3] CEBF, 'law', loc. cit.

Bahá'u'lláh's 'New World Order', itself foretold in the Bible as the promised 'new heaven' and 'new earth'.

Although Baha'i law has obvious Islamic roots, it is also significantly different, not only in matters of detail but in fundamentals. Thus, whilst Islamic law is ultimately based on the ordinances of the Qur'án and reports of the oral teachings and example of the Prophet Muḥammad, Baha'i law is based on authenticated written texts (the *Aqdas* together with its supplementary texts by Bahá'u'lláh and the subsequent interpretations of 'Abdu'l-Bahá and Shoghi Effendi) and the legislation of the Universal House of Justice. Reports of the oral teachings and practice of the Faith's successive leaders are regarded as interesting and inspiring, but they are explicitly excluded as bases for law.

A second major difference is in terms of implementation. As Islamic law has developed, its proponents have insisted that it provides the true believer with detailed prescriptions and proscriptions of every aspect of behaviour (including such matters as how to dress, eat and go to the toilet) and that a truly Islamic society is one in which a large proportion of these ordinances are socially or legally enforced. By contrast, up to the present, Baha'i law is mostly presented in the form of general principles and guidelines of conduct which each individual must then apply as they best see fit in their own lives. On many aspects of life, the Baha'i teachings are silent or say little, the successive heads of the Faith explicitly stating in some instances, that such-and-such an activity (e.g. how to dress) was a matter of individual choice and not divine decree. Again, whilst some Baha'i social laws (e.g. of marriage) are enforced, the overall emphasis is very firmly placed on individual conscience, understanding and reasoning. Baha'is are expected to obey Baha'i law because they love Bahá'u'lláh and fear God, and not because they are likely to be punished for breaking it. There is no equivalent to the Islamic practice of social regulation of prayer, fasting, and other individual obligations – in which it is a communal responsibility to ensure that every one observes the law. For Baha'is, the individual is answerable to God and is expected to regulate his or her own actions. Social sanctions for breaches of the law are not common (see later).

An example of the Baha'i approach is provided by a statement by the Universal House of Justice on the Baha'i teachings on chastity. Beyond the basic prohibition of extramarital sexual relations, the House insisted on the importance of the individual using his or her own judgment and conscience in terms of the details of their behaviour (e.g. dating, kissing). What was needed was a prayerful life oriented towards service to Bahá'u'lláh, and not a set of rigid regulations of approved and prohibited behaviours. Baha'is should realize that to become a slave to one's animal impulses brought no lasting happiness and that the present life consisted of a series of spiritual struggles and tests, in which the development of self-control was an important element in character building as well as preparing the individual soul for the next life. Individuals should by all means turn for guidance to their parents and the Baha'i institutions in working out how they should live their lives, but the House itself refused to issue a detailed set of instructions of what exactly they should or shouldn't do.[4]

A third major difference is that there is no Baha'i clerical class equivalent to the Islamic learned (*'ulamá*) empowered to authoritatively elucidate and apply the law. The job of the Baha'i 'learned' (Counsellors and Board members at the present time) is to teach, encourage, and inspire. It is the local and national spiritual assemblies that have the responsibility to apply those Baha'i laws which are socially enforced.

A fourth difference with at least most Sunni versions of Islamic law, is that Baha'is do not see their legal system as fixed and immutable.[5] Explicitly, whilst the legal pronouncements of Bahá'u'lláh, 'Abdu'l-Bahá, and Shoghi Effendi are regarded as fundamental and unchangeable, those of the House of Justice are identified as subsidiary and subject to alteration or repeal by the House itself in future times in response to changing circumstances and social developments. The Baha'i leaders have also been conscious of differences of historical and social context, such that there has been a gradualism and diversity of application of Baha'i law, Bahá'u'lláh himself stating that people should be guided to 'the ocean of true understanding' in 'a spirit of love and tolerance', and that observance of his laws should be subject to 'tact and wisdom' so as not to cause 'disturbance and dissension'. Seemingly as a result of this principle, certain Baha'i laws – such as the tithe-like payment of the *Ḥuqúqu'lláh* (see later), were initially only made applicable to Middle Eastern Baha'is, whilst even quite fundamental social laws – such as the prohibition on drinking alcohol – have been applied extremely gradually in some countries in which they go against strongly established social patterns and the majority of the Baha'is have been very new to the Faith. Shoghi Effendi also made it clear that certain laws (e.g. criminal laws) were only applicable in a future Baha'i society, and that others could not be practised if they came into conflict with the present civil law in certain countries (e.g. in the United States, Baha'is follow the requirement

---

[4] CEBF, 'chastity', loc. cit.
[5] Shi'i law includes the principle of independent judgement (*ijtihad*) by a qualified Islamic jurist which enables reasoned analysis of new situations in terms of established principles.

in many states that dead bodies be embalmed before burial even though this conflicts with Baha'i burial law). Apart from those of the Middle Eastern origin, most Baha'is were not familiar with many of the provisions of the *Aqdas* until the 1970s.[6]

3. PERSONAL OBLIGATIONS TOWARDS GOD

Bahá'u'lláh prescribed a number of spiritual obligations for his followers. These include daily prayer and reading of Baha'i scripture, an annual fast, and payment of *Ḥuqúqu'lláh*. These practices are regarded as a means for the individual to draw closer to God and to develop spiritual qualities.

Prayer and Devotionalism[7]

Prayer occupies a fundamental role in Baha'i practice, both in the form of daily obligatory prayer, individual piety and devotion, and as a central feature of Baha'i meetings. The purpose of prayer is to bring individuals closer to God and Bahá'u'lláh; to help them to purify their own conduct; and allow them to request divine assistance. Prayers express the individual's love for God and at the same time effect their inner spiritual state.

The form of prayer which is part of Baha'i law is obligatory prayer (*ṣalát*). This is a daily act of worship to be performed by the individual (unlike the Islamic equivalent, it is not congregational). There is a choice of three different prayers ('short', 'medium', and 'long'). Both the long prayer (effectively an extended meditation on the individual's relationship with God), and the short prayer need only be said once a day, whilst the medium prayer is required to be said three times a day (between dawn and noon, noon and sunset, and sunset and two hours after sunset). Some indication of the sentiments of these prayers may be gained from the short prayer:

I bear witness, O my God,
that Thou hast created me to know Thee and to worship Thee.

[6] An English translation of the *Aqdas* was made as early as c. 1900 and circulated amongst the American Baha'is of the time for a while, and a literalistic non-Baha'i translation was published in 1961 which most Baha'is deliberately chose not to read because of its hostile tone. An official Baha'i translation into English did not appear until 1992. It was accompanied by Bahá'u'lláh's answers to a series of questions about the original text, together with copious notes designed to help readers from a non-Islamic background understand aspects of the book which otherwise might have seemed alien and obscure to them. Before this, the Universal House of Justice published a *Synopsis and Codification* of the text (1973), which summarized the book's contents. See Walbridge, *Sacred*, pp. 248–52.

[7] See CEBF, 'devotionalism'; 'prayer'; and 'ablutions', loc. cit.

I testify, at this moment, to my powerlessness and to
  Thy might, to my poverty and to Thy wealth.
There is none other God but Thee, the Help in Peril, the
  Self-Subsisting.

The obligatory prayers contain some ritual elements, notably the requirements to perform ritual ablutions beforehand; to pray facing the direction
of the tomb of Bahá'u'lláh at Bahjí (the Baha'i *qiblah*);[8] and, except for
the short prayer, to make specific gestures and movements, including
prostrations (as in Islamic prayers) during the course of the prayer. These
rituals are regarded as symbolic reminders to the devotee of the importance
of purity of heart, and of the need to turn to Bahá'u'lláh and be humble
before God. Other obligations are to read from the writings of Bahá'u'lláh
every morning and evening, contemplating on what is read, and to recite
God's 'Greatest Name' – the invocation '*Alláh-u-Abhá*' (God is Most
Glorious) – ninety-five times each day.[9]

   In addition to daily obligatory prayer, Baha'is are encouraged to pray
frequently both as an individual act of devotion and when they gather
together. Large numbers of prayers by Bahá'u'lláh and 'Abdu'l-Bahá are
available for this purpose, both in their original Persian and Arabic, and
in translation, and are widely used. There are also prayers by the Báb
and Shoghi Effendi, the later not yet available outside of their original
languages. Many Baha'i prayers include petitions for divine assistance in
the development of spiritual qualities as well as requests for protection,
forgiveness, assistance, guidance, help in teaching the Faith, unity with
others, and on behalf of children, parents, and spouses. There are prayers
which may be said on awakening and going to sleep, or when embarking
on a journey, or holding a meeting, and special prayers for marriage cer-
emonies, funerals, and the annual fast. Three prayers are widely regarded
as having particular power for those in difficulty or ill health: two by
Bahá'u'lláh – '*The Tablet of Aḥmad*', and '*The Long Healing Prayer*' – and
a short prayer of the Báb's, which is often read or chanted a number of
times:

Is there any Remover of difficulties save God?
Say: Praise be God! He is God!
All are His servants, and all abide by His bidding!

---

[8] The *qiblah* (Ar.) is the 'point of adoration' to which believers turn in prayer. For Muslims, this is the
   Ka'ba in Mecca. See CEBF, '*qiblah*', loc. cit.
[9] CEBF, 'greatest name', loc. cit. In the Baha'i version of an Islamic tradition, God's greatest name is
   bahá (Glory), and various forms of this name appear in Baha'i ritual and iconography.

There are generally no set forms for such prayers, but it is recommended that individual prayer be offered in private when one was free from distractions. Stress is placed on the spirit in which the prayer is offered: the more detached the worshipper becomes, the purer and more acceptable their prayers will be.

Collective prayer – in which individuals usually take it in turn to read, chant, or sing prayers – is also encouraged, as for example, coming together at dawn for collective prayers, whether as a family or local community. Again, administrative meetings of spiritual assemblies and committees normally include the saying of some prayers, and the regular Nineteen Day Feast begins with an integral devotional period (see Chapter 15).

Fasting

Following an ordinance of the Báb, Bahá'u'lláh instructed his followers to observe a nineteen day fast during the Babi-Baha'i month of 'Alá' (normally 2–20 March.). During this month, Baha'is between the ages of fifteen and seventy are required to abstain from food, drink and smoking between sunrise and sunset. Exemptions are granted to the sick, pregnant and menstruating women, nursing mothers, and those who are engaged in heavy labour or are travelling. It is intended to be a period of meditation and prayer, during which the individual abstains from selfish desires and seeks to reorient their life, so as to reinvigorate the inner spiritual forces of their soul. Fasting is an individual spiritual obligation and responsibility and Baha'i institutions have no right to enforce it.

Ḥuqúqu'lláh

The *Ḥuqúqu'lláh* (the 'Right of God') is a monetary payment to be made to the head of the Faith by all Baha'is able to afford it.[10] It was established by Bahá'u'lláh, who described payment as a spiritual bounty which brought the individual closer to God and purified their possessions. Payment is an individual spiritual obligation, and no Baha'i is to be solicited for it. Those who are unable to pay are exempt. It is supposed to be paid when a person's property exceeds a certain value (the equivalent of 2.2 troy ounces of gold), and amounts to 19 percent of the value of all wealth other than ones' residence, place of business and household furnishings. The payment is to

---

[10] CEBF, '*Ḥuqúqu'lláh*', loc. cit. and Walbridge, *Sacred,* pp. 98–101. The *Ḥuqúq* resembles the Shi'i payment of *khums,* 'the fifth' of gained wealth, in part payable to the representatives of the Imáms.

be made only once on any particular amount, and subsequent payments become payable on further increments of wealth after necessary expenses have been deducted. The collected monies are used for such purposes as the promotion of the Baha'i religion; the upkeep of its properties; and general charity, the disbursement of the funds being determined by the head of the Faith (at the present time the Universal House of Justice).

Payment of *Ḥuqúq* was at first mostly confined to the Baha'is of the Middle East, this being one of a number of religious laws that were deliberately not applied universally throughout the Baha'i world. Information about the *Ḥuqúq* was made freely available to Baha'is elsewhere in 1985 (increasing the potential number who might pay if they wished), but the law was not made universally applicable until 1992. As the number of Baha'is paying *Ḥuqúq* has increased, a network of deputies and representatives have been appointed to receive the payments. A central Office of *Ḥuqúqu'lláh* was established in Haifa in 1991.

4. MARRIAGE AND FAMILY LIFE

The Baha'i teachings emphasize the importance and sanctity of marriage and family life, both for the individuals involved and for society as a whole.[11] Bahá'u'lláh encouraged his followers to marry, both so as to bring forth children and as an 'assistance' to themselves. Marriage was not obligatory, however. True marriage was 'a fortress for well-being and salvation'; a spiritual as well as a physical relationship which would continue through 'all the worlds of God'. Shoghi Effendi described marriage as the bedrock of the whole structure of human society. It was a divine institution.

The main requirements of modern Baha'i marriage law (which are universally applicable throughout the Baha'i world) are that: (i) marriage is dependent on the consent of both the couple and their parents – this later permission being required so as to strengthen ties between family members and to prevent any enmity in the family; (ii) both partners must have reached 'the age of maturity' (i.e. fifteen), and neither can even become

---

[11] CEBF, 'marriage'; 'divorce'; and 'family life', loc. cit. There are several volumes of Baha'i reflections on family life, indicating the importance of the topic. These include: 'Alí-Akbar Furútan, *Mothers, Fathers, and Children: Practical Advice to Parents*. Trans. Katayoon and Robert Crerar (Oxford: George Ronald, 1980); Agnes Ghaznavi, *The Family Repair and Maintenance Manual* (Oxford: George Ronald, 1989); Madeline Hellaby, *Education in the Bahá'í Family* (Oxford: George Ronald, 1987); Khalil Khavari and Sue W. Khavari, *Creating a Successful Family* (Oxford: Oneworld, 1989); Bahíyyih Nakhjavání, *When We Grow Up* (Oxford: George Ronald, 1979); and Patricia Wilcox, *Bahá'í Families: Perspectives, Principles, Practice* (Oxford: George Ronald, 1991).

engaged before this age; and (iii) the marriage should be monogamous (albeit that if polygamous marriages have been contracted prior to an individual becoming a Baha'i, then these can be continued).[12] 'Abdu'l-Bahá encouraged interracial marriages, and Baha'is are free to marry those of other religions provided that this does not involve them in any dissimulation of their own faith. Baha'is who are considering marriage are urged to gain a thorough understanding of their prospective partner's character beforehand and not to marry purely for reasons of physical attraction.

Middle Eastern Baha'is are subject to several additional stipulations (which presumably will eventually be applicable worldwide), including a limit on the length of the engagement period to a maximum of ninety-five days and the payment of a relatively small amount of money (a bridal gift) by the husband to the wife.

Modern Baha'i marriages take place under the jurisdiction of a spiritual assembly which must ensure that a proper Baha'i ceremony is held and parental consent obtained. The marriage ceremony itself consists of both partners saying a specific verse ('We will all, verily, abide by the Will of God') in the presence of two witnesses. The couple can add to this as they wish – for example by the inclusion of prayers and scriptural readings – but the ceremony should remain simple. Any other ceremony, such as a civil marriage in places where the Baha'i marriage has no legal standing, should take place on the same day as the Baha'i marriage.

Divorce

Divorce is permitted under Baha'i law, but is strongly discouraged and condemned. Baha'is should regard marriage as a sacred tie, which is only to be severed in extreme circumstances and as a last resort. The common practice of divorce in contemporary society is regarded as an indication of the decline of religion and as a major factor leading to societal breakdown. There are no specific grounds for divorce in Baha'i law other than antipathy between the partners. If antagonism arises between husband and wife, they should seek to resolve their problems through consultation, both

---

[12] The modern Baha'i prescription of monogamy has evolved. Under Islamic law, a man may marry up to four wives, and in addition may take other women into his household as concubines. In the *Kitáb-i Aqdas*, Bahá'u'lláh restricted the total possible number of wives to two, but added that having only one wife would be the cause of tranquillity for both partners. 'Abdu'l-Bahá later added that, as having a second wife was conditional upon treating both wives with justice and equality (cf. Qur'án 4:3), then multiple marriages were not possible in practice. Baha'i law also forbids concubinage and the Shi'i practice of temporary marriage (*mut'a*).

between themselves, and jointly with others who might be of assistance, such as Baha'i assemblies and marriage guidance counsellors. They should be patient with each other and avoid anger, aiming to find some way of overcoming their differences. If such endeavour is unavailing, the couple jointly or one partner alone may ask the relevant Baha'i assembly to set the date for a 'year of patience' necessary for a Baha'i divorce to be recognized. The assembly also endeavours to secure reconciliation between the couple during the year. If the couple become reconciled during this time, their marriage continues, but if they remain unreconciled at the end the year, they are considered divorced according to Baha'i law. They must also follow whatever procedures are necessary to secure a divorce according to the laws of the country in which they live.

Bahá'u'lláh specified that the husband should support the wife financially during the year of waiting (the Universal House of Justice allowed that the couple might decide upon a different arrangement if the wife had formerly been the family bread-winner). In all cases, it was the responsibility of the spiritual assembly involved to encourage and assist the divorcing couple to work out the financial details of their future lives between themselves. The couple should similarly determine suitable arrangements for the custody of children, including recognition of the continuing role of the non-custodial partner as a parent.

Family Life

Bahá'u'lláh taught that parents should raise their children to be religious (but not fanatical), God-fearing, and moral; and praised parenthood (both natural and adoptive), equating raising one's own son or the son of another with raising one of his own sons. The father was responsible to ensure that both his daughters and sons became literate and learnt about the Baha'i teachings. Children had a duty to obey their parents. Such service was equated with obeying God, and took precedence over service to Bahá'u'lláh. 'Abdu'l-Bahá stressed the importance of love, unity, and consultation between family members; stated that each member had his or her rights and prerogatives which should be respected; called on Baha'is to make their homes centres 'for the diffusion of the light of divine guidance'; and equated a mother's education of her child with worship, regarding her as the child's first teacher, who normally set the pattern of its moral and religious life. Shoghi Effendi counselled Baha'is to balance their desire to serve the Faith with their responsibilities towards their parents, spouses, and children, if necessary limiting their Baha'i activities so as to preserve family unity. This was particularly important in those cases where the spouse was not a Baha'i. He also deplored the weakening of parental control, which along with the then (1940s) rising tide of divorce in American society, he saw as evidences of moral laxity and irresponsibility.

The Universal House of Justice has noted that whilst the Baha'i teachings emphasize gender equality, this does not imply identity of function within the family, arguing that whilst the circumstances of individual families varied greatly, in general, mothers had the primary obligation to nurture their children and had a corresponding right to receive material support from their husbands. In turn, husbands would normally be considered the 'heads' of their families, although this implied no overriding authority or right of domination.

Procreation Issues

In matters relating to procreation, there are often very specific Baha'i teachings, but ultimately it is left entirely to individual couples to make their own private judgments on the basis of the Baha'i teachings involved and competent medical advice. It is recognized that the issues involved are often complex and couples are counselled to give due reflection to the ethical issues involved before making their final decisions.[13]

Thus, whilst the use of birth control methods to control the number of children a couple have is permitted, their use to completely avoid having children is seen as contradicting the belief that the primary purpose of Baha'i marriage is the procreation of children. Again, whilst abortion or the use of methods of birth control which involve the abortion of the fertilized egg are accepted for medical reasons (e.g. if there is a threat to the mother's health or the risk of severe genetic defects), abortion merely to prevent the birth of an unwanted child is seen as wrongful because it violates the sacredness of conception (Baha'is believe that the human soul appears at conception). Again, whilst it is seen as permissible for childless couples to use artificial insemination and in-vitro fertilization methods if it is the husband's own sperm which fertilizes the wife's own ovum, surrogate motherhood is rejected on account of its complex spiritual and social implications.

---

[13] CEBF, 'abortion'; 'artificial fertilization'; 'birth control'; and 'sterilization', loc. cit.

Domestic Violence

The Baha'i teachings condemn all forms of family injustice and violence. Baha'i marriage should be based on a relationship of mutual respect and equality. All forms of spousal abuse are therefore condemned. For one partner to use force to compel the other to obey them would contradict the principal of consultation on which the marriage should be based.

5. ASPECTS OF INDIVIDUAL LIFE

Alcohol, Drugs, and Tobacco[14]

Baha'is are prohibited from drinking any form of alcohol (unless prescribed by a physician) on the grounds that intoxicants lead the mind astray and weaken the body: God has endowed humans beings with reason, and intoxicants take it away. Similarly, the use of opiates and other drugs which damage the mind or body, or which make it difficult for individuals to make moral decisions (including hashish, marijuana and hallucinogens such as LSD and peyote) are explicitly forbidden – again, except when prescribed by a physician. Baha'is should also try to avoid working in jobs that involved the manufacture or large-scale sale of alcohol. Any involvement in the drugs trade is absolutely forbidden. Those who seek spiritual experience in drugs are mistaken and should turn instead to Bahá'u'lláh. The renunciation of intoxicants increases health, strength and beauty. Tobacco smoking is discouraged but not forbidden, 'Abdu'l-Bahá describing it as a habit that was both unclean, progressively injurious to health, and expensive.

Baha'is who are alcoholics or drug addicts should seek the help of doctors or organizations such as Alcoholics Anonymous. In the case of smoking, Baha'is should to be courteous and considerate to all, whether they be smokers or non-smokers.

Sex

The Baha'i leaders regarded sexual attraction and activity as a natural part of human life, of value both to the individual and for the procreation of children, but insisted that the sexual impulse could only be legitimately expressed in marriage.[15] All forms of pre- and extra-marital sexual

[14] CEBF, 'alcohol'; 'drugs'; and 'smoking', loc. cit.
[15] CEBF, 'sex'; 'adultery and fornication'; homosexuality', loc. cit.

relationships are thus forbidden, and are regarded as damaging to the spiritual progress of the soul. Sexual desire need not be suppressed, but it has to be regulated. From this standpoint, modern society is seen as overly-permissive and as over-emphasizing sex. By contrast, Baha'is should try to think and act in such a way that those appetites which can not be legitimately expressed will not be aroused – that is to exercise self-control outside of marriage.

The practice of homosexuality is also forbidden in the Faith. Baha'is who are homosexuals are counselled to regard their condition as an affliction which they should fight against, if necessary seeking medical advice. Such a struggle might be very hard – as with unmarried heterosexuals who sought to remain chaste, but it would lead to spiritual growth. It is recognized that love between two people of the same sex might be very devoted, but it is considered wrong to express this love in a sexual relationship.

Wills and Inheritance[16]

Bahá'u'lláh instructed his followers to write wills – in which they should attest to the oneness of God and their Baha'i belief – and specified that they had complete freedom to dispose of their property as they wished. In cases of intestacy, however, he provided a detailed schedule of inheritance for various categories of relatives and others adapted from the provisions set out by the Báb in the *Bayán*.

Burial[17]

Baha'is bury their dead and do not practice cremation, 'Abdu'l-Bahá teaching that just as the human body had been formed gradually, then so it should decompose slowly and naturally. There is a specific burial prayer, to which the bereaved add whatever other prayers and readings they wish for the funeral service. Baha'i law stipulates that the body of the deceased should be buried as soon as possible after death, and at a place within an hour's journey of the place of death (seemingly as a deliberate challenge to the Shi'i practice of transporting bodies for burial at the often distant shrines of the Imáms). Middle Eastern Baha'is also follow a number of other provisions, including first washing the corpse and shrouding it in silk or cotton cloth; placing a ring on its finger, with a specially inscribed verse

[16] CEBF, 'inheritance'; 'wills', loc. cit.; Walbridge, *Sacred*, pp. 83–93.
[17] CEBF, 'burial', loc. cit.; Walbridge, *Sacred*, pp. 77–82.

('I came forth from God, and return unto Him, detached from all save Him, holding fast to His name, the Merciful, the Compassionate'); using a coffin of durable wood, stone, or crystal (so as to show respect for the body as the former 'temple of the spirit'); and burying the body with its feet facing towards the Baha'i *qiblah* (i.e. the Shrine of Bahá'u'lláh at Bahjí). Many larger Baha'i communities have their own burial plots or cemeteries – in which non-Baha'is can also be buried. Baha'is can leave their bodies for medical research if they wish to, but should stipulate that they want their remains eventually to be buried and not cremated.

Rituals

The Baha'i Faith is relatively unritualistic in both official and popular religious practices.[18] The daily obligatory prayers and the ablutions that proceed them are formal rites, as are the required daily recital of the Greatest Name and the simple verses said at marriages and burials, but none of these are elaborate in nature, and it is of note that Shoghi Effendi was insistent both that prescribed practices should remain simple and that the Baha'is should not introduce rituals of their own into Baha'i practice. In 'secondary matters', the Baha'is should be flexible, such that Baha'i weddings and Nineteen Day Feasts, for example, retain a universal basic pattern, whilst varying greatly, reflecting individual and cultural preferences.

Again, in sharp contrast to Shi'i Islam, Bahá'u'lláh abolished all forms of ritual impurity, both of people and things, stressing instead the importance of physical cleanliness and purity of heart – a teaching of particular signif-icance in nineteenth century Iran, where Baha'is were willing to associate with members of non-Muslim minority groups such as Jews and Zoroastri-ans, whom Shi'is rejected as ritually polluting. Baha'is should bathe regu-larly (in clean water and not the fetid pools of traditional Iranian public bath houses) and keep their clothes clean.[19]

General Aspects of Appearance and Behaviour

In strong contrast to Islamic practice, there is no required use of Baha'i symbols of identity. Many Baha'is wear a Baha'i ring (with a Baha'i symbol

[18] CEBF, 'ritual', loc. cit.
[19] CEBF, 'cleanliness' and 'purity', loc. cit., and also Walbridge, *Sacred*, pp. 59–67. Resonant with the Baha'i teaching of gender equality, menstruation itself is not regarded as ritually impure – as it is in Islam. Menstruating women may exempt themselves from the obligations of Baha'i ritual prayer and fasting if they wish, however – presumably because of the exhaustion which some women experience during their menstrual periods.

Figure 4 The Baha'i 'ringstone symbol' (a) and the 'Greatest Name' (*Yá Bahá'u'l-Abhá*) (b).

on it, see Figure 4), place 'Abdu'l-Bahá's picture in their home, or hang a copy of a calligraphic evocation of the name *Bahá* (God's Greatest Name) on their wall, and Iranian Baha'is in particular often use the salutation *'Alláh-u-Abhá* (God is Most Glorious) when greeting each other, but none of these practices are obligatory. Nor are there special 'Baha'i' names for Baha'is to adopt – though some Baha'is name their children after heroic Baha'i figures of the past. Again, there is no distinctive Baha'i form of dress, although Baha'is are strongly encouraged to be both cleanly and modest in their dress.[20] There is no requirement that women should veil themselves or cover their hair, nor that men should grow beards (Both normal Islamic practices).[21] Male circumcision is neither encouraged nor forbidden.

Baha'is are free to eat what they wish (apart from not eating meat from an animal found dead in a trap or snare). 'Abdu'l-Bahá commended vegetarianism (because it was both healthy and avoided the cruelty to animals inherent in meat-eating), but never insisted that Baha'is become vegetarians. Nor is there a specific Baha'i dietary regimen, albeit that the Baha'i leaders advocated the value of eating simply and avoiding excessively large and lavish meals. Baha'is should be tolerant of those who ate differently from themselves and also be guided by the growing body of scientific knowledge about diet.

6. BEHAVIOUR IN CIVIL SOCIETY AND RELATIONS WITH THE STATE

Baha'is are everywhere required to follow the law of the countries in which they reside unless these laws require them to deny their faith or violate

---

[20] Baha'i pioneers to societies in which 'tribal' people traditionally wore few or no clothes were advised to be tolerant of local practices which were compatible with Baha'i morality and not to insist on changes in 'non-essentials'. There was no equivalence to the insistence made by many Christian missionaries that 'native' people adopt Western dress.

[21] Bahá'u'lláh did, however, instruct his followers not to shave their heads or (for men) to let their hair 'pass beyond the limit of the ears' – an instruction that has yet to be clarified, but might be a prohibition on the nineteenth-century Iranian custom of wearing long sidelocks (Bahá'u'lláh, *Aqdas*, pp. 35, 197).

fundamental Baha'i principles.[22] The Baha'is are to be loyal, honest and truthful in their dealings with their government; strictly avoid sedition; and not contend with those in lawful authority. They are to strictly avoid any party-political involvement, Shoghi Effendi insisting that the Faith was 'non-political', 'supra-national', and 'rigidly non-partisan'. Baha'is can vote, become members of neighbourhood councils and hold administrative office in government service if this does not entail partisan political involvement. Baha'is in public employ should be exemplary in their honesty, integrity, trustworthiness, justice, and service. Baha'is are also prohibited from join-ing any secret society (such as Masonic lodges) – presumably because of the links with politics which secret societies have had in some societies (including Qájár Iran).

Bahá'u'lláh stated that it was better to be killed than to kill, but Baha'is accept that it may be necessary to use force in some circumstances, such as to defend their own lives and those of others against attack by criminal assailants. Defence should not deteriorate into retaliation, however. At a national level, as Baha'is are loyal to the state and not absolute pacifists, they should be willing to be inducted into the military forces of their country, applying for non-combatant status (e.g. as medical orderlies) where this is possible and not being afraid to risk their own lives to try to save the lives of others.

Bahá'u'lláh clearly envisaged a future state of affairs in which aspects of Baha'i law would become enforceable by the state, stipulating specific pun-ishments for a number of criminal offences, including the death penalty or life imprisonment for both intentional arson and murder; an indemnity payment to the family of the deceased in the case of unintentional killing (manslaughter); and exile, imprisonment, and the placing of an identifica-tion mark on the forehead for theft. These punishments are entirely theo-retical at present, being intended for some future society and the details of their application are left for the future decision of the Universal House of Justice.[23]

7. SANCTIONS

At present, the only sanctions which are employed within the Baha'i com-munity are expulsion from membership and deprivation of certain rights within the community.

---

[22] CEBF, 'government, Baha'i attitude towards'; 'politics'; 'secret societies'; 'self-defence', loc. cit.
[23] CEBF, 'crime and punishment'.

As under previous heads of the Faith, expulsion may entail a declaration by the Universal House of Justice that a particular individual has broken the Baha'i Covenant and as such is a Covenant-breaker and no longer a member of the community. Such individuals are shunned by other Baha'is even at the cost of breaking family ties. As we have seen, various instances of Covenant-breaking have occurred over the course of Baha'i history, normally in association with disputes about the succession of leadership in the Faith. This is an extreme measure and is quite rare. A second form of effective expulsion has occurred recently with particular individuals being declared not to be Baha'is any longer, normally on account of their intellectual opposition to aspects of the House of Justice's authority. No shunning is involved. This is extremely rare.[24]

Deprivation of Baha'i administrative rights is applied to those who flagrantly breach certain Baha'i laws.[25] The rights are those of normal Baha'i community membership, such as the rights to attend the Nineteen Day Feast; to contribute to the Baha'i funds; to vote in Baha'i elections; to serve on Baha'i spiritual assemblies and committees; and to represent the Faith publicly (e.g. as a speaker at a public meeting). Loss of rights may be occasioned by major breaches of the Baha'i code of personal morality (e.g. drinking alcohol, drug use, sexual impropriety, active homosexuality); failure to observe Baha'i marriage laws (marrying without a Baha'i ceremony or without parental consent; marrying a third party before the 'year of patience' required for a Baha'i divorce is completed); public dissimulations of faith (e.g. making a promise to raise one's children in another religion; going through the marriage ceremony of another religion *as if* one was actually an adherent of that religion; holding religious office in another religion); refusal to dissociate oneself from political activity or office; or membership of a secret society. The decision to deprive an individual of his or her voting rights is taken by the responsible national spiritual assembly,

---

[24] Only three cases of this procedure have been widely discussed (one each in Canada [1997], New Zealand [2000], and the Netherlands [2005]). All three individuals involved had been prominent participants in internet discussion groups, maintaining views contrary to the Baha'i mainstream and critical of the Universal House of Justice. The cases are extensively reported on various websites critical of that mainstream. William Garlington. *The Bahá'í Faith in America* (Praeger, 2005), provides a brief discussion of the Canadian case (p. 168).

[25] CEBF, 'administrative rights', loc. cit. Individuals may also be deprived of voting rights in cases of severe forms of mental illness which make it impossible for them to participate in society, and of some criminal activities. In both these situations, the cause is 'external' to Baha'i law as neither mental illness nor criminality of themselves automatically debar individuals from participation in the Baha'i community, and assemblies are advised to exercise great discretion in considering such cases. In the case of severe mental illness, the deprivation of rights is simply a recognition of the individual's incapacity, and not a sanction.

normally only after extensive consultations with all involved, often including local assemblies or specialist national committees which may be charged with exercising a fact-finding and counselling role.

As deprivation of voting rights is considered to be an extremely serious action, assemblies are instructed to only undertake it as a last resort. In all cases, the matter must be thoroughly investigated before a final decision is made, each case being considered on its own merits. Particularly in cases of immorality, the assemblies should be compassionate towards human frailty, counselling and encouraging individuals to rectify their conduct and giving sufficient time for them to change their behaviour. Only if the behaviour in question is in blatant and public disregard of Baha'i law, particularly if it is becoming a matter of public scandal; or (as sometimes in the case of political activity) is endangering the Faith; or if the individual has ignored repeated warnings, should the assembly then deprive them of their rights.[26] If the individual later rectifies their conduct, then they are welcome to apply for the restoration of their rights.

---

[26] In practice, my impression is that most national spiritual assemblies tend to overlook moral breaches if they remain relatively covert. The best example is perhaps practising homosexuality, which has been extensively discussed in the American Baha'i community. Garlington, *Bahá'í Faith in America*, refers to the situation briefly (pp. 170–71).

CHAPTER 14

Baha'i Administration

The present-day organization of the Baha'i Faith is often referred to as the '*Administrative Order*'.[1] Although partially rooted in earlier institutions and in statements by Bahá'u'lláh and 'Abdu'l-Bahá, it has largely developed since the 1920s, replacing the more personalized and informal patterns of local leadership and organization which had prevailed in the early days of the Faith. Many of its major features were delineated by Shoghi Effendi, who envisioned it evolving into the future in an organic fashion and as the basis for an eventual 'Baha'i World Commonwealth'.

I. THE 'RULERS' AND 'LEARNED'

A distinction is often made between the 'rulers' and 'learned' of the Faith, and this finds expression in the two branches of modern Baha'i administration: the elected local and national spiritual assemblies which have executive power, and the appointed 'institutions of the learned' (the Hands of the Cause, the International Teaching Centre, the Continental Boards of Counsellors, Auxiliary Board Members, and their assistants), comprising 'eminent and devoted' Baha'is who are appointed to protect and propagate the Faith, and occupying a largely advisory and inspirational role. Overarching both branches is the Universal House of Justice, itself elected and empowered to direct and lead the Baha'i community as a whole. Additional elements are the various international Baha'i agencies under the direction of the Universal House of Justice (most prominently the Baha'i International Community), the departments and committees appointed by the House and by the local and national assemblies to accomplish specific tasks, and in some communities the regional Baha'i councils.

---

[1] CEBF, 'administration', loc. cit.

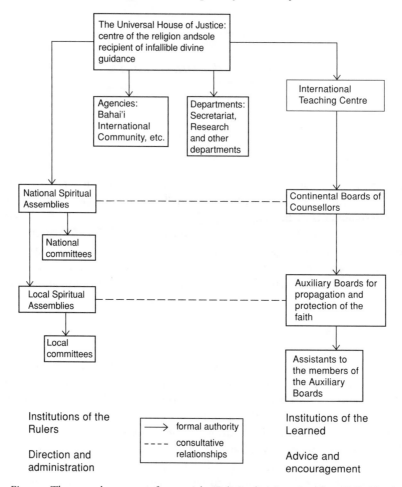

Figure 5 The general structure of present-day Baha'i administration, from P. Smith, *A Concise Encyclopedia of the Bahá'í Faith*, 2nd ed. (Oxford, Oneworld, 2002), p. 26.

The overall structure of contemporary Baha'i administration is shown in Figure 5. It will be noted that the two administrative branches are linked together by consultative relationships, the most important of which are between the Continental Counsellors and the national assemblies and regional councils, and between the Board members and the local assemblies. Further consultative links exist at the international and national conventions, with the members of all national spiritual assemblies being able to meet together for the elections of the House and the 'national' board members commonly being invited to participate in the deliberations of the national conventions.

2. THE UNIVERSAL HOUSE OF JUSTICE

At the apex of the Baha'i administrative system is the Universal House of Justice.[2] With a massive textual warrant in the writings of Bahá'u'lláh, 'Abdu'l-Bahá and Shoghi Effendi, it stands unchallenged as the supreme institution in the contemporary Baha'i world, its decisions being regarded as divinely guided and infallible. Obedience to it by Baha'is is seen as obligatory (see Chapter 5).

In its Constitution (26 November 1972), the House outlined its own powers and duties.[3] These included the administration of the affairs of the Baha'i community globally; the guidance, organization and coordination of all community activities; the oversight of the Baha'i funds and properties for which it is responsible; and the safeguarding of 'the personal rights, freedom and initiative of individuals', ensuring that no Baha'i body or institution 'abuse its privileges or decline in the exercise of its rights and prerogatives'. The House is empowered to establish whatever institutions it deems necessary, and to review and approve, modify, or reverse the decisions or actions of any national or local spiritual assembly in the world. It can also intervene in any matter in which a spiritual assembly is failing to take action or make a decision, either requiring the assembly to take action or itself taking action directly.

As to the manner of its election and functioning, the House reaffirmed that its membership was to consist of nine men elected from the Baha'i community by secret ballot by the members of all national spiritual assemblies, and that in their own legislative work, the House members ultimately had to reserve for themselves 'the right of unfettered decision': they were not to be governed by the feelings, opinions and convictions of those whom they represented, but were strictly to follow the 'dictates and promptings' of their own consciences, aware that as a collectivity they alone had been made the recipients of divine guidance in the contemporary Baha'i world.

The House also specified that the elections for the House would normally be held at an 'International Baha'i Convention' or by some alternative means

---

[2] 'Abdu'l-Bahá and Shoghi Effendi had both envisaged the Guardianship and the Universal House of Justice functioning together in overall leadership of the Faith.

[3] Universal House of Justice, *Constitution.*

if that was not possible,[4] and that for the present these elections would be held quinquenially. Vacancies in membership of the House would be filled by by-elections. In addition to electing the members of the House, the main business of the Convention would be to deliberate on the worldwide affairs of the Faith and 'to make recommendations and suggestion' for the House of Justice's consideration.

3. THE ASSEMBLY SYSTEM

The modern system of locally and nationally elected spiritual assemblies was largely established by Shoghi Effendi in the early 1920s. Together with the Universal House of Justice at the international level, these assemblies are vested with 'legislative, executive and judicial powers over the Baha'i community'. An additional element has recently been introduced in the form of regional Baha'i councils (formally established by the Universal House of Justice in May 1997, but existing in essentially experimental form in some countries from 1986 onwards). All these bodies are able to establish specialist committees to help them with their work.[5]

Local spiritual assemblies can be established anywhere where there are at least nine Baha'is aged twenty-one or over, subject to the approval of the responsible national spiritual assembly and in geographical areas determined by the national assembly in consultation with the Universal House of Justice (e.g. in a village, town, or rural or urban district). The assembly can be formed either by joint declaration (if there are only nine adult Baha'is resident locally) or in an annual election. All local assemblies are normally formed on the first day of the Baha'i Ridván festival (usually 21 April) and subsequently re-formed on the same date in each succeeding year, their members holding office until their successors are elected. The local assemblies exercise 'full jurisdiction' over 'all Baha'i activities and affairs' within their localities subject to the provisions of their 'Local Baha'i Constitution'[6] and their 'general powers and duties' as defined in the Baha'i writings and the pronouncements of the House of Justice.

National and Regional spiritual assemblies can only be established by the decision of the Universal House of Justice, and their areas of geographical

---

[4] A postal ballot was employed on the one occasion (2003) when the House decided that an International Convention could not be held due to unsettled conditions in the Middle East.

[5] CC2, pp. 29–60, 83–136; CC3, pp. 60–91; CEBF, 'assemblies'; 'convention'; 'regional Baha'i councils', loc. cit.

[6] This refers to the by-laws of a local spiritual assembly, the prototype of which was adopted by the New York local assembly in November 1931 (*Bahá'í World*, vol. 4, pp. 159–65).

jurisdiction are determined by the House. The national spiritual assembly itself (again with nine adult members) is elected by a body of locally elected delegates at a National Convention in accordance with the provisions of the 'National Baha'i Constitution',[7] and its members remain in office until their successors have been elected. The conventions are normally held annually during the Riḍván period (21 April–2 May). The total number of delegates is determined by the Universal House of Justice (in rough proportion to the numerical size of the national Baha'i community). Individuals can not serve as both Board members or Counsellors and national assembly members at the same time. In addition to the election of a national spiritual assembly, each national convention is concerned with consultation on national Baha'i activities, plans, and policies.

The 'general powers and duties' of the national assemblies include 'exclusive jurisdiction and authority' over all Baha'i activities and affairs throughout their defined areas of jurisdiction, and they are charged with seeking 'to stimulate, unify and coordinate' the 'manifold activities' of all the local spiritual assemblies and individual Baha'is under their jurisdiction. Each national assembly represents its national Baha'i community in relation to other such communities and to the Universal House of Justice.

Regional Baha'i councils have been established in several countries as an intermediate level of administration between the national and local spiritual assemblies so as to provide a means of decentralized decision-making where this is desirable: often because the sheer size of the country involved (e.g. India, the United States). Whilst possessing considerable autonomy, the councils remain subordinate to their national spiritual assembly. The councils can either be elected (by the members of all local assemblies in their region) or appointed by the national assembly on the basis of a confidential list of nominees proposed by regional electors and Auxiliary Board members. Individual national assemblies can only form such councils following consultations with the Universal House of Justice and with its permission.

Local and national assembly committees are established as and when they are needed. In all cases, the committees are appointed by the responsible assembly and are under its supervision. They are commonly required to

[7] This refers to Declaration of Trust and By-Laws of a National Spiritual Assembly given in model form in the successive volumes of the old series of *Bahá'í World*. The prototype of all national Baha'i constitutions was the Declaration of Trust and its associated by-laws adopted by the National Spiritual Assembly of the Baha'is of the United States and Canada in 1927 (*Bahá'í World*, vol. 3, pp. 95–104). The delegates are selected at local or regional conventions in electoral 'unit' areas determined by the national spiritual assembly. All adult Baha'is of good standing resident in the unit may participate as electors.

submit regular reports of the work they accomplish to their assembly. At a national level, assemblies vary in the committees they establish, but there are often committees concerned with Baha'i teaching work, youth activities, educational institutions, and publications.[8]

4. THE 'INSTITUTIONS OF THE LEARNED'

Apart from the Báb, most Babi leaders were members of the Islamic learned class, the *'ulamá*, and many of the secondary Baha'i leaders during the nineteenth century also came from a clerical background, including all four of the Hands of the Cause appointed by Bahá'u'lláh. Indeed, these appointments indicate that Bahá'u'lláh intended for there to be a group of Baha'i 'learned' with something of the status of Islamic clerics, and he specifically blessed 'the learned among the people of Baha', describing them as his 'trustees', 'the daysprings of Divine Utterance' and 'the stars of the firmament of Glory'. It seems very unlikely that he intended for there to be a Baha'i clerical order similar to the Shi'i hierarchy, however, he himself making reference to future 'Houses of Justice' as Baha'i governing bodies. The Baha'i 'learned' were instead to be teachers of the Faith, dedicating themselves 'to the education of the world' and 'the edification of its peoples'.[9]

Later, both 'Abdu'l-Bahá and Shoghi Effendi made use of eminent Iranian Baha'i 'learned' as propagandists and 'trouble-shooters' both in Iran and internationally, whilst at the same time building up the system of elected assemblies. More recently, formal institutions of the Baha'i 'learned' have been established with the renewed appointment of functioning Hands (1951–7) and of supporting Auxiliary Boards (from 1954), and then of the various institutions created by the Universal House of Justice.

International Institutions

With the House of Justice's 1964 ruling that no more Hands of the Cause could be appointed, the House in consultation with the remaining Hands

---

[8] In the United Kingdom, for example, where much Baha'i administrative work has now been decentralized to four regional elected councils (for England, Wales, Scotland, and Northern Ireland), each with their own specialist committees, there are still some eighteen national committees, responsible for such activities as pioneering and travel teaching within the country and internationally, children's activities, youth service projects, services for the visually impaired, and residential schools. The British national spiritual assembly also has offices for public information, religious and educational affairs, the advancement of women, and social and economic development.

[9] Bahá'u'lláh, *Aqdas*, p. 82; *Tablets*, pp. 35, 221. See also Cole, 'The evolution of charismatic authority'.

set about devising means of continuing the functions of the Hands into the future. The result was the creation of the Continental Boards of Counsellors (1968) and an International Teaching Centre (June 1973) as new international 'institutions of the learned' with responsibilities respectively parallelling those of the Hands in the various continents and those working at the Baha'i World Centre.[10] Thus, the Continental Boards of Counsellors were made responsible for overseeing the protection and propagation of the Faith at a continental level: supervising the work of the Auxiliary Boards; consulting and collaborating with the national spiritual assemblies; and informing the Hands and the House of Justice of developments in their areas. For its part, the International Teaching Centre was initially charged with: (i) directing and coordinating the work of the Continental Boards of Counsellors and acting as liaison between these Boards and the Universal House of Justice; (ii) being fully informed of the situation of the Faith in all parts of the world, and on the basis of that knowledge making recommendations to the House of Justice and advising the Continental Counsellors; (iii) being alert to the possibilities for the extension of Baha'i teaching activity; and (iv) determining and anticipating needs for literature, pioneers, and travelling teachers, and working out regional and global teaching plans for approval by the House of Justice. It has also come to direct the work of the Continental Pioneer Committees and assume an increasingly important role in routine matters of Baha'i activity, leaving the members of the Universal House of Justice with more time to concentrate on their own specific responsibilities. The Centre is directly responsible to the House of Justice.

Originally, eleven Continental Boards were formed (three each in Africa, the Americas and Asia; one each for Australasia and Europe) with a total of thirty-six Counsellors, but the Boards were later reduced to five (one each for Africa, the Americas, Asia, Australasia, and Europe) and the number of counsellors progressively raised (it is now eighty-one). There were originally three Counsellor members of the International Teaching Centre, but subsequent increases have raised the number to nine (since 1988). Both Continental and International Counsellors are now appointed for five-year (reappointable) terms of office by the Universal House of Justice, and since 1985–6, a number of international conferences have been held in Haifa for all Counsellors to consult on all issues of concern.

[10] CEBF, 'Continental Boards of Counsellors'; 'International Teaching Centre', loc. cit.

The Auxiliary Board Members and Their Assistants[11]

Shoghi Effendi first established the Auxiliary Boards to support the work of the Hands of the Cause, with separate Boards being formed on a continental basis for the propagation and protection of the Faith, and individual Board members assuming responsibility for specific geographical areas. This structure has remained essentially unchanged under the Universal House of Justice, albeit that overall direction of the Boards was transferred to the Continental Boards of Counsellors after their appointment. The House also freed the Board members from national assembly membership (1963), so that they had more time to focus on their own tasks and the distinction between the two branches of the administration was made more clear cut; introduced (reappointable) five year term of service (1986) for Board members; and enormously expanded their total number (now with almost a thousand worldwide – from seventy-two in 1957). Even with more Board members, the rapid increase in the number of Baha'is in some areas made it increasingly difficult for many Board members to maintain adequate contact with all the assemblies and Baha'is in their areas, however, the House therefore permitting the Board members to appoint assistants (1973. There are now about twelve thousand assistants).[12]

The specific function of the Board members at the present is to help arouse and release the energies of the Baha'is to accomplish the goals of the Faith, enthusing the Baha'is in activities such as teaching and striving to deepen their understanding of their religion and to consolidate local Baha'i communities. They are bidden to strictly observe the 'separation of powers' between the two branches of the administration, working to reinforce the work of the local assemblies and committees whilst avoiding impinging on their administrative authority. The assistants (who may include both youth and local spiritual assembly members) work under the direction of particular Board members, and are normally given specific duties (such as encouraging the greater involvement of women in Baha'i administration in some parts of the world) or responsibility for a particular geographical area.

Overall Role

Although the Baha'i 'learned' originally developed in an Islamic context, it is clear that their modern role is very different from that of the *'ulamá*, most

---

[11] CEBF, 'Auxiliary Boards'; 'assistants', loc. cit.
[12] Email communication to the author from the Office of Public Information at the Baha'i World Centre, dated 4 August 2006.

importantly in that they are strictly subordinate to the Universal House of Justice; do not have a separate 'power base'; are given carefully defined advisory roles, leaving executive power in the hands of the national and local assemblies; and individually serve for fixed-term periods. Nor are they comparable to the various Christian priesthoods, in that whilst appointed to provide spiritual guidance and encouragement, they are not given any sacramental role. Again, whilst respected as individuals of high rank, their statements are not regarded as authoritative in their own right.

In terms of the overall functioning of the Baha'i administrative system, the 'learned' provide more than merely encouragement and moral leadership, however. By not being part of the assembly system, they provide a separate perspective on conditions, events and opportunities. Thus, administrative and teaching activities can be assessed and compared and problems and weaknesses in assembly functioning identified. For the House of Justice, the institutions of the learned provide an additional means of assessing the state of the global Baha'i community as well as of the threats and challenges it might face. The consultative relationships between national assemblies and Counsellors and between local assemblies and Board members provide additional input for assembly decision-making (The assemblies do not have to take the advice of the 'learned', but in extreme cases, the learned can report problems of administrative functioning to their own 'superiors' – assistants to Board members; Board members to the Counsellors; Continental Counsellors to the International Teaching Centre).

It should be noted that there are no formal qualifications for appointment to one of the institutions of the learned, other than the implicit quality of dedication to the Baha'i Faith. Particularly active involvement in teaching the Faith seems to be a common quality of many of those appointed (perhaps more at the present time than in the past). Those appointed to these institutions are likely to be invited to participate in meetings which may include discussion of their new responsibilities, but there is no formal training programme or educational requirements.

5. THE ADMINISTRATION AND THE BAHA'I COMMUNITY

The Baha'i writings frequently emphasize the need for the Baha'i administration to embody a specific 'spirit' and not operate purely as a bureaucratic structure. This is particularly stressed in relationship to the assembly system, assembly members being reminded of the spiritual responsibilities of their work (including 'extreme humility' and selfless devotion), and warned of the dangers of personalistic leadership and of over-administration. Thus, whilst strictly adhering to basic principles, they should be flexible in 'secondary matters' avoid excessive rule-making and regulation. Again, in dealing with the Baha'i community as a whole, Baha'i administrators should endeavour to gain the support, respect, and affection of their fellow believers; observe the principle of consultation (see later); and remember that the right of individual self-expression lay 'at the very root of the Cause', and that only through the support of the 'rank and file' Baha'is could the administration function effectively.[13]

Consultation

Consultation is stressed as an essential principle of administration.[14] It is intended both as a system to enable individual voices to be heard and as a means to study a variety of views – in the belief that it is always better to seek the views of many than just to have the views of a few and that true consultation leads to fresh insights. The principle of consultation is also greatly emphasized in the Baha'i writings in relationship to government, community affairs, business, family life, and individual decision-making.

In the Baha'i view, consultation does not consist of the mere voicing of personal opinions – which could lead to altercation and useless quibbling destructive to truth ('Abdu'l-Bahá attended a meeting of the French Senate, which he criticized on these grounds). Rather, those who consult together need to have a sense of mutual fellowship and unity; humbly seek the truth; express their own views with the greatest courtesy, dignity, care, and moderation; carefully, calmly, and patiently weigh all the views expressed; and willingly abandon their own prior opinions if an alternative view seems better. Everyone should be able to express their views with 'absolute free-dom'. No one should belittle the thoughts of another, or feel hurt if others opposed their own views. Only if matters were fully discussed would the right way be found, and the 'shining spark of truth' might only emerge out of the 'clash of differing opinions'. Only if a unanimity of views did not emerge, should a majority vote prevail.

At a formal level, all Baha'i have the right to consult with their local assembly about matters of concern. The local community is also able to make its views known to the national assembly through its own local assembly and the regular Nineteen Day Feasts. Again, for a short period every year, locally elected delegates are able to consult directly together about matters of concern to the whole national Baha'i community, meeting with

[13] Shoghi Effendi, *Bahá'í Administration*, pp. 63–4; idem, *Citadel*, pp. 130–31.
[14] CCI, pp. 93–110; CEBF, 'consultation', loc. cit.

the members of the outgoing national spiritual assembly as well as electing and advising their successors at the national convention.

Consent and Appeal

In the Baha'i system, whilst the local and national assemblies retain the 'sacred right of final decision', they are duty bound to try to lead by consent, seeking to win the confidence and affection of 'those whom it is their privilege to serve'; acquainting themselves with their views and sentiments; welcoming advice, discussion and the expression of grievances; avoiding aloofness and secrecy in their own deliberations; and fostering a sense of interdependence and co-partnership with the rank-and-file of the Baha'is.

Any individual Baha'i also has the right of appeal against the decisions of his or her local or national spiritual assembly. Local assemblies have the right of appeal against the decisions of their responsible national assembly and of adjudication in the case of unresolvable problems between themselves and other local assemblies. In each instance, the appeal should be made to the next highest authority (i.e. against a local assembly to the national assembly; against a national assembly to the Universal House of Justice), which would then decide whether to take jurisdiction over the matter or refer it back to the original assembly for reconsideration. In all cases, however, the appellants should initially try to resolve the difficulties they had with the assembly in question, and only make their appeal if resolution was not possible.

Elections

Elections are a very common aspect of Baha'i life, whether it be for members of assemblies, regional councils, or the Universal House of Justice; delegates for conventions; or assembly or committee officers. In all cases, the elections are carried out by secret ballot by the eligible electors. Nominations, canvassing, or any form of electioneering are prohibited, as is any discussion of personalities before the election. Instead, each individual elector is required to prayerfully follow the dictates of his or her own conscience in determining who to vote for. In countries where universal literacy prevails, the electors write down the names of those they wish to vote for, and appointed tellers then count up the votes.[15]

---

[15] CCi, pp. 315–18; CEBF, 'elections', loc. cit. In situations in which there are illiterate electors, a variety of local solutions seem to be practised, the most common being the appointment of some trusted outsider to record the illiterate person's vote (personal communications).

6. FUNDING

Bahá'u'lláh noted that 'the progress and promotion of the cause of God depend on material means', and called upon his followers to support the activities of the Faith financially. This they did, both through the formal system of the *Ḥuqúqu'lláh*; gifts to Bahá'u'lláh and 'Abdu'l-Bahá; and support for particular projects such as the Ashkhabad and Chicago temples. Later, a formalized system of funding developed as part of the regularization and expansion of the administrative order under Shoghi Effendi and the Universal House of Justice.[16]

Several different funds are now in existence, including local and national funds administered by the various spiritual assemblies; an 'International Baha'i Fund' administered by the Universal House of Justice; 'continental funds' to support the work of the Counsellors and the Auxiliary Boards; and an 'International Deputization Fund' to support pioneering. Whilst individuals are encouraged to support these funds as a spiritual blessing to themselves, all contributions are a strictly personal matter, determined purely by dictates of conscience. No solicitation of contributions is allowed other than general appeals for donations. Baha'is are advised to exercise wisdom, and not incur debts or cause suffering to others in order to donate. Baha'i assemblies are directed to be wise and careful in their expenditures, adopting proper measures of auditing and control.

Only Baha'is are allowed to contribute to funds supporting the direct work of the Faith (e.g. administration and teaching projects), but non-Baha'is are able to contribute to separate Baha'i funds devoted solely to charitable and socio-economic development work.

[16] CC1, pp. 529–50; CEBF, 'funds', loc. cit.

CHAPTER 15

Aspects of Baha'i Community Life

I. THE IDEAL OF BAHA'I COMMUNITY LIFE

The ideal of Baha'i community life is an important part of the Baha'i teachings.[1] Indeed, the frequency with which Baha'is use the term 'community' to refer to their local congregations and national memberships, or indeed to the 'worldwide Baha'i community', is itself of note, indicating an aspiration that being a Baha'i should involve more than just individual religious practice or attendance at Baha'i meetings, but lead to a strong sense of shared identity with fellow believers, expressed in mutual concern and care. Given the enormous diversity of the Baha'i community worldwide, it is difficult to generalize about the actual practice of Baha'i community life, of course, and without numerous local studies it is impossible to judge to what extent individual communities have been able to express the ideal portrayed in the Baha'i writings – it may well be easier to develop such a sense of communal solidarity in the large Baha'i congregations in some African, Asian and Latin American villages than among a small scattering of Baha'is in a large city, but it is clear that throughout the world, active Baha'i communities seek to enhance their solidarity through the meetings they organize and, where possible, practices such as communal dawn prayers or the Ruhi Deepening program so popular in recent years.

An important part of the Baha'i ideal is the establishment and maintenance of unity within their own communities. For the individual, this should involve learning to overlook the faults of others with a 'sin-covering eye'; to be loving, forbearing, patient, and merciful; to resolutely abstain from gossip and backbiting (a practice described by 'Abdu'l-Bahá as 'the most great sin and as the cause of divine wrath);[2] to overcome personal differences and petty preoccupations; to use consultation to solve problems; to take responsibility for their own lives rather than focussing on the faults

---

[1] CEBF, 'community', loc. cit.   [2] CEBF, 'backbiting', loc. cit.

of others; and to avoid criticizing others and using harsh language against them. The Baha'is should strive daily to become more united and loving – to be 'as one being and one soul'. Correspondingly, one of the primary duties of the various Baha'i administrative institutions is to work to maintain unity amongst the Baha'is. The spiritual assemblies should be at the heart of community life, and the Counsellors, Board members and assistants should strive to inspire the Baha'is to greater communal activity as well as identifying situations in which the ideal is not being realized.

2. THE BAHA'I YEAR

One focus for Baha'i identity is the variety of activities organized by local Baha'i communities. Of particular formal importance are the regular Nineteen Day Feasts and the commemorations of the Baha'i holy days (see later), but many communities also organize devotional and social meetings; children's, youth and adult study classes; informal discussion groups for enquirers; and public meetings and other campaigns for proclaiming the Baha'i teachings. Neighbouring local communities may also collaborate in organizing joint meetings and activities, whilst national assemblies and their committees organize national and regional conferences and schools. Many Baha'is also meet regularly as members of local spiritual assemblies and their various committees.

The Calendar

Many Baha'i activities – including the Nineteen Day Feasts – follow a special Baha'i (*Badí'*, 'wondrous') calendar first devised by the Báb and subsequently amended slightly by Bahá'u'lláh. Beginning at the spring equinox – the ancient Iranian new year (*Naw-Rúz*, Pers. 'New Day'), normally 21 March, the year is divided into nineteen months, each of nineteen days, with four intercalary days (five in a leap year) being added to make up a solar year of 365 days (19 × 19 = 361).[3] The last month ('Alá') is the Baha'i month of fasting, and the intercalary days (*Ayyám-i Há*, 'days of five') – a period of celebration, charity, hospitality, and gift-giving – are placed just prior to the Fast. Each month is named after a divine quality or

---

[3] Various aspects of the Babi religion were structured in units of nineteen in accordance with the occult numerology used by the Báb, in which nineteen was the numerical value of the words for '(divine) unity' (*wáhid*) and 'absolute being' (*wujúd*), as well as comprising the number of letters in the Islamic formulae, *Bismi'lláh ar-rahmán ar-rahím* ('In the name of God, the Merciful, the Compassionate'). See CEBF, 'numbers', loc. cit.

attribute.[4] The first year of the calendar is 1844, the year of the Báb's declaration (the *Badí'* year 164 began at Naw-Rúz 2007).

The Nineteen Day Feasts –so named because they are normally held every nineteen days on the first day of each Baha'i month (see Table 3) – are the main regular communal gatherings of Baha'is.[5] They now combine three distinct sections: an initial devotional, with prayers and other writings from Bahá'u'lláh, 'Abdu'l-Bahá, and the Báb being read or chanted; an administrative period for local community consultation and reports from the local spiritual assembly; and a final social section with fellowship between the Baha'is. The idea goes back to the Báb, who instructed his followers to offer hospitality once in nineteen days, and was subsequently confirmed by Bahá'u'lláh in order to 'bind hearts together'. Later, 'Abdu'l-Bahá developed the feast into a regular monthly meeting at which the Baha'is prayed and ate together (explicitly identifying these gatherings with the Christian Lord's Supper), whilst Shoghi Effendi introduced the administrative section of the Feast so as to provide regular opportunity for consultation between the local Baha'i community and its assembly. Details of the feast vary from one place to another. Although the simple serving of water is deemed sufficient as a symbol of fellowship, in most communities the social section of the feast includes the sharing of light refreshments, whilst in others a meal may be eaten. In some communities, there is music and singing.

Holy Days

There are eleven holy days over the course of the year, including the new year festival of *Naw-Rúz*.[6] These comprise nine 'major' holy days – the commemorations of the births of the Báb and Bahá'u'lláh (20 October and 12 November in the Gregorian calendar), their declarations of mission (22/23 May and three of the days during the Riḍván period: the first, ninth, and twelfth days (21, 29 April, 2 May), marking the arrival

---

[4] CEBF, '*Ayyám-i-Há*', 'calendar', and '*Naw-Rúz*', loc. cit. See also Walbridge, *Sacred*, pp. 181–205. Walbridge discusses the significance of the names of the various months, days, and years in the Baha'i calendar. *Naw-Rúz* is also the ancient Zoroastrian new year, and is still celebrated as the new year in Iran, Kurdistan, Afghanistan and Tajikistan. It occurs on the first day of the spring equinox in the northern hemisphere, which is normally 21 March, but may sometimes occur on the 20th or the 22nd. At present, Baha'is in the Middle East celebrate it on the equinox, but those elsewhere always celebrate it on the 21st. Many Baha'is exchange greetings cards at this time, whilst those of Iranian background often follow some of the traditional Iranian (non-Baha'i) customs associated with the festival (e.g. growing a dish of sprouting green lentils or beans). See Walbridge, *Sacred*, pp. 213–16.

[5] CEBF, 'feast, nineteen day', loc. cit. See further Walbridge, *Sacred*, pp. 206–211.

[6] CEBF, 'holy days', '*Naw-Rúz*', and '*Riḍván*', loc. cit. See further Forghani; Walbridge, *Sacred*, pp. 183–4, 213–47.

Table 3. *Baha'i holy days and feast days*

21 March	***Naw-Rúz*** (Baha'i New Year). Feast of *Bahá* (Splendour [#1]).
9 April	Feast of *Jalál* (Glory [#2]).
21 April–2 May	**The Ridván Festival**, with the first, ninth, and twelfth days (21, 29 April, 2 May), being specifically marked as holy days. The celebration of the first day of Ridván should be at 3 o'clock in the afternoon, marking the time of Bahá'u'lláh's arrival.
28 April	Feast of *Jamál* (Beauty [#3]).
17 May	Feast of *'Azamat* (Grandeur [#4]).
22/23 May	***Declaration of the Báb***. Commemorated at about two hours after sunset on the 22nd May.
29 May	***Ascension of Bahá'u'lláh***. Commemorated at 3 o'clock in the morning.
5 June	Feast of *Núr* (Light [#5]).
24 June	Feast of *Raḥmat* (Mercy [#6]).
9 July	***Martyrdom of the Báb***. Commemorated at noon.
13 July	Feast of *Kalimát* (Words [#7]).
1 August	Feast of *Kamál* (Perfection [#8]).
20 August	Feast of *Asmá'* (Names [#9]).
8 September	Feast of *'Izzat* (Might [#10]).
27 September	Feast of *Mashíyyat* (Will [#11]).
16 October	Feast of *'Ilm* (Knowledge [#12]).
20 October	***Birth of the Báb***.
4 November	Feast of *Qudrat* (Power [#13]).
12 November	***Birth of Bahá'u'lláh***.
23 November	Feast of *Qawl* (Speech [#14]).
26 November	***Day of the Covenant***.
28 November	***Passing of 'Abdu'l-Bahá***. Commemorated at about 1 o'clock in the morning.
12 December	Feast of *Masá'il* (Questions [#15]).
31 December	Feast of *Sharaf* (Honour [#16]).
19 January	Feast of *Sulṭán* (Sovereignty [#17]).
7 February	Feast of *Mulk* (Dominion [#18]).
26 February–1 March	*Ayyám-i Há*.
2 March	Feast of *'Alá'* (Loftiness [#19]). Month of fasting begins.

of Bahá'u'lláh at the 'Ridván' Garden in Baghdad, the arrival of his family, and his final departure); the martyrdom of the Báb (9 July); the passing ('Ascension') of Bahá'u'lláh (29 May), and two 'minor' holy days – the establishment of Bahá'u'lláh's covenant of succession (the Day of the Covenant, 26 November); and the passing of 'Abdu'l-Bahá (28 November). At Shoghi Effendi's explicit instructions, there are no holy days linked to his life. The nine 'major' holy days are given particular emphasis, and Baha'is who are able to abstain from work on those days.

There are specific times of observance for several of the holy days, including two which may involve night-time vigils (the ascension of Bahá'u'lláh and the passing of 'Abdu'l-Bahá), but there is no set format for these various commemorations, and Baha'i communities organize their own meetings for them as they see fit. Devotional programmes of prayers and specific writings for the holy day are commonly arranged – Bahá'u'lláh's 'Tablet of Visitation' being widely used on the day of his passing and for the martyrdom of the Báb, and public celebrations and communal dinners are often held for Naw-Rúz and the Birthday of Bahá'u'lláh. The Riḍván period is also the time of most Baha'i elections, a practice begun during the ministry of 'Abdu'l-Bahá, with local spiritual assemblies (on the first day of Riḍván), national assemblies and the Universal House of Justice normally being elected during this time. Both Shoghi Effendi and the Universal House of Justice have frequently sent special messages to the Baha'is at Riḍván, effectively marking the period as one of annual reflection on the progress of the Faith.

3. CONFERENCES, 'SUMMER SCHOOLS', AND INSTITUTES

Contacts between Baha'is of different local communities have long been an important part of Baha'i life, whether it be visits of individual Baha'is from one community to another; the thirty-eight international conferences which Shoghi Effendi and the Universal House of Justice organized between 1953 and 1982; or the countless regional, national, and continental conferences organized by various Baha'i bodies.[7] Two world congresses have also been held (in London, 1963 and New York, 1992). Such contacts reflect and reinforce the self-consciously global sense of identity felt by many Baha'is. In addition to the formal programmes of these meetings (talks, musical entertainments, etc.), they provide a setting for Baha'is of different backgrounds to meet, socialize and discuss matters of common concern. With improvements in communications technology, link-ups between conferences have now become common, further enhancing the sense of the Baha'is being members of a single global community. In addition, there have been various conferences concerned with specific issues and interests – such as the arts, music, education, women, youth, development, health, and scholarship.

---

[7] For a list see CEBF, 'conferences and congresses', loc. cit.

Baha'is also often meet each other outside their local communities at institutes and courses of learning where they can study their religion in more depth, as well as socialize and pray together. Dating back to the Green Acre Summer conferences in New England in the early 1900s, such 'schools' have been a common feature of Baha'i life in many national communities since the 1930s.[8] They may be held in either purpose-built institutions or in rented property, and typically last for a week or two during the holiday season (hence 'Summer schools'). Shorter weekend and youth schools are also held. Given that in many countries, the local Baha'i groups are small and scattered, these schools also offer some experience of a more intensive Baha'i community life.

Since the 1960s, rural-based 'teaching institutes' have been an important means of integrating large numbers of new Baha'is in the 'Third World' into the Faith. Held in the areas where the new Baha'is live, these institutes are often based in modest buildings newly constructed to serve as village Baha'i centres. Visiting or local tutors then present courses covering the basic rudiments of Baha'i belief and practice as well as sometimes starting literacy classes and fostering programmes of human resource development.[9]

4. HOLY PLACES AND PILGRIMAGE[10]

Various sites associated with the Báb, Bahá'u'lláh, and 'Abdu'l-Bahá are considered holy by Baha'is, most particularly the site of the House of the Báb in Shíráz; the House of Bahá'u'lláh in Baghdad; the Shrine of Bahá'u'lláh at Bahjí, and the Shrine of the Báb (including the Shrine of 'Abdu'l-Bahá) in Haifa. As the Shíráz house (where the Báb first declared his mission in 1844) was demolished by Islamic revolutionaries in September 1979 and the Baghdad house was taken over by Iraqi Shi'ites in the 1920s, only the shrines in Bahjí and Haifa are at present places of pilgrimage. Pilgrimage to these sites is not a religious obligation, but many Baha'is wish to visit the shrines at least once in their lives. The Shrine of Bahá'u'lláh is also the *qiblah* – the 'point of adoration' – to which Baha'is throughout the world turn when the say their daily obligatory prayers.

When Bahá'u'lláh designated the Shiraz and Baghdad houses as places of Baha'i pilgrimage, he also specified ritual observances for those who visited them, but given present circumstances, these are not now applicable. By contrast, there are no ritual requirements for those who visit the shrines at the Baha'i World Centre, apart from a general injunction to observe physical

---

[8] CEBF, 'Green Acre' and 'summer schools', loc. cit.   [9] CEBF, 'institutes', loc. cit.
[10] CEBF, 'pilgrimage'; 'shrines and holy places', loc. cit.

and emotional reverence. In practice, this involves being quiet in manner, dignified in dress, and removing one's shoes before entering the shrines. When large groups of Baha'is visit the shrines there is often a prearranged programme of prayers and other writings which are recited or chanted by individuals within the group. On some special occasions large groups of Baha'is circumambulate Bahá'u'lláh's Shrine at Bahjí or that of the Báb in Haifa. Individuals who visit the holy places on their own will commonly pray (in whatever manner they wish: standing, kneeling, sitting), and many will prostrate themselves, particularly at the 'holy thresholds' separating the outer rooms where pilgrims gather from the inner shrines where the holy remains are buried.

Pilgrimages to the Haifa-Akka area have always been carefully controlled so as to ensure that the pilgrims are well-received and are able to make their visitations in an orderly fashion that gives them the best opportunity to pray, meditate and gain a sense of linkage with the Baha'i World Centre whilst simultaneously not disrupting the administrative work of the Centre. Pilgrimage groups are accordingly limited in numbers and the duration of their stay (at present, in groups of 150 people in a succession of nine-day visits spread over most of the year). All pilgrims are required to gain advance permission before arrival and their pilgrimage programme during their visit is coordinated by a pilgrim reception centre in Haifa. Up until the early 1960s, whilst pilgrim groups were still very small, pilgrims were accommodated in Baha'i properties, but with larger numbers they now have to make their own accommodation arrangements. In addition to the pilgrims, the general public are able to visit some of the Baha'i sites and gardens at designated times – the Baha'i gardens in Haifa in particular being a major tourist site – with about 250,000 visitors per year by 2000–01.

For those on pilgrimage, additional places of importance which they may visit in and around Akka include the cell in the old citadel in which Bahá'u'lláh was confined and various houses in which Bahá'u'lláh and 'Abdu'l-Bahá lived, most importantly, the Mansion of Bahjí. In Haifa, pilgrims may also visit the former House of 'Abdu'l-Bahá and Shoghi Effendi; the International Archives Building, containing Babi and Baha'i relics – including a photograph of Bahá'u'lláh and a miniature portrait of the Báb; the 'Monument Gardens' containing the memorials to the various members of 'Abdu'l-Bahá's family; the Seat of the Universal House of Justice and the other buildings of the Arc; and the designated site for a future Baha'i House of Worship at the head of Mount Carmel. The pilgrims also have opportunities to meet with members of the World Centre staff, often including members of the Universal House of Justice, and are invited to attend meetings addressed by Baha'i dignitaries.

Outside of the World Centre, there are many lesser Baha'i holy places in Iran, including the site of the Síyáh Chál prison in Tehran; the fortress-prisons of the Báb in Mákú and Chihríq; the House of Bahá'u'lláh in Tehran; the Shaykh Ṭabarsí shrine, and the grave of Quddús. As almost all Baha'i holy sites in Iran were seized by the authorities in the aftermath of the Islamic Revolution of 1979, and several subsequently destroyed, visitations by would-be pilgrims are either difficult or impossible. Other sites in the Middle East include the Riḍván (Najíbiyya) garden in Baghdad and one of the houses which Bahá'u'lláh occupied in Edirne. Elsewhere the grave of Shoghi Effendi in London, the Maxwell home in which 'Abdu'l-Bahá stayed when he visited Montreal, and the grave of the early Baha'i Sayyid Muṣṭafá Rúmí in Burma are all regarded by Baha'is as having a special significance, and are places of visitation.

5. HOUSES OF WORSHIP[11]

Although as yet few in number, the institution of the Baha'i House of Worship (the *Mashriqu'l-Adhkár*) represents an important ideal of Baha'i community life, the central temple structures being intended to provide a spiritual focus for the various philanthropic institutions (including hospitals, drug dispensaries, homes for the elderly, traveller's hospices, schools, and universities) to be built around them. Ultimately, it is intended that Houses of Worship should be built throughout the world, each one serving as a symbolic centre for communal unity and prayer, the temples and the associated service institutions being open to people of all religions. The seven temples presently standing (Wilmette, Kampala, Sydney, Frankfurt, Panama, Apia, and New Delhi) are largely limited to their role as places of prayer for their local Baha'i communities and the occasional national gathering. Only the Wilmette and Frankfurt temples have service institutions (homes for the elderly) associated with them. Both the Wilmette and New Delhi Houses of Worship are also important tourist sites.

6. MUSIC AND THE ARTS[12]

The Baha'i leaders were generally sympathetic to the arts, Bahá'u'lláh praising craftsmanship as reflecting a divine quality, describing it as a form of

---

[11] CEBF, '*Mashriqu'l-Adhkár*', loc. cit. See also Julie Badiee, *An Earthly Paradise: Bahá'í Houses of Worship Around the World* (Oxford: George Ronald, 1992).

[12] CC1, pp. 1–8; CC2, pp. 73–82; CC3, pp. 18–45; CEBF, 'art'; 'calligraphy'; 'cinema and film'; 'craftsmanship'; 'drama and dance'; 'iconography'; 'music'; 'poetry', loc. cit. See also Michael Fitzgerald (ed.), *The Creative Circle: Art, Literature, and Music in Bahá'í Perspective* (Los Angeles, CA: Kalimát Press, 1989).

worship, and calling upon those who followed a particular craft or art to attain the greatest proficiency in it. There is as yet no 'Bahá'í art' – or music, literature, and architecture, albeit that the arts play an important role in the lives of many Bahá'ís and their communal activities. Shoghi Effendi noted that the spirit of every religion came to be expressed in art and predicted that when the Bahá'í Faith played a larger role in society, its spirit would find fuller expression in the work of artists and would act to ennoble peoples' sentiments and attract them to the Faith.

Of the traditional Iranian arts, three – religious chanting, religious poetry, and calligraphy – were particularly valued by the Central Figures of the Faith and remain a strong part of the Babi-Iranian Bahá'í tradition. Thus, amongst the Iranian and Arab Bahá'ís, the tradition of chanting the Bahá'í prayers and other writings is very strong and is part of everyday life, with children being taught to chant by their parents and many 'performances' being rendered of great beauty and strength; there have been a number of Babi and Iranian Bahá'í poets of note, must famously the Babi leader Ṭáhirih; and there have also been a number of eminent Iranian Bahá'ís who were gifted calligraphers – indeed, both the Báb and Bahá'u'lláh were famed for the beauty of their handwriting and praised calligraphic skill.

Of the other arts, it is of note that in the context of traditional Islamic culture, the attitude of Bahá'u'lláh and 'Abdu'l-Bahá towards music was distinctively positive: unlike many conservative Muslims who regard music other than religious chanting as satanic in nature and condemn listening to it, the Bahá'í leaders praised music in general as a potential 'ladder for the soul', affecting the emotions and enabling the individual to become spiritually uplifted – inflamed with the love of God – a view similar to that of many Islamic Sufis. Similarly, 'Abdu'l-Bahá referred to the educational potential of drama, and gave one of the Bahá'ís an outline of a religious play,[13] whilst Shoghi Effendi noted the value of stage productions in awakening noble sentiments among the mass of the people and attracting them to the Faith, and noting that this could include the portrayal of Bahá'í historical episodes – as long as there was no portrayal of any of the Manifestations of God as this would be irreverent from a Bahá'í perspective.

This said, the views of the Bahá'í leaders were conservative in terms of much of modern culture. For example, they warned that the emotional impact of music could also inflame the passions in a harmful way and called on the Bahá'ís to ensure that music did not lead them to 'overstep the bounds of propriety and dignity'. Again, Shoghi Effendi deplored the

---

[13] '*The Drama of the Kingdom*'. See Balyuzi, '*Abdu'l-Bahá*, pp. 497–502.

excessive corruption that prevailed in the cinema industry and therefore discouraged movie acting as a career.

In terms of practice, music, drama, and dance performances have become an increasingly common element in Baha'i meetings and conferences in recent years, and amateur Baha'i choirs, singing and dance groups have proliferated in various parts of the world, frequently being engaged to present Baha'i ideas to wider audiences. The development of 'Baha'i music' has been particularly important. This has been extremely diverse in nature, reflecting different cultural and musical traditions. The practice of chanting prayers, which is so strongly embedded in Middle Eastern Baha'i culture, is relatively unusual in other parts of the world, but the composition of Baha'i-themed songs reflecting various indigenous styles of music has become widespread. One Baha'i singing group – *El Viento Canta* from South America – has become particularly well-known internationally, and has toured widely in Europe, Asia, and Africa, as well as in the Americas. In Africa, national or regional Baha'i music festivals have been held in a number of countries. Several Baha'i arts associations have also been established, both at national and international levels.

There have been a number of Baha'is who were eminent figures in the arts, including the English potter Bernard Leach (1887–1979); the American painter Mark Tobey (1890–1976); the jazz trumpeter Dizzy Gillespie (1917–93); the Russian poet Izabella Grinevskaya (1864–1944); the African-American laureate, Robert Hayden (1913–80); and the 1930s Hollywood movie star Carole Lombard (1908–1942), several of whom expressed Baha'i ideas and motifs in their work.[14] There have also been a number of well-known Iranian Baha'i musicians and singers, both in traditional and modern styles.

7. ARCHITECTURE[15]

There is no distinctive style of Baha'i architecture, although Shoghi Effendi's liking for what he saw as the beauty and dignity of Classical Greek styles (as expressed in the International Archives Building) has had an obvious impact on the style of the recent buildings of the Baha'i World Centre. The eight Baha'i Houses of Worship built to date (including the now demolished temple at Ashkhabad) are quite diverse in style, despite conforming to the same basic pattern of being nine-sided buildings with domes. The Houses of

[14] There are CEBF articles on Gillespie, Grinevskaya, Hayden, Leach, and Tobey.
[15] CEBF, 'architecture', loc. cit.

Worship do not contain any figurative representations. Several incorporate indigenous elements and motifs – notably the Kampala, Panama, Apia, and New Delhi temples. The Wilmette and New Delhi temples, together with the Chilean temple currently under construction, have attracted considerable interest among architects for their originality of construction. Other Baha'i buildings in various parts of the world, such as national and local Baha'i centres, are again varied in style. Shoghi Effendi also had a great love of gardens, devoting much energy to establishing and expanding gardens around the various Baha'i holy sites, and we might anticipate that many Baha'i buildings would emulate this example.

CHAPTER 16

Baha'i Activities and the Wider World

I. THE MISSION OF EXPANSION

The Baha'i Faith is a 'missionary' religion in the sense both of advocating energetic endeavour on the part of its adherents to 'promote the Faith' and gain new adherents and in seeing planned expansion as a central objective or mission of activity leading ultimately to a world in which Baha'is and Baha'i institutions are the predominant element. The Baha'i leaders taught that the propagation of their religion should be peaceful and non-disputatious.

Teaching and Pioneering[1]

In modern Baha'i parlance, those who promote the Faith are described as 'teachers' and 'pioneers', 'teaching' referring to the endeavour to attract more people to the Baha'i Faith, and 'pioneering' to the act of leaving one's own home to establish residence in another locality or country in order to propagate the Faith. The term 'missionary', with its implications of a professional religious specialist, is avoided. All Baha'is are encouraged to become teachers of the Faith, whilst pioneering is much praised and encouraged – being described as 'the prince of all goodly deeds'. Teaching and pioneering should not be looked upon as 'jobs', individual pioneers are sometime given financial assistance to settle into a new territory and funding may be provided for short-term teaching projects, but all Baha'is should aim to be self-supporting, and to combine their Baha'i activities with following a profession.

The central importance of spirituality in teaching and pioneering is much emphasized in the Baha'i writings. Ultimately, it is only the moral quality of Baha'i teachers which will vindicate the claims of the Faith and attract

---

[1] CEBF, 'teaching'; 'pioneers, pioneering', loc. cit. Claire Vreeland (comp.), *And the Trees Clapped Their Hands: Stories of Bahá'í Pioneers* (Oxford: George Ronald, 1994) provides a number of stories of pioneers.

outsiders to it. The Baha'i teacher should trust in God and be detached, pure in heart, prayerful, loving, humble, wise, patient, forgiving and coura-geous. He or she should avoid disputation and show due consideration for everyone they encountered, regardless of their interlocutor's age, level of education or social status. Other qualities are also important, however: the Baha'i teacher should become ablaze with 'the fire of the love of God' and thus speak with 'penetrating power' and 'set on fire' those who heard them; make teaching the 'dominating passion' of their lives and be as 'unrestrained as the wind' in their teaching endeavour; strive to become knowledgeable about the Faith and its scriptures; and be sensitive to those they taught, exer-cising moderation, kindliness, tact and wisdom in what they said, leaving to themselves and to God those who rejected their message.[2]

Different Baha'is teach their religion in different ways – there is no one right method of teaching as what is considered to be of primary importance is the 'spirit' and dedication of the teacher. In some places, public meetings are used as a means of securing initial publicity for the Faith, and informal meetings in homes – 'firesides' – with discussions and hospitality, have proven particularly effective in various parts of the world. Some Baha'is spend often considerable periods of time as 'travel teachers', travelling from one place to another to teach their faith. Effective organization has long been stressed, with systematic expansion plans a characteristic of the Faith. Practicalities, such as the need for pioneers and travel teachers to learn the language of the people they wished to teach and to remain in close contact with the responsible Baha'i administrative bodies, are also emphasized.

The entry of large numbers of new Baha'is in various 'Third World' coun-tries from the 1950s onwards changed conceptions of teaching, the Universal House of Justice emphasizing the importance of 'teaching the masses' as a means of achieving continued large-scale expansion. Given the dire poverty of many of the people they were now contacting, Baha'i teachers were specif-ically warned not to give the impression that conversion would lead to any material advantage to those who responded to their message. Baha'i service and socio-economic development projects were to be available to all people in a locality and not just to newly converted Baha'is.

Consolidation and 'Deepening'

In any religious movement, gaining converts ('new believers' in Baha'i parlance) is not sufficient: methods of maintaining and enhancing the

---

[2] For compilations of Baha'i writings on teaching, see CC2, pp. 61–71, 293–326; CC3, pp. 154–225.

commitment of all members are needed to ensure the continued sociological existence and success of the group. In the Baha'i Faith, such mechanisms
are both communal – through the effective consolidation of united and
active local Baha'i communities, and individual – through the processes of
study, discussion, prayer and meditation which the Baha'is term 'deepening'. Aspects of Baha'i community life are described earlier (Chapter 15),
but a brief description of deepening can be given here.[3]

All Baha'is are encouraged to deepen their knowledge and understanding
of the Baha'i Faith, as well as their level of involvement and commitment.
Key here is prayerful study of the Baha'i scriptures, Bahá'u'lláh bidding his
followers to 'immerse' themselves in 'the ocean' of his words, and requiring
them to read passages from his writings every morning and evening so as
to uplift their own souls. This should not be a passive process, the Baha'is
should reflect and meditate on what they read and strive to translate it into
action. True understanding depended on purity of heart, and not acquired
learning, a message reiterated by the subsequent leaders of the Faith.

Beyond this, Shoghi Effendi also encouraged the Baha'is to undertake
formal study of the history, teachings and administration of the Faith;
strive to better understand the significance of Bahá'u'lláh's revelation; and
to widen their vision – including gaining a knowledge of Islam and the
Qur'án as a background to the Faith and some awareness of comparative
religion and of contemporary social and religious thinking. A high spiritual
and intellectual standard should be maintained. The Baha'is should study
the actual writings of Bahá'u'lláh and 'Abdu'l-Bahá rather than summaries
and second-hand accounts. To study was a 'sacred obligation', and there
was no limit to the study of the Faith. Without deepening, he believed, the
teaching work would be ineffective, and new Baha'is would not become
firmly committed to the Faith.

During Shoghi Effendi's guardianship, the main ways of deepening were
private study, local study classes and 'Summer schools' and similar institutes
held during the holiday season (which he hoped would eventually evolve
into Baha'i universities).[4] Following the massive expansion of the Faith
amongst often poorly educated people of the 'Third World' from the 1950s
onwards, several Baha'i communities have experimented with techniques to
help Baha'is of all educational levels to become both more familiar with the
Baha'i scriptures as part of their spiritual life and more involved in the work
of teaching the Faith, one of the most successful being the series of '*Rúhí*

[3] CEBF, 'deepening'; 'consolidation', loc. cit. On deepening see CC1, pp. 187–234.
[4] CEBF, 'summer schools'; 'institutes'; CC1, pp. 25–44.

books, which came to prominence in the Colombian Baha'i community in the 1980s and thereafter were widely adopted throughout the Baha'i world, gaining the praise of the Universal House of Justice. As a highly structured method of learning and activity, study circles based on the Rúhí books focus on group consultations on the meanings of selected Baha'i writings and their significance for individual and collective action. The holding of children's classes and devotionals is also much encouraged.

Opposition[5]

Bahá'u'lláh regarded opposition to God's messengers as a recurrent feature of religion, well evidenced by the responses to previous Manifestations of God and again in his day. Religious leaders bore a particular responsibility in this regard, as they often saw a new prophet as a challenge to their established power, or could not reconcile his teachings with their own limited ideas. Opposition to the Baha'i cause was thus to be expected. The Baha'is should not be deterred by it, even when it led to persecution. They should put their trust in God, assured of eventual victory. God's purpose could not be thwarted. His signs had encompassed the world. The 'ascendancy of the oppressor' would be temporary and unavailing. God would give those who remained steadfast such power that they would be able to withstand all the forces of the earth. They should teach the Faith with wisdom and tolerance, and if they could, defend it from its opponents in their writings. Martyrdom was a glorious station and should be embraced if it was completely unavoidable, but Baha'is should not seek it out deliberately. Those who opposed his Faith were ignorant and heedless.

2. SOCIAL INVOLVEMENT

Bahá'u'lláh gave his followers a powerful and multi-faceted vision of social reconstruction (see Chapter 11), some elements of which Baha'is seek to implement within their own communities, whilst others require wider governmental and societal changes to occur. Social advocacy therefore constitutes part of what Baha'is see as their mission in the world. Inevitably, social advocacy also has political dimensions, albeit that Baha'is strictly follow policies of avoiding involvement in partisan politics and of being loyal to established governments. Areas of particular concern include internationalism and support for the United Nations; religious tolerance and the

[5] CEBF, 'opposition'; 'persecution'; 'martyrdom', loc cit. On opposition see CC2, pp. 137–50.

coexistence of ethnic groups; the advancement of women; education; and socio-economic development.

Involvement with the United Nations[6]

Baha'is support the work of the United Nations (UN), seeing the UN institutions as an important, albeit inadequate move towards the Faith's internationalist objectives. They are also actively involved in the work of several UN agencies, as well as advocating revisions to the UN charter to strengthen its role vis-à-vis the constituent member states. Pragmatically, the Baha'is see the UN as a body that can sometimes exert influence to prevent or minimize persecution of Baha'is in various parts of the world, appealing for its help on a number of occasions.

Tolerance and Unity in Diversity

Baha'is stress the essential unity of the human race and the essential need for cultural and religious tolerance of diversity. Within the Baha'i community itself, the Baha'is celebrate their own enormous ethnic diversity, but a key test of the success of the Baha'i teachings, of course, is the extent to which individual Baha'i communities have achieved integration between their own component ethnic elements. In this regard, whilst there is a general lack of sociological studies of Baha'i communities, such evidence as there is suggests a significant degree of integration over time, both in Iran (among Baha'is of Muslim, Jewish, and Zoroastrian background) and the United States (among black, white, and Amerindian Baha'is), with many cases of intermarriage. It is also of note that indigenous tribal peoples have become a significant presence in a number of national Baha'i communities, community life subsequently evolving to reflect their concerns, as with the establishment of Baha'i radio stations in Latin America, which cater for local needs and promote Amerindian culture.

Baha'is have also had some impact outside their own community. Thus, whilst eschewing political involvement, American Baha'is have a long history of activism in work to promote racial unity, holding a variety of seminars, local parades, children's conferences, picnics, concerts, arts festivals, dance-dramas, and exhibitions over the years.[7] More recently, Baha's have

---

[6] CEBF, 'United Nations, League of Nations', loc. cit.
[7] See Gayle Morrison, *To Move the World: Louis G. Gregory and the Advancement of Racial Unity in America* (Wilmette, IL: Bahá'í Publishing Trust, 1982); Nathan Rutstein, *To Be One: A Battle Against*

also become involved in the public debate about racism and other forms of social division in countries as diverse as Bermuda, South Africa and Switzerland, in some cases achieving a wider social impact with their ideas, as in India, where a Baha'is booklet on '*Communal Harmony*', which called for Indians to overcome the complex of religious, linguistic and caste-based tensions found in their country, was later praised and extensively quoted by the Indian Supreme Court. Baha'is have also supported the work of the United Nations on these issues, participating in such events as the International Year for the World's Indigenous Peoples (1993) and the International Decade for Indigenous Peoples (1994–2004), as well as local initiatives by such groups as the Australian Aboriginal Reconciliation Council.[8]

The Advancement of Women[9]

Baha'is have a long history of activism in promoting the social advancement of women, particularly in Iran and more recently in some parts of the 'Third World'. Thus, in matters of Baha'i law, Bahá'u'lláh significantly challenged contemporary Iranian cultural norms and commonly accepted social practices by making it an obligation for fathers to educate their daughters as well as their sons; forbidding the purchase of women, the taking of concubines or temporary wives, betrothal or marriage to girls under the age of fifteen, and instant divorce; and denying men any sexual rights over their female servants. For his part, 'Abdu'l-Bahá stated that in cases of financial difficulty, parents should give priority to the education of their daughters over that of their sons as the girls were potential mothers, and as such their own children's first educators who could lead their children to wisdom and morality – women who were ignorant and illiterate having a potentially adverse effect on their children. Meanwhile, from the late nineteenth century onwards, under the influence of the Baha'i teachings, an increasing number of Iranian Baha'i women began to assume a significant role in the Baha'i community and to achieve higher levels of education.

More recently, the advancement of women has again become an important issue in the Baha'i community in recent years, particularly following

Racism (Oxford: George Ronald, 1988); Richard W. Thomas, 'A long and thorny path: Race relations in the American Bahá'í community'. In *Circle of Unity: Bahá'í Approaches to Current Social Issues*, ed. Anthony A. Lee, pp. 37–65 (Los Angeles, CA: Kalimát Press, 1984); idem, *Racial Unity: An Imperative for Progress* (Wilmette, IL: National Spiritual Assembly of the Bahá'ís of the United States, 1992).

8 CEBF, 'race', loc. cit.
9 CEBF, 'women', loc. cit. See Peggy Caton (ed.), *Equal Circles: Women and Men in the Bahá'í Community* (Los Angeles, CA: Kalimát Press, 1987); Susan S. Maneck, 'Women in the Baha'i Faith'. In *Religion and Women*, ed. Arvind Sharma (Albany: State University of New York Press, 1994).

the large-scale influx of poor Third World villagers into the Faith (including many illiterate women) and the debates engendered by the modern feminist movement. International Women's Year (1975) marked a particular focus for Baha'i activity in this regard, the Universal House of Justice subsequently repeatedly calling for national Baha'i communities to implement programmes to promote the full and equal participation of women in their activities, as well as seeking to sensitize Baha'is regarding the implications of the principle of gender equality for community life, as in its issuance of a compilation of Baha'i writings on *Women* in January 1986.[10] International institutional developments have included the establishment of a European Task Force on Women by the continent's Board of Counsellors in 1992 and of a Baha'i International Community Office for the Advancement of Women in New York in 1993. Some national communities have also now established their own offices for the advancement of women or their equivalent and numerous conferences on the advancement of women and related issues have also been held.

Activities to advance the role of women within Baha'i communities have included the promotion of girls' education and of adult female literacy, training in health and income-generating skills for poor rural women, and consultation on gender roles in the community (specifically involving men, the change of whose attitudes is seen as essential to any meaningful change in women's status).

In addition to furthering gender equality amongst the Baha'is, there has been increasing contact and work with non-Baha'i women's organizations, both internationally and locally, and a number of major projects have been organized which have reached out beyond the Baha'is to involve the wider community, in some cases gaining governmental or UN agency support.[11]

Gender Differentiation

The strong Baha'i advocacy of the advancement of women noted, some important elements of differentiation remain. In this regard, the Baha'i position regarding female emancipation has clearly strengthened over time, a trend often seen by modern Baha'is in progressive developmentalist terms

---

[10] See CC2, pp. 355–406.

[11] Two projects which have received particular attention are the Indore Baha'i Vocational Institute for Rural Women in India (1983–) and a multinational Baha'i-UNIFEM Project on using traditional song, dance and drama as an agency of social change (1991–) (*The Bahá'í World, 1993–94*, pp. 255–63).

as with other aspects of the Baha'i teachings. Thus, Bahá'u'lláh himself allowed for significant inequalities, notably in following the Báb in permitting men to take two wives (rather than four as in Islam). At the same time, however, he strongly encouraged Baha'i men to content themselves with only one wife for the sake of domestic harmony.[12] Subsequently, 'Abdu'l-Bahá argued that as it was impossible for a man to treat two wives equally, the Baha'i teachings implicitly demanded monogamy, and Shoghi Effendi forbade polygamy altogether.

Bahá'u'lláh also referred to 'the men' of the House of Justice, and the Universal House of Justice has confirmed that it is official Baha'i policy for its own membership to be confined to men – a policy to which a few Western Baha'i intellectuals have voiced their opposition.[13] All other contemporary Baha'i administrative bodies are equally open to both sexes, and it is of note that an increasing number of women have been appointed or elected to Baha'i administrative positions (by 1993, for example, 28 percent of national spiritual assembly membership worldwide was female – with generally higher figures in richer countries and lower figures in much of Africa and Asia).

Educational Involvement[14]

In addition to the Baha'i leaders' teachings on education, there has been Baha'i involvement in the practicalities of schooling since the late nineteenth century, and in recent years, an increasing number of Baha'i schools, colleges, preschools and basic 'tutorial' schools (teaching rural development skills such as literacy) have been established in various parts of the world, including both official Baha'i institutions, such as the New Era School in India (effectively dating back to 1953) and the Maxwell International School in Canada (1988) – both high status international schools, and institutions established by groups of Baha'is incorporating Baha'i principles, such as the

---

[12] Bahá'u'lláh also prescribed that the husband should pay a relatively small amount of money as a bridal gift (*mahr*) to his wife (not to her family) and discriminated between male and female inheritors in the case of intestacy – including stating that the father's residence should be inherited in the male line and following the Babi ordinance that mothers and sisters were to inherit slightly less than fathers and brothers. As what would seem to be a matter of simple practicality in the conditions of the time, he exempted women from the obligation of formal pilgrimage, as well as allowing menstruating and pregnant women to exempt themselves from fasting if they so choose.

[13] See Cole (*Modernity*, pp. 182–4). No reason is given for this exception, but 'Abdu'l-Bahá stated that the wisdom of it would eventually become clear (CC2, pp. 369–70).

[14] CEBF, 'education', loc. cit.

Universidad Núr and the Private Technical University of Santa Cruz (both in Bolivia).[15]

There is no one single pattern of contemporary Baha'i involvement in education beyond the attempt to combine moral and the best available 'secular' education and to open Baha'i educational institutions to students of all religions. The Baha'i teachings on education provide a general framework of ideas rather than a single program of action, and as with other Baha'i social projects, there is a ready tolerance of diversity in application. At the same time, as the number of Baha'i educational institutions increases, there is increasing dialogue amongst Baha'i educationalists regarding the theory and practice of what they are doing, and it seems reasonable to expect that this process will lead to a more explicit and integrated framework of ideas on the subject.[16]

It is of note that as Baha'i communities in many countries have become larger and more visible, there has been increasing involvement in wider educational debates and projects concerned with such matters as moral and religious education, education for rural development and peace education, with Baha'i initiatives gaining support and approval in countries as diverse as India, Honduras and the Marshall Islands.

Socio-Economic Development[17]

Development issues have assumed increasing importance in the Baha'i community since the large-scale expansion of the Faith into the countries of the 'Third World' has fundamentally changed the global Baha'i demographic. Beginning in earnest in the 1970s with the establishment of a growing number of Baha'i schools and rural development programmes, this trend was given focus and impetus by the Universal House in October 1983, when it called for the more systematic application of Baha'i principles to upraise 'the quality of human life' and established an Office of Social and Economic Development in Haifa to 'promote and coordinate' Baha'i development activities worldwide. The number of projects increased rapidly, with most being developed in the poorer countries of the world. A variety of Baha'i

---

[15] By 1992, there were 178 academic Baha'i schools and 488 tutorial schools worldwide (*The Bahá'í World, 1992–3*, p. 313).

[16] For examples of Baha'i educational thinking, see Nikjoo and Vickers, and Rost, *Brilliant Stars*.

[17] CEBF, 'socio-economic development', loc. cit. *The Bahá'í World* volumes provide details of recent Baha'i development projects. For general discussions, see Moojan Momen, *Bahá'í Focus on Development* (London: Bahá'í Publishing Trust, 1988), and Holly Hanson Vick, *Social and Economic Development: A Bahá'í Approach* (Oxford: George Ronald, 1989).

agencies and institutes have been accordingly established to promote development, either as institutions of a particular Baha'i national spiritual assembly or as separate non-governmental organizations. By 2003, there were about five hundred major Baha'i development projects in operation worldwide, with over twenty-five hundred small-scale temporary projects also organized and forty-five Baha'i development institutions including some of the Baha'i schools. Many of these projects were multi-faceted, combining various aspects of development. Concerns range from education and literacy, to dealing with social problems such as substance abuse, and to the promotion of agriculture, health care, immunization, child care and microenterprise. Common features of implementation include an emphasis on the importance of grass-roots initiatives and knowledge; consultation with and amongst the local community; ideas of empowerment (particularly of women) and human resource development; the essential need for wider social and moral issues to form part of development process (for example, the fostering of trustworthiness); an ethos of community service (Baha'i projects are non-sectarian in their focus, and not confined to the Baha'is); and a valuing of local minority cultures. The several Baha'i radio stations have also been employed to promote local community development. A considerable body of experience has being built up, and some projects have evidently been highly successful, several gaining the support of government and international donor agencies – including the Canadian International Development Agency (CIDA) and the Norwegian Agency for International Development Cooperation (NORAD). There have also been a number of national and international conferences for Baha'is interested in development issues, where they can share ideas and develop perspectives.

Baha'is have also begun to try to elaborate and apply their teachings to work and business, with an increasing number of Baha'i-based business and professional organizations formed in recent years. One of the best-known of these is the European Baha'i Business Forum (est. 1990), which provides a forum for the discussion of Baha'i approaches to business matters; holds seminars on raising the standards of business ethics; and has established contacts with educational centres in several countries, including Albania, Bulgaria, and Rumania. Other associations have been established in Australia and Hong Kong. There are also a number of organizations for Baha'is involved in medicine and health care,[18] and there is growing Baha'i interest in environmental issues.

---

[18] CEBF, 'business and professional organizations', loc. cit. For a listing of some of the main Baha'i professional and voluntary organizations, see *The Bahá'í World, 2001–2002*, pp. 320–21.

3. LEARNING AND SCHOLARSHIP

Learning and knowledge are highly praised in the Baha'i writings, and both Shoghi Effendi and the Universal House of Justice encouraged the development of Baha'i scholarship, highlighting its importance for the Faith. This appeal is multifaceted. Thus, learning more about the Faith is linked to the belief that true religion can be supported by rational proofs, and so to both the lifelong project of 'deepening' and becoming a more committed and understanding Baha'i and the mission of effective teaching of the Faith. More generally, the Baha'i concern with societal reconstruction and improvement includes an appeal for Baha'is to learn about all the 'arts and sciences' that can contribute to the progress of the human race.

In relationship to teaching, an extensive Baha'i apologetic literature has developed.[19] In this regard, Baha'is are reminded that in order to teach educated people, they should themselves be well informed so that they can discuss contemporary issues intelligently. Indeed, as early as the 1940s, Shoghi Effendi noted that the thinking world had already 'caught up' with the universal principles enunciated by Bahá'u'lláh and that these no longer seemed new to them. It was necessary therefore both for there to be more Baha'i scholars and for 'a more profound and co-ordinated Baha'i scholarship' so that the Baha'i teachings could be better communicated to intelligent and educated people. At least some Baha'is needed both to know not just the Baha'i teachings in depth, but have a sound knowledge of general and religious history, economics, sociology, science, and the like. Thus they would be able to correlate the thinking of modern thinkers and progressive movements with the Baha'i teachings.

The pressing needs of teaching and administrative consolidation meant that little attention was given to the development of this conception of scholarship by the Baha'i community until the 1970s, by which time the increasing extent of Baha'i interest in issues of social reform considerably broadened its range.[20] A key development here was the establishment of the Canadian Association for Studies on the Baha'i Faith in 1975 – in response to a call by the Universal House of Justice. This body aimed to promote lectures and conferences relating to the Baha'i Faith at Canadian universities. Reflecting international interest, the organization was renamed the Association for Baha'i Studies (ABS) in 1981, and a large number of national or regional affiliate associations have now been established (twenty-four by 2001, including ten in the Americas, five in Europe, four in

---

[19] CEBF, 'apologetics', loc. cit.   [20] CEBF, 'Bábí and Bahá'í Studies'; 'scholarship', loc. cit.

Africa, three in Asia, and two in Australasia). Various special interest groups have also been formed under the ABS umbrella, including an international Baha'i Health Agency (1982). Regarding all Baha'is as potential scholars, the ABS associations have sought both to present the Baha'i Faith and its ideals to a wider intellectual audience and to explore the implications and possible application of the Baha'i teachings in all aspects of human life, including social issues, moral education, the search for a global ethic, the environment, law and the arts. ABS-linked publications include a series of *Baha'i Studies* volumes (1976–, mostly monographs) and *The Journal of Baha'i Studies* (1988–). Other institutional developments within the Baha'i community have included the establishment of a Baha'i University (Universidad Núr) in Santa Cruz, Bolivia in 1984; the sponsorship of Baha'i Chairs at the Universities of Maryland in the United States and Indore in India (both in 1990); and the introduction of a three-year Certificate Programme in Baha'i Studies in Australia (1995).

More or less at the same time as these developments, there has been a renewal of interest in the more narrowly academic study of the Babi and Baha'i religions. Although most of those involved in this movement have been Baha'is or former Baha'is, this renewal has been to a considerable extent independent of the Baha'i community as such, albeit that there is also some significant overlap, with a few branches of the ABS network sponsoring academic scholarship (most notably with the British-based *Baha'i Studies Review* [1990–]); private and official Baha'i publishers producing academic monographs and series; some prominent academic Baha'is simultaneously playing a significant role in faith-based Baha'i deepening programmes and even the production of apologetic literature; and, most recently, the Baha'i sponsorship of an academic Chair of Baha'i Studies at Hebrew University in Jerusalem (1999). There have also been major tensions, however, in part at least because of the difference of approach between academic scholarship and the more faith-based activities encouraged by the Baha'i institutions. These tensions have been evident in a number of well-known cases of Baha'i academics becoming disaffected with Baha'i institutions or experiencing crises of faith and leaving the Baha'i community altogether, in some cases then writing extensively against the Faith.[21] Again, an American *Baha'i Encyclopedia* project started in the 1980s has been endlessly delayed, seemingly because the academic style adopted by many of the

---

[21] Notably Dr. Denis MacEoin, presently Royal Literary Fund Fellow at the University of Newcastle-upon-Tyne in England and Juan Cole, a Professor of History at the University of Michigan. See also the discussion in Garlington, *'Baha'i Faith' in America*, pp. 162–6.

contributors was incompatible with the faith-based approach favoured by the Baha'i institutions. The extent to which academic viewpoints can be accommodated with these faith-based perspectives will be significant for the future nature and development of Baha'i Studies and its role within the Faith.

Some Final Comments

The successive heads of the Baha'i Faith have claimed that the Baha'i example and teachings are particularly appropriate for the modern world, ultimately providing the only effective solution to the problems of the present age and offering a path forward to a better future. In commenting on these ambitious claims, four concluding points may perhaps be usefully made.

Firstly, although the Baha'i leaders asserted the particularity and importance of the Baha'i Faith as a distinctive religious movement, they also placed this particularity in a wider and more inclusive framework, effectively arguing that all human beings are commonly involved in the necessity of dealing with the modern world and its problems, and offering the Baha'i vision as one element in what must be an ongoing consultation as to what should be done in dealing with the urgent issues that face the world and its peoples. The Baha'is do not see themselves as separated from the wider world. Genuine collaboration between people of different viewpoints and religions is seen as a fundamental part of forward progress towards the Baha'i millennial vision.

Secondly, the Baha'i leaders have described the process of economic, political and cultural globalization which is so characteristic of the modern age as an inevitable spiritual impulse in humanity's ongoing progress. Historically, the globalization process was in full flood in the late nineteenth century and formed part of the environing world for the initial development of the Baha'i Faith. In this context, Bahá'u'lláh and 'Abdu'l-Bahá insisted that the whole world had to be seen as a single country and all of the world's peoples as members of a single human race. Quite explicitly, they rejected the intense nationalism of their age and presented an internationalist vision of an ideal world which is perhaps even more challenging today than it was then, both internationally and within individual societies. Thus, no nation can now be independent from the rest of world and it is essential for all nations to find ways of dealing with this reality. Similarly, almost every nation in the world now faces the challenge of finding ways of enabling

peoples of different ethnicities, religions and cultures to live together peacefully and even harmoniously in a single society. In both these concerns, the
Baha'i vision is clearly relevant.

Thirdly, the Baha'i vision is also of interest in relationship to the role of
religion in the modern world. At a time when both strident secularism and
crass commercialism on the one hand and various extreme and sometimes
violent and fanatical movements of religious conservatism and reaction on
the other vie with each other for influence, the Baha'i vision is part of a
wider but often unheeded movement asserting the vital relevance of liberal,
tolerant and compassionate religiosity to the very survival of human society,
and warning of the moral and societal dangers posed both by the secularist
rejection of all forms of religiosity and by prejudiced religious fanaticism.

Finally, it can be argued that the great social shift of the past fifty years
or so has been the empowerment of women (with a sometimes vicious
reaction to this process on the part of some men). The moderate feminism
espoused by the Baha'i leaders since the late nineteenth century is again
of interest here, perhaps particularly in terms of their assertion that female
emancipation should be espoused by men as well as by women, and that
societies themselves can not develop effectively in material as well as spiritual
terms unless women and men are able to play an equal and united role in
their development.

Some speculation on the future development of the Baha'i movement is
also appropriate. In this regard, the major developments of the past half-
century seems particularly important, with the Baha'i Faith now becoming
a genuinely global religion embracing adherents of an enormous diversity of
religious and ethnic groups. Individual Baha'i communities probably face
somewhat different futures, however. Thus, for the present, the Baha'is in
the Middle East would seem likely to face continuing problems, whether
in the form of overt persecution or the necessity of remaining quiet and
relatively invisible so as to avoid opposition from religious conservatives.
The recent court proceedings in Egypt are a useful reminder here that there
are many liberal non-Baha'is in the region who are sometimes passionately
concerned about the well-being of the Baha'is on human rights grounds,
but whilst such individuals are an important indicator of possible future
developments, they remain for the present a relatively marginal grouping
in their environing societies. It is difficult to see any dramatic change in
this situation occurring in the near future.

The situation is quite different in North America, Europe (including Turkey), and the 'Anglo-Pacific' (collectively 'the West'). Here, there
are strong and often deeply rooted Baha'i communities, existing in an

environment in which freedom of speech, association and activity are all common political givens. In this context, whilst the Baha'i communities are often extremely small, their 'voice' can often be loud and influential. For the immediate future, Baha'is in the West – including the large numbers of Baha'is of Iranian origin who now live there – are likely to play a major role in articulating Baha'i ideas to the wider world. At the same time, the chances of large-scale increases in Baha'i numbers in these societies – many of which are now determinedly secular – does not seem to me to be great, apart perhaps amongst some minority groups.

The situation in the rest of the world (the Baha'i 'Third World') is enormously varied, and so impossible to summarize in a few words. This said, in terms of numbers and possible social impact, the immediate Baha'i future would seem to rest in some of the countries of this wider world. Although born in the Middle East and receiving its vital initial internationalization in the West, the Baha'i Faith can no longer be described as either 'neo-Islamic' or 'Western'. The success – or failure – of individual Baha'i communities in this wider world to establish themselves firmly; integrate and deepen their often new adherents; and develop constructive ties with the governments and peoples of their societies seems to me to be absolutely fundamental to the overall progress of the Baha'i 'project'. Necessarily, it will see a greater cultural diversity amongst the Baha'is as hitherto dominant Iranian, Arab and Western voices become balanced by those from Africa, Latin America, the Caribbean, Asia, and the Pacific.

Recent Baha'i Leaders

I. HANDS OF THE CAUSE OF GOD APPOINTED BY SHOGHI EFFENDI, 1951–7

(A) First Contingent, 24 December 1951

-1. Dorothy B. Baker   (1898–1954, American).
-2. Amelia E. Collins   (1873–1962, American).
-3. 'Alí-Akbar Furútan   (1905–2003, Iranian).
-4. Ugo Giachery   (1896–1989, Italian).
-5. Hermann Grossman   (1899–1968, German).
-6. Horace Holley   (1887–1960, American).
-7. Leroy Ioas   (1896–1965, American).
-8. William Sutherland Maxwell   (1874–1952, Canadian).
-9. Charles Mason Remey   (1874–1974, American).
-10. Ṭarázu'lláh Samandarí   (1874–1968, Iranian).
-11. George Townshend   (1876–1957, Irish).
-12. Valíyu'lláh Varqá   (1884–1955, Iranian).

(B) Second Contingent, 29 February 1952

-13. Shu'á'u'lláh 'Alá'í   (1889–1984, Iranian).
-14. Músá Banání   (1886–1971, Iranian).
-15. Clara Dunn   (1869–1960, Australian).
-16. Dhikru'lláh Khádem   (1904–86, Iranian).
-17. Adelbert Muhlschlegal   (1897–1980, German).
-18. Siegfried Schopflocher   (1877–1953, Canadian).
-19. Corinne True   (1861–1961, American).

(C) Appointed Individually (Dates of appointment in parenthesis)

-20. Rúḥiyyih Khánum	(1910–2000, American) (26 March 1952). Daughter of William Sutherland Maxwell (above).
-21. Jalál Kházeh	(1897–1990, Iranian) (7 December 1953).
-22. Paul E. Haney	(1909–1982, American) (19 March 1954).
-23. 'Alí-Muḥammad Varqá	(b. 1911–2007. Iranian) (15 November 1955). Son of Valíyu'lláh Varqá (above).
-24. Agnes Baldwin Alexander	(1875–1971, American) (27 March 1957).

(D) Third Contingent, October 1957

-25. Hasan Balyuzi	(1908–80, Iranian British).
-26. Abu'l-Qásim Faizí	(1906–80, Iranian).
-27. Collis Featherstone	(1913–90, Australian).
-28. John Ferraby	(1914–73, British).
-29. Raḥmatu'lláh Muhájir	(1923–79, Iranian).
-30. Enoch Olinga	(1926–79, Ugandan).
-31. John Robarts	(1901–91, Canadian).
-32. William Sears	(1911–92, American).

II. MEMBERS OF THE UNIVERSAL HOUSE OF JUSTICE

Members	Previous Position	Year of Election/ Years of Service:
Mr. Hugh Chance	US	1963–93
Mr. Húshmand Fathe-Azam	IN	1963–2003
Mr. Amos Gibson	US	1963–82 (d.)
Dr. Luṭfu'lláh Ḥakím	IBC	1963–67 (Resigned, d. 1968)
Mr. David Hofman	Brit	1963–88 (Resigned)
Mr. H. Borrah Kavelin	IBC	1963–88 (Resigned, d. 1988)
Mr. 'Alí Nakhjavání	IBC	1963–2003
Mr. Ian Semple	IBC	1963–2005
Mr. Charles Wolcott	IBC	1963–87 (d.)
Dr. David Ruhe	US	1968–93

Mr. Glenford Mitchell	US	1982*
Dr. Peter Khan	ITC	1987*
Mr. Hooper Dunbar	ITC	1988
Mr. Adib Taherzadeh	EuC	1988–2000 (d.)
Dr. Farzam Arbab	ITC	1993
Mr. Douglas Martin	OPI	1993–2005
Mr. Kaiser Barnes	ITC	2000*
Mr. Hartmut Grossman	ITC	2003
Dr. Firaydoun Javaheri	ITC	2003
Dr. Payman Mohajer	ITC	2005*
Mr. Paul Lample	ITC	2005*

*By-election

Previous position:

Brit	British National Spiritual Assembly
EuC	European Board of Counsellors
IBC	International Baha'i Council
IN	Indian National Spiritual Assembly
ITC	International Teaching Centre
OPI	Office of Public Information (BIC)
US	US National Spiritual Assembly.

Select Bibliography

There are several useful introductions to the Babi and Baha'i religions written from a Baha'i perspective. These include: John E. Esslemont, *Bahá'u'lláh and the New Era*. 4th ed. (London: Bahá'í Publishing Trust, 1974 [1st ed. 1923]); John Ferraby, *All Things Made New: A Comprehensive Outline of the Bahá'í Faith*. Rev. ed. ([London]: Bahá'í Publishing Trust, 1987); William S. Hatcher and J. Douglas Martin, *The Bahá'í Faith: The Emerging Global Religion* (New York: Harper & Row, 1984); and John Huddlestone, *The Earth is But One Country* (London: Bahá'í Publishing Trust, 1976).

More critical and historical accounts are provided by Peter Smith, *The Babi and Baha'i Religions: From Messianic Shi'ism to a World Religion* (Cambridge: Cambridge University Press, 1987), which includes an extended guide to further reading (pp. 225–38), and Margit Warburg, *Citizens of the World: A History and Sociology of the Baha'is from a Globalization Perspective* (Leiden: Brill, 2006). For reference to specific topics, see Peter Smith, *A Concise Encyclopedia of the Bahá'í Faith* (Oxford: Oneworld, 2000, 2nd ed., 2002 [Hereinafter CEBF]), which includes an extensive bibliography. For short introductions, see Moojan Momen, *The Baha'i Faith: A Short Introduction* (Oxford: Oneworld, 1996); Margit Warburg, *Baha'i* (N.p: Signature Books, [2001]); Peter Smith, *The Bahá'í Religion: A Short Introduction to its History and Teachings* (Oxford: George Ronald, 1988); and, idem, *The Bahá'í Faith: A Short History*. 2nd ed. (Oxford: Oneworld, 1999). William P. Collins, *Bibliography of English-Language Works on the Bábí and Bahá'í Faiths, 1844–1985* (Oxford: George Ronald, 1990) is invaluable (Joel Bjorling, *The Baha'i Faith: A Historical Bibliography* [New York: Garland, 1985] is less useful).

Websites with Baha'i related material vary enormously in quality and objectivity (pro- and anti-sites abound). The 'Baha'i Library Online' (bahai-library.com) provides much useful material, as do three official sites related to the Bahá'í International Community: the Bahá'í Reference Library (reference.bahai.org); Bahá'í World News Service (bahaiworldnews.org); and One Country (onecountry.org). Of periodicals, the UK-based *Baha'i Studies Review* is consistently useful, as is Kalimát Press's *Studies in Bábí and Bahá'í History / Studies in the Bábí and Bahá'í Religions* series (Los Angeles, 1982–).

Babi-Baha'i History. There is as yet no other overall academic account of Babi-Baha'i history apart from my own works and some unpublished dissertations (see Smith, *Babi and Baha'i Religions*). The standard Baha'i account is by Shoghi Effendi, *God Passes By*. Rev. ed. (Wilmette, IL: Bahá'í Publishing Trust, 1974). Moojan Momen (ed.), *The Bábí and Bahá'í Religions, 1844–1944: Some Contemporary Western Accounts* (Oxford: George Ronald, 1981) provides an invaluable collection of sources. The two *Bahá'í World* series, *Vol. I: Bahá'í Yearbook*, Vols. II–XII (Wilmette IL: Bahá'í Publishing Trust, 1980–81 (1st publ. 1926–56); Vols. XIII–XVIII. Haifa: Bahá'í World Centre, 1970–86; new series. 1992/93–. Haifa: Bahá'í World Centre, 1993–) include useful materials and surveys from the 1920s onwards. For dates, see Glenn Cameron and Wendi Momen, *A Basic Bahá'í Chronology* (Oxford: George Ronald, 1996) (less good for the Babi period). The works of Edward Granville Browne are still of value, notably his *The Táríkh-i-Jadíd, or New History of Mírzá 'Alí Muḥammad the Báb, by Mírzá Ḥusayn of Hamadán* (ed. and trans. Cambridge: Cambridge University Press, 1893); *A Traveller's Narrative, Written to Illustrate the Episode of the Báb*. 2 vols. (ed. and trans. Cambridge: Cambridge University Press, 1891); *Materials for the Study of the Bábí Religion* (comp. Cambridge: Cambridge University Press, 1918); and *Selections from the Writings of E. G. Browne on the Bábí and Bahá'í Religions*, ed. Moojan Momen (Oxford: George Ronald, 1987).

For more specific studies, excluding unpublished dissertations and a recent plethora of articles (some referred to in the endnotes), the only recent academic account of Babism is Abbas Amanat, *Resurrection and Renewal: The Making of the Babi Movement in Iran, 1844–1850* (Ithaca, NY: Cornell University Press, 1989). Denis MacEoin, *The Sources for Early Babi Doctrine and History: A Survey* (Leiden: Brill, 1992) provides a detailed survey of sources. What is now seen as the standard Baha'i account is Nabíl, *The Dawn-Breakers: Nabíl's Narrative of the Early Days of the Bahá'í Revelation*. Trans. Shoghi Effendi (Wilmette, IL: Bahá'í Publishing Trust, 1932).

For Baha'i history, there is nothing comparable to the works by Amanat and MacEoin on Babism. On the life of Bahá'u'lláh, see H. M. Balyuzi, *Bahá'u'lláh: The King of Glory* (Oxford: George Ronald, 1980), and Moojan Momen, *Baha'u'llah: A Short Biography* (Oxford: Oneworld, 2006). On Bahá'u'lláh's writings and teachings, Adib Taherzadeh, *The Revelation of Bahá'u'lláh*. 4 vols. (Oxford: George Ronald, 1974–87) provides an overview from a Baha'i perspective, whilst Juan Cole, *Modernity and the Millennium: The Genesis of the Bahai Faith in the Nineteenth-Century Middle East* (New York: Columbia University Press, 1998) and Nader Saiedi, *Logos and Civilization: Spirit, History, and Order in the Writings of Bahá'u'lláh* (Bethesda: University Press of Maryland, 2000) offer two stimulating, controversial and highly contrasting accounts, Cole partly in terms of possible European influences on Bahá'u'lláh's thought and Saiedi rigorously excluding all external influences – in part as a rebuttal to Cole. For later Baha'i leaderships, we have H. M. Balyuzi, *'Abdu'l-Bahá: The Centre of the Covenant of Bahá'u'lláh* (London, George Ronald, 1971) on 'Abdu'l-Bahá, and on Shoghi Effendi accounts by his widow, Ruhiyyih Rabbani, *The Priceless Pearl* (London: Bahá'í Publishing Trust, 1969), and by Ugo Giachery, *Shoghi Effendi: Recollections* (Oxford: George Ronald, 1973). There is also an extremely useful collection of documents for the period of leadership by the Hands of the Cause, Universal House of Justice, *The Ministry of the Custodians: An Account of the Stewardship of the Hands of the Cause* (Haifa: Bahá'í World Centre, 1992).

There are several useful histories of particular countries, although at the time of writing no general survey on Iran apart from Vahid Rafati's article, 'The Baha'i community of Iran', *Encyclopaedia Iranica*, loc. cit. See also Smith, *Concise Encyclopedia* [CEBF], 'Iran', loc. cit. Dominic Parviz Brookshaw and Seena Fazel (ed.), *The Baha'is of Iran: Socio-Historical Studies* (London and New York: Routledge, 2008) provides a number of useful essays. There are several studies of the persecutions of the Iranian Baha'is, mostly on those since 1979, including the Bahá'í International Community, *The Bahá'ís of Iran: A Report on the Persecution of a Religious Minority*. Rev. ed. (New York: Bahá'í International Community, 1982), and a supplement: *Major Developments, July 1982–July 1983*; Roger Cooper, *The Baha'is of Iran*. Rev. ed. (London: Minority Rights Group, 1985); Douglas Martin, *The Persecution of the Bahá'ís of Iran, 1844–1984* (*Bahá'í Studies*, vol. 12/13, 1984); and Margit Warburg, *Iranske dokumenter: Forfølgelsen af Bahá'íerne i Iran* (Copenhagen: Rhodos, 1985). Updated accounts of events are provided in the successive volumes of the Bahá'í World series. Earlier attacks are described in A. L. M. Nicolas, *Massacres de Babis en Perse* (Paris: Adrien-Maisonneuve, Libraire d'Amérique et d'Orient, 1936), and Muhammad Labib, *The Seven Martyrs of Hurmuzak*. Trans. M. Momen (Oxford: George Ronald, 1981).

Overall developments elsewhere are summarized in Smith, *Babi and Baha'i Religions*, pp. 157–95, and CEBF, 'expansion', loc. cit. There are a few detailed studies of Western Baha'i communities, notably Robert H. Stockman, *The Bahá'í Faith in America*. 2 vols. to date (Vol. 1. *Origins, 1892–1900*. Wilmette IL: Bahá'í Publishing Trust, 1985; Vol. 2. *Early Expansion, 1900–1912*. Oxford: George Ronald, 1995); and Will Van den Hoonaard, *The Origins of the Bahá'í Community of Canada, 1898–1948* (Waterloo, ON: Wilfrid Laurier University Press, 1996). See also R. Jackson Armstrong-Ingram, *Music, Devotions, and Mashriqu'l-Adhkár* (Los Angeles, CA: Kalimát Press, 1987); Bruce W. Whitmore, *The Dawning Place: The Building of a Temple, the Forging of the North American Bahá'í Community* (Wilmette, IL: Bahá'í Publishing Trust, 1984); and the essays in Richard Hollinger (ed.), *Community Histories* (Los Angeles, CA: Kalimát Press, 1992) and Peter Smith (ed.), *Bahá'ís in the West* (Los Angeles, CA: Kalimát Press, 2004). Pioneering studies of Asian Baha'i history include A. Manisegaran, *Jewel Among Nations: An Account of the Early Days of the Bahá'í Faith in West Malaysia* (Ampang: Splendour Publications, 2003), and Jimmy Ewe Huat Seow, *The Pure in Heart: The Historical Development of the Baha'i Faith in China, Southeast Asia and Far East* (Mona Vale, NSW: Baha'i Publications Australia, 1991).

Beliefs and Practices. The Baha'is have now published an extensive body of the writings of their successive leaders, but as yet only one volume from the Báb, *Selections from the Writings of the Báb*. Trans. Habib Taherzadeh et al. (Haifa: Bahá'í World Centre, 1976).

For the writings of Bahá'u'lláh see: *Epistle to the Son of the Wolf*. Trans. Shoghi Effendi (Wilmette, IL: Bahá'í Publishing Trust, 1962); *Gems of Divine Mysteries: Javáhiru'l-Asrár* ([Haifa]: Bahá'í World Centre, 2002); *Gleanings from the Writings of Bahá'u'lláh*. Trans. Shoghi Effendi. Rev. ed. (London: Bahá'í Publishing Trust, 1978); *The Hidden Words of Bahá'u'lláh*. Trans. Shoghi Effendi (London: Bahá'í Publishing Trust, 1966); *The Kitáb-i-Aqdas: The Most Holy Book* (Haifa: Bahá'í World Centre, 1992); *The Kitáb-i-Iqan: The Book of Certitude*. Trans. Shoghi Effendi. 3rd ed. (London: Bahá'í Publishing Trust, 1982); *Prayers and Meditations by Bahá'u'lláh*. Comp. and trans. Shoghi Effendi. Rev. ed. (London: Bahá'í Publishing Trust, 1978); *The Proclamation of Bahá'u'lláh to the Kings and Leaders of the World* (Haifa: Bahá'í World Centre, 1967); *The Seven Valleys and the Four Valleys*. Trans. Ali Kuli Khan and Marzieh Gail. 3rd rev. ed. (Wilmette, IL: Bahá'í Publishing Trust, 1978); *The Summons of the Lord of Hosts: Tablets of Bahá'u'lláh* (Haifa: Bahá'í World Centre, 2002); *The Tabernacle of Unity* (Haifa: Bahá'í World Centre, 2006); *Tablets of Bahá'u'lláh Revealed After the Kitáb-i-Aqdas*. Trans. Habib Taherzadeh et al. (Haifa: Bahá'í World Centre, 1978); and *Writings of Bahá'u'lláh* (New Delhi: Bahá'í Publishing Trust, 1986).

For those of 'Abdu'l-Bahá, see *Memorials of the Faithful*. Trans. Marzieh Gail (Wilmette IL: Bahá'í Publishing Trust, 1971); *Paris Talks: Addresses Given by 'Abdu'l-Bahá in 1911*. 12th ed. (London: Bahá'í Publishing Trust, 1995); *Promulgation of Universal Peace*. Comp. Howard MacNutt. 2nd ed. (Wilmette, IL: Bahá'í Publishing Trust, 1982); *The Secret of Divine Civilization*. Trans. Marzieh Gail. 3rd ed. (Wilmette, IL: Bahá'í Publishing Trust, 1979); *Selections from the Writings of 'Abdu'l-Bahá*. Trans. Marzieh Gail et al. (Haifa: Bahá'í World Centre, 1978); *Some Answered Questions* (Wilmette, IL: Bahá'í Publishing Trust, 1981); *The Tablets of the Divine Plan*. Rev. ed. (Wilmette, IL: Bahá'í Publishing Trust, 1977); and *The Will and Testament of 'Abdu'l-Bahá* (Wilmette, IL: Bahá'í Publishing Committee, 1944).

For Shoghi Effendi, see *The Advent of Divine Justice*. Rev. ed. (Wilmette, IL: Bahá'í Publishing Trust, 1963); *Bahá'í Administration*. 5th ed. (Wilmette, IL: Bahá'í Publishing Trust, 1945); *Citadel of Faith: Messages to America, 1947–1957* (Wilmette, IL: Bahá'í Publishing Trust, 1965); 'The Faith of Bahá'u'lláh, A World Religion'. In *Guidance for Today and Tomorrow* (London: Bahá'í Publishing Trust, 1953), pp. 1–10; *God Passes By*. Rev. ed. (Wilmette, IL: Bahá'í Publishing Trust, 1974); *High Endeavours: Messages to Alaska* ([Anchorage:] National Spiritual Assembly of the Bahá'ís of Alaska, 1976); *The Light of Divine Guidance: The Messages of the Guardian of the Bahá'í Faith to the Bahá'ís of Germany and Austria*. 2 vols. (Langenhain: Bahá'í-Verlag, 1982–5); *Messages to America: Selected Letters and Cablegrams Addressed to the Bahá'ís of North America, 1932–1946* (Wilmette, IL: Bahá'í Publishing Trust, 1947); *Messages to the Antipodes: Communications from Shoghi Effendi to the Bahá'í Communities of Australasia*, ed. Graham Hassall (Mona Vale: Bahá'í Publications Australia, 1997); *Messages to the Bahá'í World, 1950–1957*. 2nd ed. (Wilmette IL: Bahá'í Publishing Trust, 1971); *Messages to Canada* ([Toronto, ON:] National Spiritual Assembly of the Bahá'ís of Canada, 1965); *Messages of Shoghi Effendi to the Indian Subcontinent, 1923–1957*. Comp. I. F. Muhajir (New Delhi: Bahá'í Publishing Trust, 1995); *The Promised Day is Come*. Rev. ed. (Wilmette, IL: Bahá'í Publishing Trust, 1980); *The Unfolding Destiny of the British Bahá'í Community* (London: Bahá'í Publishing Trust, 1981); and *The World Order of Bahá'u'lláh*. Rev. ed. (Wilmette, IL: Bahá'í Publishing Trust, 1965).

For the Universal House of Justice, see *The Constitution of the Universal House of Justice* (Haifa: Bahá'í World Centre); *The Four Year Plan* (Riviera Beach, FL: Palabra, 1996); *Individual Rights and Freedoms in the World Order of Bahá'u'lláh* (Wilmette, IL: Bahá'í Publishing Trust, 1989); *Messages from the Universal House of Justice, 1963–1986: The Third Epoch of the Formative Age*. Comp. Geoffry W. Marks (Wilmette, IL: Bahá'í Publishing Trust, 1996); *The Promise of World Peace* (Haifa: Bahá'í World Centre, 1985); and *A Wider Horizon: Selected Messages of the Universal House of Justice, 1983–1992* (Riviera Beach, FL: Palabra, 1992).

For compilations of material from the successive leaders of the Baha'i Faith, see Universal House of Justice, *Compilation of Compilations*. 3 vols. [Sydney]: Bahá'í Publications Australia, 1991–2000), and Helen Hornby (comp.), *Lights of Guidance: A Bahá'í Reference File*. 2nd ed. (New Delhi: Bahá'í Publishing Trust, 1988).

Overviews of various Baha'i beliefs and practices are provided by John Walbridge, *Sacred Acts; Sacred Space; Sacred Time. Bahá'í Studies, vol. 1* (Oxford: George Ronald, 1996); Denis MacEoin, *Rituals in Babism and Baha'ism* (London: I. B. Tauris, British Academic Press, 1994); Jack A. McLean, *Dimensions in Spirituality: Reflections on the Meaning of Spiritual Life and Transformation in Light of the Bahá'í Faith* (Oxford: George Ronald, 1994), and (ed.), *Revisioning the Sacred: New Perspectives on a Bahá'í Theology* (Los Angeles, CA: Kalimát Press, 1997); and Julio Savi, *The Eternal Quest for God: An Introduction to the Divine Philosophy of 'Abdu'l-Bahá* (Oxford: George Ronald, 1989). Books dealing with specific topics are referenced in the endnotes.

ABBREVIATIONS

CC   Universal House of Justice. *Compilation of Compilations*.
CEBF Smith, *Concise Encyclopedia*.

Index